WORK, CHANGE AND WORKERS

Work, Change and Workers

STEPHEN BILLETT

Griffith University, Australia

 Springer

A C.I.P. Catalogue record for this book is available from the Library of Congress.

ISBN-10 1-4020-4643-X (HB)
ISBN-13 978-1-4020-4643-8 (HB)
ISBN-10 1-4020-4651-0 (e-book)
ISBN-13 978-1-4020-4651-3 (e-book)

Published by Springer,
P.O. Box 17, 3300 AA Dordrecht, The Netherlands.

www.springer.com

Printed on acid-free paper

Printed in the Netherlands.

Dedication

This book is dedicated to Alison Lee Jackson and Hannah Grace Billett

Contents

viii   *Contents*

Preface

This book aims to provide a fresh account of the changing nature of work and how workers are changing as result of the requirements of contemporary working life. It also identifies implications for preparing individuals for work and then maintaining their skills throughout working life. It does this by examining the relations between the changing requirements for working life and how individuals engage in work through an analysis that engages a range of disciplinary perspectives. These include the psychological, sociological, philosophical and anthropological literatures as they relate to work and empirical research that represents both the perspectives of work and work practice as social institutions and as a vocation that individuals exercise with intentionality and agency. This body of work is also used to identify implications for vocational education, professional development and on-going learning throughout working life.

This book is the product of a now long-term project to understand contemporary working life and its implications for learning throughout working life. Along the way it has benefited from a range of contributions. It commenced with research from the early to the late 1990s that sought to understand how people learn through their work. The Australian Research Council, state government funding, private enterprise sponsorships and the National Research and Evaluation Committee of the Australian National Training Authority supported these investigations, as did the many workplaces and workers who contributed time, insights and sometimes patience. This research concluded that there was little that separated individuals' engagement in work and their learning. Hence, to understand learning through and for work required a better understanding of what constitutes work and how individuals engage with paid work.

Building on this earlier research, a Fulbright scholarship taken in 1999 had as its key purpose to understand what constitutes 'new work' which was much on the minds of governments, governmental agencies and many academics. This scholarship engaged working at and utilising the resources of the Rand Corporation (Santa Monica) hosted by Cathy Stasz, the University of California, Berkeley hosted by David Stern and Norton Grubb, the University of Pittsburgh hosted by Lauren Resnick and Colombia University in New York hosted by Tom Bailey. The foundations of the first part of this book are derived from work conducted in those institutions.

More recently, the project to understand work and learning throughout working life has comprised a series of small-scale but detailed studies of the working lives of a few individuals working in diverse occupations. Recent projects funded by grants from the Australian Research Council and Griffith University's internal grants focused in detail on individuals working lives and richly complement the earlier phases of the inquiry that identified key trends in the changing nature of work, and its implications for learning throughout working life. This research also examined relations between individuals' life outside of work as well as their working lives. Here, issues of personal agency and the negotiations with the social practice comprising their work came to the forefront of the analysis. It is this recent work that largely shapes the second part of this book. A six-month period of sabbatical in 2004 supported by Griffith University assisted advancing the conceptual basis of interactions between social and individual agency, which is referred to here as being relationally interdependent. Earlier versions of some of this work have been published in journals and presented at conferences in the United Kingdom, the United States of America, Canada and Europe.

Along the way, discussions with colleagues such as Margaret Somerville from the University of New England, Tara Fenwick from the University of Alberta, Phil Hodkinson and Miriam Zukas from Leeds University and Tarja Tikkanen from Norway have been essential in formulating the ideas presented here, as have the many authors whose work is referred to throughout the chapters of this book, and those anonymous reviewers of previously published papers. However, the journey taken so far has been rich and informative, and at times confronting. Working across both practical investigations yielding significant bodies of data from interviews and observations and then engaging with diverse perspectives within the literature has been a stimulating, energising and rewarding process. Yet, boundary crossing or perhaps trespassing, can lead to contestations and deliberations that are confronting and energising in a different kind of way. Responses to seminars given at the University of Leicester, University College London and the University of Technology, Sydney all stand as moments that led to careful reflection and consideration of such boundary crossing. Towards the end, Jill Ryan and Darryl Dymock provided much needed help and support in completing the manuscript.

Stephen Billett

SECTION 1: INTRODUCTION

Chapter 1

WORK, CHANGE AND WORKERS

Globalisation and the intensified economic competition it engenders are profoundly altering the way we live and relate to each other. For a start, work is undergoing such transformation that in future the notion of a job may change its meaning entirely. (Carnoy, 2001: 306)

1. CONTEMPORARY ACCOUNTS OF WORK LIFE

There is a widely held view that, in the last quarter of the last century and now spilling into this century, there have been considerable changes to the kinds of work available, how they are practised and who engages in them. The world of work has become unstable with changes to global economic activity, technology and cultural practices (e.g. McBrier and Wilson, 2004). In many recent accounts of work, work practice and career development much is made of the disempowerment and anxiety caused by the constantly turbulent and uncertain nature of contemporary work (e.g. Bauman, 1998; Beck, 1992; Giddens, 1991). For instance, a common claim is that a continuous and logically coherent working life is now less available, thereby making continuity of work skills and identity problematic. Many new jobs are held to be contingent—fixed term and part-time (Carnoy, 1999), making work insecure and insufficient.

According to Rifkin (1995) more than 75 per cent of the labour force in industrialised nations engages in work that is little more than simple repetitive tasks that do not provide any gratifying and meaningful identity for the workers. Leicht (1998) claims that contemporary workplaces are characterised as featuring: (a) flatter organizational hierarchies, as new information technologies eliminate the need for most layers of middle management; (b) the growing use of temporary workers employed on an 'as-needed' basis to perform specific jobs for the duration of single projects; (c) the extensive use of subcontracting and outsourcing to small firms; (d) massive down-sizing of the permanent workforce resulting from flatter hierarchies and the replacement of skilled workers by machine tenders; (e) a post-unionised bargaining environment where unions have no place and no structural ability to gain a foothold to bargain with employers; and (f) virtual organisations that exist not as distinctive structural locations but as webs of technologically driven interactions. Such characteristics are presented as significant trends that are transforming existing conceptions and practices of paid work that individuals encounter in their working life.

Beyond the unpredictability of what constitutes much contemporary work is the claim that the kinds of work we engage in are increasingly subject to change. It is popularly claimed that individuals will need to engage in multiple careers and will be required to reinvent their occupational identity a number of times throughout their working lives.

These work-related manifestations of change are held by some to reflect a broader and more ubiquitous set of conditions that create great uncertainty. Beck (1992) proposes that contemporary (modern) society presents greater risks than in former times, rendering a greater sense of insecurity and uncertainty. Giddens (1991) proposes that contemporary society is generative of anxiety and has individuals standing before it as anxiety ridden. Work and working life are not exceptions to this general claim, particularly if Leicht's (1998) six claims outlined above are upheld. So, finding continuity in working life in late modernity is held to be a precarious enterprise for individuals because of its turbulent and transformative character (e.g. O'Doherty and Willmot, 2001).

All this fuels the notion that paid work which provides adequate and consistent remuneration, personal fulfilment, and pathways to self-identity and sense of self is becoming less likely, and that jobs which are both secure and well regarded are becoming a rarity (Bauman, 1998). This suggests, rather bleakly, that high salary levels, the ability to enact social good, personal discretion in how individuals engage in work, for how long and to what level of intensity, and the prospect of engaging in interesting work, in the humanist tradition, may be becoming the privilege of fewer workers.

Such propositions emanate most strongly from theoretical accounts of work that might be described as social theorising, and are admittedly speculative. Often, such accounts are premised in theoretical rather than empirical analyses. That is, these accounts are based on propositions deducted from the authors' theoretical (Giddens, 1991) or ideological stance (Beck, 1992) or their observations of the past and present, and speculations about the future (Bauman, 1998). These analyses extend from meta-analysis about changing societal conditions through to accounts that explain how individuals and society come together. For instance, the social structuring of work is often the key premise, with individuals by degree being viewed as captive, subjugated or resistant to these socially derived practices. So, the degree to which an individual is free to make decisions and act autonomously in work is subject to diverse viewpoints.

For instance, in the risky and uncertain era of late modernity, it is suggested that individuals have become 'enterprising selves' (Du Gay, 1996; Rose, 1990), engaging in self-regulation as they act in ways against their preferred sense of self. In so doing, they adopt an almost Machiavellian persona that seeks to project a self that meets the requirements of their work, while fostering quite different personal beliefs. Hence, in this view, it is suggested that individuals direct their critical faculties in ways that subvert and bury their real selves in efforts to secure continuity and advancement in their employment (Grey, 1994). The theoretical view here would be to see these individuals as socialised subjects, engaged in self-deception and regulation generative of a false consciousness. Clearly, this perspective privileges the social world and positions it as objective and comprising potent institutional facts (Searle, 1995), the press of social institutions that cannot be wished away.

Wright Mills (1973) suggested that in identifying the close relationship between human development and work, Marx proposed that the essence of being a human rests upon work. What comprises a human being "coincides with their production, both what they produce and with how they produce" (p. 8). Within this perspective the nature of individuals, their conditions, their prospects and their rewards depend on "the material conditions determining their production" (Wright Mills, 1973: 8). Here, individuals are held to be dependent upon these social structures both materially and for their identity. The work, working life and sense of self of those engaged in paid work are therefore dependent upon the social structures that shape their work and behaviour. Given that many of these theorists report erosion in the conditions of work and working life, they extrapolate directly their propositions to the quality of an individual's working life and the prospect for a positive sense of self.

Yet to what degree are both of the conditions and conclusions supported by empirical accounts of work and workplace activities?

2. QUALITIES AND BENEFITS OF WORKING LIFE

There is evidence to support some of what is suggested in these theoretical accounts. The immediate post-war period was a time of economic development, stable employment and declining inequality. However, the period since the mid 1970s has featured increasing global competition, pressure on labour to be more productive and the assertion of management practices in Western countries such as the USA (Handel, 2005), the United Kingdom (Carnoy, 1999), Canada (Livingstone, 2001), many European states and Australia (Pusey, 2003). According to Carnoy (2001: 306), in the face of intense global competition, work is being reorganised around "... the centralised management, customised products, and work differentiation, such that work has become individualised and workers differentiated."

The consequences of this reorganisation are to make work more readily sub-contracted, undertaken by part-time and temporary workers, while core work becomes more broadly skilled and conducted in teams. These actions separate workers from the kinds of stable work and work identities that have become accepted in modern industrialised societies (Carnoy, 2001). These practices and their consequences are likely to be felt in different ways, degrees and at different times and paces, across and within countries. For instance, some kinds of work (e.g. garment and automobile manufacturing and steel production) were exported from some countries having particular, and sometimes, devastating effects within communities usually sustained by those industries. Then there are changes that pervade these countries more generally and broadly across a range of industry sectors. For instance, in considering the increasing erosion of job security, drawing upon empirical data, Handel (2005) proposes that

> ... there is now a general agreement that job security and internal labour markets also eroded in the 1990s, but the effect fell disproportionately on white-collar and more educated workers, narrowing some of the insecurity gap between the more and less privileged workers ... (p. 69)

This suggests that it is not only exported work that has caused job losses and uncertainty, but also more widespread adjustments about work, its standing and its regard within the community. In this way, some of the claims of social theorists previously mentioned appear to be upheld and these extend to the worth of the available work.

Indeed, those employed part-time and contractually often report contemporary work to now be more unsatisfactory in terms of remuneration, security and opportunities for advancement (Bolle, 2001, McGovern Smeaton and Hill, 2004). Moreover, although women workers are now participating in greater numbers in the American, British and Australian workforces, there is a tendency for work that is highly regarded, remunerated and that offers advancement to experience reductions in conditions and opportunities when occupied by women (Skuratowicz and Hunter, 2004). So the pursuit of worthwhile work is, in part, frustrated by such changes. Analogously, Skinner (2004) and others (e.g. McNair, Flynn, Owen,

Humpreys and Woodfield, 2004) have noted that a polarisation of employment patterns has arisen through shifts from manufacturing to service work and transformations brought about by technology. This polarisation sees a hollowing out of mid-skilled work and a concentration in both high and low skill occupations. Yet, the impact of this hollowing-out may be different across populations. McBrier and Wilson (2004) claim that any falls in the occupational mobility of white-collar workers are likely to be more extreme for African-Americans than their white counterparts. The shift to low skill and less secure forms of work had particularly negative impacts for African-Americans. So there is some empirical evidence to support the theorising and speculation of the grand social theorists of general erosion in the quality of work and work life.

Nevertheless, much of this evidence is premised on quantitative accounts, using surveys and other measures, albeit with some consideration for the individual's satisfaction with what is being proposed. However, in all of these evidence based accounts, the appraisal of the changes to and impacts of work is through socially and culturally derived measures, rather than more subjective accounts of an individual's experience of work (Handel, 2005). Consequently, conceptions of what constitutes good work and an effective working life are shaped by these kinds of objective accounts, rather than those that accommodate individual subjective experience.

3. SUBJECTIVE ACCOUNTS OF WORK LIFE

However, the experience of work needs also to be understood from personal or subjective viewpoints. From interviews with Australian workers, Pusey (2003) found the centrality of work for humans was both rehearsed and reinforced: "For nearly everyone work is a social protein, a buttress for identity and not a tradeable commodity" (p. 2). This suggests that it is important to understand work not only from the perspective of objective measures, but also individual subjective experience of what constitutes work and working life. For instance, Noon and Blyton (1997) propose that the majority of people in all categories of jobs would continue to work even if there is no financial need, because of social contact and its purposefulness in sustaining an identity. This suggests either wholesale social subjugation (i.e. the individual becomes socialised to engaging in work) or individuals finding meaning and sense of self within their work which is personally fulfilling. In studies examining the lived experience of contemporary workers (e.g. Billett et al., 2004; Billett and Pavlova, 2005; Fenwick, 1998, 2002, 2004; Somerville, 2002; Somerville and Abrahamsson, 2003), a more complex pattern emerges. That is, there is an intertwining between the press of the social world and an individual's agency and intentionality that shapes and is shaped by their sense of self.

For instance, fire fighters who are required to be highly agentic and exercise discretion in their work revel in their identities as fire fighters yet are subject to a command and control work organisation in which subordinates are required to unquestioningly obey instructions from a superior (Billett et al., 2005). Coalminers are immersed in a culture that provides identity as a worker and member of a community yet also engages them in behaviours that are potentially deleterious to the health (Somerville, 2002).

It seems that, for the workers in these studies, work is important and central to their sense of self, yet their sense of it, engagement with it and control over it is not so readily characterised by social subjugation or even localised press. Instead, there is a rich interplay between what the workplace and the social world affords these workers and how they engage with (i.e. construe, construct and respond to) what is afforded them. While their degree of autonomy and prospect of exercising their self is in part contingent upon the kind of work they undertake and their prospects for discretion and autonomy, the underlying condition that emerges is of these workers being able to make a space for themselves and to exercise their self in different ways (Billett and Pavlova, 2005; Billett et al., 2005; Fenwick, 2002, 2004; Somerville, 2002). Indeed, Giddens (1991) advancing from his theory of structuration suggests a space for individuals to negotiate with the social world and positions them as being agentic. He offers a view of individuals engaging with the world of work to be seen as more personally agentic than views that hold individuals as being socially subjugated. Therefore, beyond objective accounts, more personally based perspectives (i.e. how work relates to an individual's needs) are warranted, as they articulate salient qualities about work and workers' identity, and the worth of working life to individuals.

In response to Giddens' (1991) proposal that individuals exercise agency when confronted by the anxiety creating, socially subjugating conditions of contemporary working life, Fenwick (1998) counters by suggesting that individuals are not cowering and anxiety ridden. Instead they engage with changing circumstances agentically. Fenwick (1998) identifies this agency, discretion and personal intentionality in the actions and agency of small business operators in their working lives. The women in her study were able to exercise their preference for the kinds of businesses they wanted to pursue and the ways they pursued their business goals. In this way, they were able to demonstrate that rather than being captive to business orthodoxy and entrepreneurialism, they could pursue their own goals and develop their own practices. Similarly, Billett, Ehrich and Hernon-Tinning (2003) in examining how small business operators learnt to implement a goods and service tax, identified the central role of individual agency in learning new practices, in the relative isolation of small-business settings. Here, small business operators' learning of new practice was characterised through the enactment of their personal initiative and a reflective approach to learning, not only in deciding what and how to learn, but also how they elected to engage with the support that was available to them.

4. WORK AND SENSE OF SELF

In extending this emphasis of personal agency, some claim individual agency is not directed towards individuals 'being themselves', as humanists propose, but towards constructing a 'sense of self' albeit constrained by the parameters of their work and working life (e.g. Knights and Willmott, 1989). These views suggest that individuals are negotiating and exercising agency in their work practices, albeit constrained in different degrees by the requirements of the workplace and conditions of their working lives. Through analyses of the working lives of three workers (Billett et al., 2004), then another five workers (Billett and Pavlova, 2005) over periods of six months and a year respectively, and then groups of workers in the same workplace (Billett et al., 2005) the following was noted: not only were these workers able to adapt to the changing circumstances of their work, but these changes, in the main, supported the individuals' personal workplace goals. For instance, changes in circumstances in a small business within a fruit and vegetable wholesaler permitted a casual part-time employee to establish a role for herself at work and in doing so realise her goal of securing an identity outside of the home, as a care giver to her children (Billett and Pavlova, 2005).

Also challenging the view advanced earlier about the disempowerment experienced by workers, survey data offers a different picture. For instance, surveys of Australian employees identify the contribution of workplace support for their workplace-based learning (ABS, 2002) to be at a higher level than their employers report providing it (ABS, 2003). This is surprising given that in a country which previously had a national training levy and required employers to report their expenditure to a prescribed level (or pay the equivalent in additional tax), employers may be under-reporting their learning support. Furthermore, as much learning support in the workplace is not always obvious or appreciated by employees, there might be an expectation that employees would under-report. The data across these two surveys then calls into question claims that contemporary workplaces are inherently hostile towards and non-supportive of employees.

Consequently, rather than seeing contemporary work as turbulent, inevitably disempowering and causing anxiety, the evidence from these studies suggests more differentiated outcomes. This is not to say that all workers are able to exercise discretion and secure workplace outcomes that are suited to and driven by the personal goals. However, the studies reported above challenge the view that all workers are inherently captive to the press of the immediate social experience, which at this time makes working life seem more insecure and less rewarding or supportive. In seeking to understand workers' engagement with their paid employment, the investigations of working life experiences, referred to in this section capture something of the role of individuals in negotiating the changing character of contemporary working life. They proceed in quite a different way from the studies reflecting social theories and based on more quantitative measures of the quality of working life. Although the small-scale investigations are only illustrative, referring to their specific populations rather then offering any kind of generalisation, they provide a particular and different perspective that warrants further consideration. In particular, it could be concluded that the accounts of contemporary working life provided through theoretical and objectively based socially derived measures may not be providing the complete picture of contemporary and emerging working life.

4.1   Changing work and its impacts

The perspectives discussed in the previous two sections offer quite different, although not always contradictory views of working life, and its consequences for workers. Each makes important contributions to under-standing work life. Yet, the gulf between them is such that there needs to be some reconciliation in order to advance a more comprehensive and viable account of work and working life. These distinctions are only reconcilable, in part, through an acceptance of their representing different levels of analysis or methods of analysis, or research orientations. They suggest something quite different in how we understand how individuals might come to experience, make sense of and engage in working life. Certainly the differences in these views suggest the need for a more comprehensive view of working life. On the one hand, and consistent with economic and sociological accounts of work, judgements about the worth of contemporary working life have been premised on objective and socially valued measures (e.g. level of remuneration, other benefits, employment security, opportunities for promotion). On the other hand, the more subjective accounts focusing on how work meets the needs and desires of individuals may provide a different kind of account. It seems that both kinds of accounts are important in particular ways. Yet, it is perhaps only when their contributions are integrated, attempts made to reconcile and examine them together that a fuller and more comprehensive account of contemporary working life and its impact upon individuals can be advanced.

Such a task requires engaging with theoretical and empirical work that can address the complexity and relatedness of the kinds of issues that have emerged in the overview presented above. In essence, it is necessary to understand and account for, firstly, the institutional facts that constitute the experience of work and working life that individuals encounter; secondly, the experience that individuals have in their encounters with paid work; and, thirdly, how the agency of the social and individual are negotiated through participation in working life, and the remaking of the work in which workers engage. At its heart, the central concern is to understand the relations between the socially structured world in which work and working life occur and how individuals make sense (construe), construct meaning and engage with the social world.

This task is set within an existing and long-standing debate within the social sciences about structure and agency, and their relations. This book has a particular purpose and focus for engaging in that debate and using its deliberations to elaborate a more comprehensive and complex understanding of work, working life and the processes of learning and remaking the cultural practice of work. The next section introduces this debate.

4.2   Interdependency between affordances and agency

The bases of relations between individuals' agency (i.e. their directed and intentional thinking and acting) and their engagement in social practice are multiple, complex and overlapping. In considering relations between the personal and social, Valsiner (1994) refers to the 'relatedness' between an individual's values and the mores of the social practice. Individuals' agentic actions are directed to sustaining and extending their work practice, for instance, in ways that are not always consistent with the goals of their workplace). The exercise of their agentic action might even lead individuals to disassociate or dis-identify with the practices (e.g. Hodges, 1998) of their workplace. Tensions arise when the kinds of participation individuals desire are not afforded by the workplace. A workers' pursuit of promotion and learning the kinds of skills required for promotion might be inhibited by workplace practices, resulted in tensions between the individuals' goals for the continuity of their practice and the workplace's practices that are directed to its continuity (e.g. the need for certain skills, numbers of workers, achieving service or production goals). For instance, in one study a qualified fitter employed as a production worker, was highly agentic in his efforts to become a fitter in this workplace. Yet he was frustrated by the lack of available positions and the greater he exercised his agency (e.g. following fitters to off-limit work areas) the more he eroded his prospects of achieving his goal, because he became perceived as a nuisance by the fitters and a risk by his supervisors.

Understanding further these reciprocal processes contributes to key discussions within psychological theorising about the relations between individual cognition and the socio-geneses of knowledge (e.g. Cobb, 1998; Rogoff, 1995; Scribner, 1997; Valsiner and Van de Veer, 2000). Valsiner (1994) refers to this process as the co-construction of knowledge, the reciprocal act of knowledge construction through which both the object and the subject are transformed. Analogously, engagement in work activities are held to be co-participative (Billett, 2004)—constituted by the relationship between how the work practice affords participation and how individuals elect to participate in the work practice and engage with what is afforded. More than just influencing engagement in work, these co-participative practices are also held to mediate individuals' learning (Billett, 2001a). That is, if change arises through engagement in goal-directed activity, the basis of that engagement (e.g. whether it was full-bodied or not), and the purposes of individuals' engagement (e.g. superficial compliance or relating to core interests) will influence the learning that transpires and how work is remade. When engaging in work individuals are both learning and remaking practice through the constructive processes that accompany their engagement.

This conception of co-participation may help to understand the emerging concepts of the social geneses of human cognition. This is because these conceptual premises assist understanding how: (a) the social practice (e.g. workplace) affords opportunities for participation, learning and remaking practice; (b) individuals' decisions to engage in social practice influence their learning; and (c) the interdependent relations between (a) and (b) make useful contributions to understanding the relations between social practice and individuals' learning through work.

5.   UNDERSTANDING WORK AND WORKERS

From the discussions above, it is important to understand paid work both as an institutional fact (Searle, 1995) that individuals will encounter, and experience its changes and transformations, as well as something which is experienced more subjectively by individuals. Commencing by considering work as an institutional fact, it is possible to identify three dimensions of the changing character of work likely to be experienced in the contemporary world of work and which cannot be wished away.

5.1   Changes in work

There are changes to the kinds of work to be done and participation in occupational categories that reflect this work. Some industries and occupations are in the ascendancy, as employment in them flourishes, and the scope of their applications broadens. Others are in decline or changing forms. There are also changes to what constitutes the categories of work. Technical work may need to be redefined, for instance, as diverse forms of work embrace information technology, thereby potentially rendering individuals increasingly as technicians (Barley, 1996). However, other forms of work are being discarded as they are no longer required (e.g. hot metal printing, watch repairing), or have been transformed in ways that makes existing skills redundant (e.g. typesetting). The cultural practices that comprise paid work are in need of transformation when cultural need changes. Shifting demands for particular kinds of work are likely to reflect changes in cultural needs, albeit initiated by technical innovation, new forms of social organisation or new and emerging cultural needs.

5.2   Changes in work participation

How individuals participate in work is also in transformation in current times. Full-time workers are working longer and with greater intensity in many countries. Consequently, for instance, there is a need for older workers to maintain their competence as workers, even in the face of a societal preference for youth that is reflected in how enterprises distribute their resources for developing workers' skills. Workers with disabilities are also participating in the workforce. Yet again their participation is complicated by their need to be seen as competent without making too many demands upon their employers (Church, 2004). Women workers are now almost a majority in many Western nations' workforces, yet still experience lower wages and poorer (Jacobsen, 2004). Moreover, it seems a greater percentage of the workforce is now involuntarily contingent (part-time, contracted and temporary) even in buoyant labour markets.

Also, and compared with previous times, more work is perhaps being conducted in relative social and geographical isolation, such as from home. Consequently, the kinds of engagement between workers and workplaces are being transformed. While employers exercise less of an interest in an individual's progression and development because of the breakdown of (traditional) relations between workers and employers (Carnoy, 1999), employees themselves may well be exercising a greater commitment to managing more uncertain work lives. That is, the 'enterprising self' and efforts directed to being oneself through work is now replacing the concept of the faithful and loyal employee, particularly when work and workers are contingent.

5.3   Changing work performance requirements

It follows from the previous two factors that the requirements for performing effectively in working life are also changing. The capacities and competencies that individuals require to be effective in their work practice are being transformed by the different means of conducting and organising work, as well as the specific occupational skills required to achieve work goals. As the organisation of work and its requirements change, as cultural need proposes particular ways of working, the use of technology and the knowledge, practices and capacities or ways of knowing required for work also change. Certainly, the debate about whether work is being up-skilled or down-skilled by technology and new ways of working is still open to debate, because it differs widely and is person-dependant in part. However, given the frequency of change, work tasks are likely to be less routine, yet more intense, complex and requiring greater levels of interactions with others and artefacts, which all bring additional demands.

These sets of changes reflect the world of work that individuals will encounter as presented by social theory and research that identifies significant trends in the changing nature of contemporary work. However, there is also a need to consider the more subjective experience that arises from these conditions and, importantly, the negotiations between the two that constitute an individual's experience of work, and how they participate in and learn about work.

6.   WORK AS RELATIONAL INTERDEPENDENCE

Contemporary work and workers can be seen as comprising a relational interdependence between the institutional facts that constitute the work individuals encounter and how these are shaped as individuals participate in work. This is not to posit the individual against the social, because individuals are socially shaped, albeit uniquely through an idiosyncratic set of experiences. Instead, this interdependence is characterised not so much by a strong emphasis on either the social institutions that comprise the sites for paid work or an individual's vocational practice but in terms of a dualistic interdependence between the two.

Indeed, rather than being reciprocal or mutual, these relationships are negotiated and differ in intensity: they are relational (Billett, 2003a). For one worker, the workplace may well be highly invitational and supportive of their development and career progression. As a result, this individual may elect to engage effortfully in the workplace. They might also take advantage of their privileged position. For another worker, the same workplace might afford fewer opportunities, perhaps being denied what others are granted and excluded from opportunities for maintaining the currency of their skills let alone developing them further. This worker may elect to withdraw and only participate reluctantly or strategically for their own purposes. Conversely, they might engage effortfully and intensely to secure opportunities and acknowledgement despite the limited affordances being advanced. Importantly, the interdependence between socially constructed individuals and socially constructed workplaces is central to the continuity of both. That is, both individual development and the making of cultural practices that comprise paid work activities, depend upon the interaction between the individual and social contributions. The social suggestion is not comprehensive enough, pervasive nor uniformly applicable to secure socialised outcomes. Therefore, if for no other reason, individuals are required to be agentic to understand what is being proposed socially and in enacting and remaking what is encountered in work.

Of course, the issues addressed in discussing work and workers are wide, diverse and differentiated. While it is necessary to refer to work and workers in general terms, this risks masking the diversity of work, workers and working lives. The ideas in this book are drawn from national surveys of employment patterns, accounts of work based on specific instances, and detailed analyses of individuals' working lives. Yet as Darrah (1997) proposed, work can be so diverse as to obviate generalisations about its requirements. This sentiment can be extended to categories of work, categories of workers and the diverse circumstances of individuals' working lives, and the bases by which workers construct meaning within their working lives. So while the accounts of work presented here, can at best be selective, partial and notably incomplete, an attempt has been made to not restrict the analysis to just the so-called objective accounts of work and working life. Instead, richer accounts of individuals' working lives need including in consideration of work, work life and how it is transformed.

7.   STRUCTURE OF THE BOOK

This book seeks to understand the contemporary and changing experience of work. It comprises four sections. Following the introductory chapter, the second section, *Social and individual bases for understanding work life*, establishes the conceptual case for understanding the requirements for work and its transformation. Its three chapters focus on the cultural, social and individual genesis of knowledge required for work (Chapter 2: Cultural, situational and individual geneses of work life); an elaboration of the relational interdependence between social and individual factors (Chapter 3: A relational basis for understanding working life); and conceptions of the worth of work (Chapter 4: The worth of work).

The third section of the book, *Changing concepts and requirements of work,* has four chapters which focus on the changing availability and categorisations of paid work (Chapter 5: Changes in available work); practices of participation in work (Chapter 6: Changing participation in work); character of those participating in work (Chapter 7: Changing composition of paid workforces); and the requirements for work performance (Chapter 8: Changing requirements for work performance).

The fourth section of the book, *Describing and elaborating work,* consists of three chapters. The first offers a framework to describe and illuminate work (Chapter 9: A framework for describing work), the next elaborates the factors shaping working life (Chapter 10: Changing work practice and work requirements: Case studies), with the conceptual contributions synthesised in the final chapter (Chapter 11: Work, learning and identity).

This first chapter—Work, change and workers—has aimed to outline the case for the need for and an approach to examine changing work and the experience of work for workers (i.e. changing workers). It has argued that without an understanding of relationships between the changing character of work and the changing basis by which individuals engage in work in Western economies, work and working life will remain misunderstood and unclear. In this way, the chapter outlines what constitutes work, how work practice might best proceed, on what bases individuals engage in work and learn through work. The chapter has also introduced the conceptual terrain that is traversed within the book and foreshadows the case it makes throughout. In particular, relations between the social and the individual are held to be a way of understanding the contributions of both and how they are negotiated between the agency of the social and the individual through working life.

7.1   Structuring of chapters

The structuring of each chapter and sections of this book are premised on the assumption that few readers will work through the text in a linear fashion. Rather, it is assumed that readers will focus on areas of specific interest. Consequently, each chapter is intended to be largely self sufficient, as in the structure and organisation of a chapter within an edited collection. Hence, each chapter provides examples and instances of concepts, which may well be repeated elsewhere. Moreover, the sections of the book em-phasise particular interests. The first section comprises conceptual accounts which are illuminated through the use of examples, trails of which can be found in other sections. The second section comprises the products of a broadly based review of literature on work and work life. The third section focuses more strongly on empirical evidence. In order to assist the reader utilise the contents of the book to greatest effect, in addition to the contents pages and index to guide the reader to particular areas of interest, notes are made about were else within the book particular concepts can be found.

This means that, if you read across the chapters in a linear fashion there may be some instances of repetition and redundancy. However, the structure and design of the book is intended to accommodate what is assumed to be the most likely use of the book: selective and targeted engagement with its contents.

SECTION 2: SOCIAL AND INDIVIDUAL BASES FOR UNDERSTANDING WORK LIFE

The second section is entitled 'Social and individual bases for understanding work life'. It establishes the conceptual case for understanding the requirements for work and its transformation. Its three chapters focus on the cultural, social and individual genesis of knowledge required for work (Chapter 2); an elaboration of the relational interdependence between social and individual factors (Chapter 3); and conceptions of the worth of work (Chapter 4).

Chapter 2—Cultural, situational and individual geneses of work life—proposes that, in order to understand the requirements for work, their transforming character and the factors that shape their manifestation in a particular workplace setting, it is important to understand the historical and cultural genesis of that knowledge, and situational factors that shape work life and its transformation. The knowledge required for work, it is proposed, arises from the practices and services that are required by cultures to meet their needs. This knowledge has developed over time, and therefore has historical bases. Yet, as cultural need changes, so do the requirements for work. Changing requirements lead to particular kinds of work becoming more or less available, and to the kinds of workers and their means of engaging with work changing. Therefore, these requirements are inherently dynamic. It is only in their enactment in a particular workplace that the requirements are manifested in practice. So, what counts as competence in particular workplace settings is likely to be highly situational. However, beyond situational requirements there is also what counts as competence for the individual. That is, there is also a personal dimension to conceptions of competence and what constitutes work performance, as well as the learning and remaking of the work practices that individuals engage in.

Chapter 3—A relational basis for understanding work life—elaborates the bases for considering work, vocations and identity as having both social and cultural, and individual dimensions. Importantly, the chapter proposes that what constitutes work, vocations and identity needs to be understood in terms of relations between social perceptions and individual agency and intentionality. Vocations, drawing upon Dewey (1916), are held to be life directions whose meaning is found not wholly in social classifications of worth but in individuals' goals and aspirations. They constitute life directions and, as such, can have significance for individuals, and how they construe, participate in and remake work practices. While individuals' sense of vocations and work identity may be important it is also relational insofar as how individuals may elect to exercise their agency in their paid work. Another relational dimension is that of workers' struggle to overcome their contingent work status. The degree by which they might have to exercise their agency and the constraints that they might have to confront, likely have an array of relational dimensions. For instance, given that workplaces are highly contested environments the exercise of individuals' agentic action will be relational to the kinds of workplace affordances (i.e. support and interactions) that they might experience. Beyond these cultural and situational factors, and at a more general level is the ongoing everyday process of engaging in and making sense of experiences encountered in working life. These experiences are not construed and constructed in uniform ways. Instead, they are shaped by what individuals know and how they perceive these experiences.

Chapter 4—The worth of work—discusses perspectives on how work might be valued. It proposes going beyond the consideration of a set of societally-sanctioned occupational hierarchies as a means to value work. Instead, it is proposed that there are values based perspectives, those of the communities in which individuals live and work, those associated with benefits accrued to individuals and the worth of work to individuals' sense of self and identity. These perspectives are offered as an adjunct to the relational argument that is being made throughout the book. They emphasise the different bases by which societal press and individual agency might motivate and guide individuals' engagement in work and its associations with their needs to participate in paid employment. Ultimately, both the more objective and relational premises for understanding work and work life emerge as important bases for knowing and valuing the worth of work.

Chapter 2

CULTURAL, SITUATIONAL AND INDIVIDUAL GENESES OF WORK LIFE

> Work forms the bedrock of all economic systems. When the nature and social organisation of work change, so does the fabric of society. (Barley and Orr, 1997: 1)

To understand the requirements for work and work life, their transforming character and the factors that shape their manifestation and transformation in a particular workplace setting, it is important to understand the historical and cultural genesis of the knowledge required for work and the situational factors that shape the enactment and transformation of work, and also how individuals construe and construct that knowledge. The knowledge required for work and working life arises from the practices and services that are required by cultures (i.e. particular countries) to meet their needs. It has developed over time, and therefore has historical bases. As cultural needs change so do the requirements for work. The changing requirements lead to particular kinds of work becoming more or less available with the means of engaging in work also changing, as are the kinds of people who are working. All this leads to work requirements—the capacities required for work—that are inherently dynamic. Yet, it is only in their enactment in a particular workplace that these requirements are manifest in practice and can be understood.

So, what counts as work requirements in particular workplace settings is likely to be both dynamic and highly situational. However, beyond socially objective views of work and issues associated with what counts as competence for the individual, there is a need to consider more personally subjective accounts of what constitutes work and working life for those engaged in it. That is, there is also a personal dimension to these conceptions. This chapter sets out to elaborate the historical, cultural and situational origins of the requirements for work and their transformations. They are discussed, with consideration to the role of individuals in that process, in order to more fully understand changing work and work requirements from the subjective perspective of individuals and more objective accounts of work.

1.   CULTURAL AND SITUATIONAL GENESES OF WORK KNOWLEDGE

In considering how best to understand the requirements for work and work life in particular occupations and how they change over time, there is a need to account for and elaborate the historical, cultural and situational geneses of the knowledge required for vocational practice at the occupational, situational and individual level. This is because the knowledge required for performance in work reflects a historically derived cultural need that is generative of occupational requirements and their transformation over time. Yet, although shaped by cultural need, judgments about require ments for work performance are situated in particular workplaces and work settings. These represent their manifestation of the vocational practice as shaped by localised factors and constraints. This situational perspective becomes prominent because the actual requirements for work and their change over time are socially and culturally situated (Resnick, Säljö, Pontecorvo and Burge, 1997). So, beyond cultural and historical development there will be particular sets of localised social factors that shape the requirements for work performance and their transformation: how they are both enacted and remade.

1.1   Socio-historic genesis of work knowledge

To understand the nature of work and performance at work it is necessary to account for the historical and sociocultural practices that have led to the need for culturally distinct activities (Scribner, 1985b), referred to here as vocations or occupations. How people learn the kinds of knowledge required to perform occupations is culturally shaped since beyond involuntary behaviours, higher order capacities required for work are socially shaped (Vygotsky, 1987; Wertsch, 1991). In particular, the Vygotskian view holds that higher orders of knowledge are culturally sourced, rather than a product of individual biological determination or highly individualistic constructivism. Because of their origins, securing these forms of knowledge is likely to require interactions with social partners and sources (e.g. language, tools and artefacts). Consequently, the social basis for vocational knowledge is central to understanding the requirements of work and working life as it: (i) informs how the practice itself is shaped by social factors; (ii) its requirements for performance; and (iii) the means by which individuals are likely to learn the knowledge required to perform at work. The sociocultural constructivist approach provides a way of understanding the complex of historical, cultural and situational factors that shape work life, its geneses and means of transformation. It is explained as follows.

> The basic tenet of the sociocultural approach to mind is that human mental functioning is inherently situated in social interactional, cultural, institutional and historical contexts. Such a tenet contrasts with approaches that assume implicitly or explicitly, that it is possible to examine mental processes such as thinking or memory independently of the sociocultural setting in which individuals and groups function. (Wertsch, 1991: 85)

In this way, a sociocultural constructivist approach emphasises the need to engage and interact with social sources of knowledge that comprise the social gift of work and individuals engagement in and learning of it.

2. SOURCES OF CHANGES TO WORK LIFE REQUIREMENTS

Sociocultural constructivist theory proposes that the activities individuals engage in have historical and cultural geneses. Four lines of development are advanced within this theory (Cole, 1998; Rogoff, 1990; Scribner, 1985b): (i) phylogenetic—the evolving history of the human species; (ii) sociocultural—development that reflects a particular cultural need; (iii) microgenetic—the moment-through-moment learning occurring as individuals engage with the social world; and (iv) ontogeneses—the development of individuals' knowledge throughout their life histories (Scribner, 1985b). These have been augmented by including in this scheme the situated level of practice—its genesis (Billett, 1998, 2001b), manifestation of cultural practice (Suchman, 1997a) and contributions to learning (Engeström and Middleton, 1996; Goodnow, 1996; Lave, 1993; Rogoff, 1995). Together, these five lines of development offer bases for appraising how competence in working life is constituted and enacted in practice and learnt. In other words, how the requirements for work are formulated, constituted, remade and transformed. Figure 2.1 depicts relations between these lines of development. It positions the phylogenetic level as being supra-cultural: across cultures. At the next level, sociocultural development reflects the particular practices (e.g., tools, norms and processes as manifested by that practice) required to meet cultural needs. However, these requirements are manifested in a particular work practice, comprising a particular complex of situational factors. It is at this level, that individuals negotiate meaning and remake practice. For the individual, this is the source of their ongoing ontogenetic development.

2.1   Phylogenetic level of development

The knowledge required for work is one part of the evolving and cumulative efforts of humans to know and act. The phylogenetic level of development represents the accumulated and evolving knowledge and practices of human development: the development of the species (which Vygotsky and Baldwin aimed to transform from a biological to social concept (Valsiner, 1998)). The accumulation of knowledge at the phylo-genetic level likely has applicability across a range of cultural activities. For instance, the human need for communicating has led to the purposes and practice of literacy, as has the need for calculations led to mathematics, which are applied in different ways across cultures.

Cultures require and employ oral and written communication forms, including rules for organising language and writing. This is because these concepts and practices have to be enacted to achieve a manifestation. Yet this enactment is shaped in particular ways by factors that influence their enactment at that particular point in time and place. For instance, the culture and genre of the particular focus of communication serve to shape and constrain the particular form of language use and its rules for practice. Equally, calculations while containing universal processes (i.e. adding, subtraction, multiplication, division) are shaped by the purposes and forms. The requirement for a vocational practice such as caring for the health of others arise historically and might include the heuristics of diagnosing a condition before responding with treatment, or the evolving concept of hygienic practice being economical for all health care practices. However, while contributing to how work will be conducted through the development and carriage of particular sets of practices, goals and values, these need to be understood within the context of particular cultural practices that constitute the occupations individuals engage in and where these evolving concepts and practices are manifested.

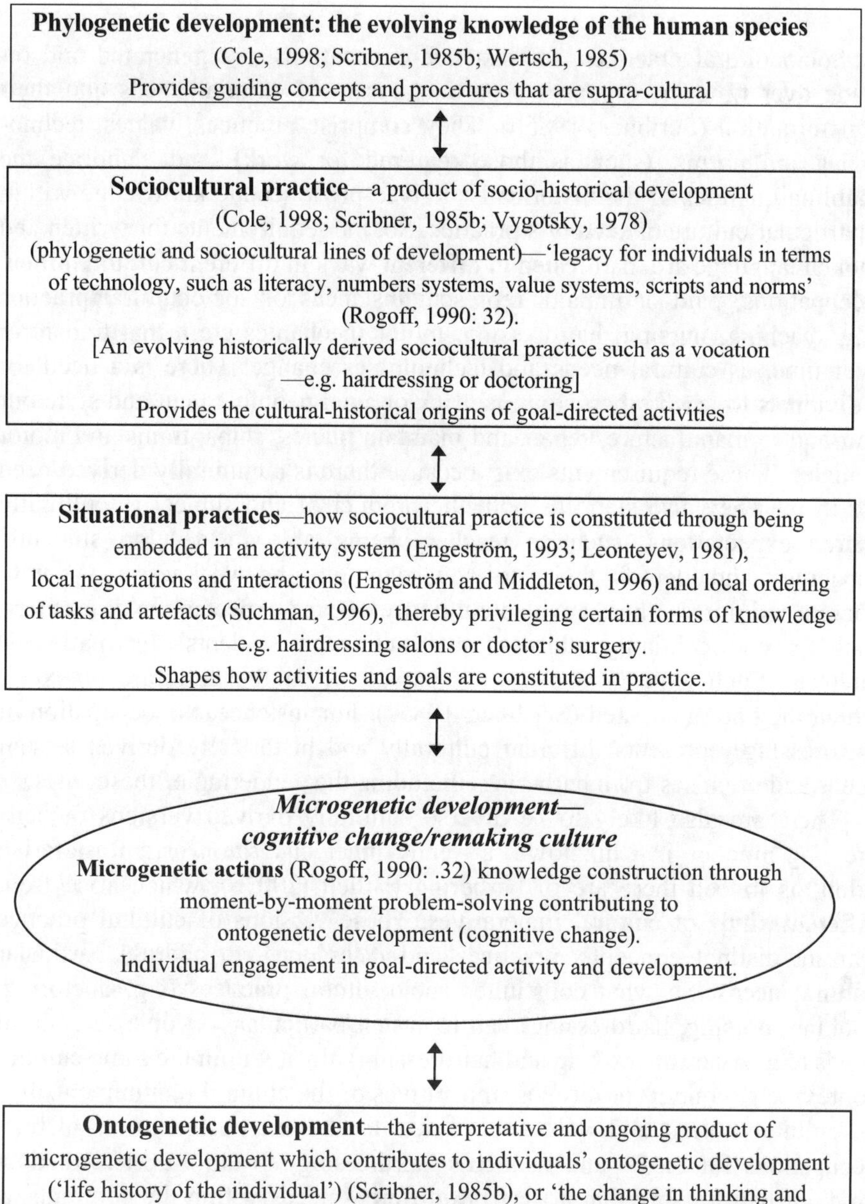

Phylogenetic development: the evolving knowledge of the human species
(Cole, 1998; Scribner, 1985b; Wertsch, 1985)
Provides guiding concepts and procedures that are supra-cultural

Sociocultural practice—a product of socio-historical development
(Cole, 1998; Scribner, 1985b; Vygotsky, 1978)
(phylogenetic and sociocultural lines of development)—'legacy for individuals in terms of technology, such as literacy, numbers systems, value systems, scripts and norms'
(Rogoff, 1990: 32).
[An evolving historically derived sociocultural practice such as a vocation
—e.g. hairdressing or doctoring]
Provides the cultural-historical origins of goal-directed activities

Situational practices—how sociocultural practice is constituted through being embedded in an activity system (Engeström, 1993; Leonteyev, 1981),
local negotiations and interactions (Engeström and Middleton, 1996) and local ordering of tasks and artefacts (Suchman, 1996), thereby privileging certain forms of knowledge
—e.g. hairdressing salons or doctor's surgery.
Shapes how activities and goals are constituted in practice.

Microgenetic development—
cognitive change/remaking culture
Microgenetic actions (Rogoff, 1990: .32) knowledge construction through
moment-by-moment problem-solving contributing to
ontogenetic development (cognitive change).
Individual engagement in goal-directed activity and development.

Ontogenetic development—the interpretative and ongoing product of microgenetic development which contributes to individuals' ontogenetic development
('life history of the individual') (Scribner, 1985b), or 'the change in thinking and behaving arising in the history of individuals' (Rogoff, 1990: 32)
Mediates participation in goal-directed activity.

Figure 2-1. The sociogeneses and remaking of vocational practice

2.2   Sociocultural practice

Sociocultural practices, for instance occupations, are generated and remade over time in response to particular sets of cultural needs and their
transformation (Scribner, 1985b). They comprise practices, values, technologies and norms, (such as those required for work), and elaborate the
enabling qualities of the historically derived phylogenetic knowledge within
a particular culture or society's practice. So, the requirements for written and
spoken language are manifested in different ways in different cultural milieu.
Occupations, paid or unpaid, represent instances of sociocultural practice
(e.g. teaching, nursing, hairdressing, motor mechanics etc.). that transform
over time, as cultural needs and technologies change. There is a need for
individuals to teach others, to nurse sick or aged people, to cut and style our
hair and to manufacture, repair and maintain planes, ships, trains and motor
vehicles. These requirements exist because there is a culturally derived need
for them. They also stand as both the product of and subject to culturally
shared expectations, such as teachers being able to develop students'
capacities, and identify their individual strength and weaknesses. As with
doctors and nurses, there are also culturally derived expectations of teachers,
such as confidentiality, fairness and acting in students' (or patients')
interests. Such expectations are inseparable from the cultural context in
which they are generated (Scribner, 1985a). For instance, the occupation of
hairdressing represents different culturally and historically derived sets of
needs and premises from barbering, including the gendering of these roles.

There are also likely to be diverse culturally derived versions of hairdressing practice in Chinatown, a trendy inner city salon or a Rastafarian
salon, as indeed there are of barbering (Billett, 2003b), which arise from
different kinds of cultural imperatives. These versions of cultural practice
warrant distinct concepts, practices and techniques, to address particular
cultural needs. So what constitutes sociocultural practices (e.g. doctoring,
cooking, nursing, hairdressing) can represent particular, yet diverse cultural
needs (e.g. styles of cooking and hairdressing) albeit within the same cultural
context (e.g. country or city) as imperatives of the cultural requirement. Just
as cultural norms and values have led to the establishment of distinct
occupations for men's and women's hairdressing, so too are there distinct
kinds of hairdressing that arise from different needs within the community.
Taking this example a step further, as the population of a particular
community changes it is easy to understand how the requirements for paid
work change (see Chapter 5). For instance, as younger men begin to frequent
hairdressing salons for treatments that are not provided in barbershops, there
may well be a decline in the number of barbering jobs. However, this trend
might be reversed if hairstyles change back to shorter and simpler styles that

can be performed through barbering. Similarly, as a growing number of individuals in the community want particular or diverse kinds of food, the scope of food preparation and the skills required for preparing food might change, leading to a demand for some skills and a decline in others.

Consequently, the sociocultural level of development provides an important basis for considering the dynamic requirements for work and work practice, perhaps most commonly understood as an occupation. What actually constitutes the requirement for an occupation within a particular country, for instance, is used for the regulation of practice and learning of that occupation. The requirements to be a teacher, electrician, doctor, or nurse are codified and need to be met by novices before they are permitted to practice independently. The level of codification is likely to be premised upon factors associated with the risks to the community associated with its conduct. So, some forms are work are required to be certified (e.g. electricians, pilots, doctors and nurses) whereas some other occupations are not.

Moreover, it is these requirements generated at this sociocultural level (e.g. within a country) that are used to organise and regulate the access to and learning of an occupation. For instance, surveys of the skills required for occupations are gathered to produce standards and curriculum for the preparation of these occupations. Some occupations are seen as having higher or lower status in the community; with their standing being shaped by community values and norms. These socially constructed measures of status will likely differ across cultures and in different ways at different times (see also Chapter Eight). For instance, doctors' work is seen to be high status in most communities. In some cultures, the work of dentists is seen as being of lower status than doctors. Yet, even within a category of occupations, skilled workers such as trades people (e.g. carpenters, plumbers, builders, steelworkers, hairdressers) enjoy different status across and within countries. For instance, in the countries in northern Europe (Germany, Switzerland, Austria) some trade work is held in higher esteem probably than in countries such as Britain and Australia. Yet, there are also likely to be differences in the standing of trades work with a hierarchy based more on a cultural valuing than an objective assessment of relative skills. For instance, electricians and plumbers are often seen as high status trades, while hairdressing and barbering are seen to have lower status in some countries, yet may be valued by some young people in the community (e.g. the numbers of young women who want to be hairdressers).

Then, there are strong and enduring societal and cultural sentiments that prefer office-based occupations to those that have a connotation of manual work. So, the distinction between 'white-collar' (i.e. clerical, administrative and managerial) and 'blue-collar' (i.e. manual, trade) work emphasizes the erroneous, but popular distinction between mental and manual work. For instance, Cho and Apple (1998) report how the government in Korea attempted to encourage more young people to work in manufacturing because of difficulties in securing an adequate workforce. However, manufacturing work was seen as unfashionable by many young people and undesirable by many parents and teachers. Their study reports how government efforts to increase the labour force for manufacturing were stifled by the actions of parents and teachers. So, while some young Koreans followed the advice of parents and teachers and sought clerical work, some elected to engage in manufacturing work, but for personal goals such as earning sufficient funds to travel overseas.

Thus, the sociocultural level of development articulates a need for a particular occupation, its standing and critical requirements within a particular cultural context, yet is subject to factors that shape their standing and transformation. The means for this cultural need to be enacted are supported by concepts and practices that have evolved over time through practice and are often quite robust because there have been tested and refined through practice over time. Yet, this level of development, because it expresses cultural needs and requirements, is subject to change as technologies transform and the requirements for securing occupational goals are modified. It represents a dynamic form of practice that has particular meaning within a culture, community or nation.

However, while informing about particular values, practices and expectations, the sociocultural level remains disembedded from actual practice within a workplace. Ultimately, although shaped by cultural need, practices and norms, situational factors shape how a culturally-derived occupational practice is constituted and enacted in particular work contexts (Billett, 2001b), as are the performance requirements (see Chapter 8). Each workplace represents a unique instance of a vocational practice that is a product of historical development and changing cultural need yet is constituted by a particular and transforming set of situational factors. These permit the manifestation of practice in a particular workplace's setting.

2.3   Situational factors

Given the array of factors that shape its enactment (e.g. individuals, division of labour, clients, location, layout etc) it is not surprising that a hairdressing practice in a particular salon at a particular point in time is in some ways a unique instance of culturally-derived occupational practice shaped by situational factors (Billett, 2001b). In an investigation of work activities in four hairdressing salons, the goals for and bases of participation in hairdressing work were determined by factors comprising the internal press of the workplace and external demands of the client community (Billett, 2003b). In each salon, the goals for hairdressing had distinctive features. Given the same set of hairdressing problems to resolve, hairdressers in each salon fashioned responses that had consistency across and within the salons, yet with some significant individual variations. Therefore, some components of the responses were consonant with the goals and norms of the sociocultural practice (i.e. the historically derived practices of hairdressing), while others were products of the particular salons (i.e. situational manifestations of practice—'what we do here is') or some idiosyncrasies arising from the hairdressers' personal histories or ontogenies.

Observations revealed the diverse characteristics of what comprised the performance requirements for vocational practice in each salon. In a fashionable inner city salon, the key goals for performance were to transform the client's appearance, and to offer new cuts and colours. The interactions with clients in this salon were a product of the types of clientele and the interests and values (lifestyle) of the hairdressers. In a salon in a low socioeconomic suburb, the requirements for performance were to manage a precarious business with an absent owner, two part-time senior hairdressers and a clientele that included those who demanded complex treatments, yet did not subsequently care for their hair. A key requirement was to manage these 'awkward' customers when they returned complaining vociferously and forcefully about their treatments. In another salon, the clientele comprised elderly women who came for companionship as much as for hair treatments. Here, the hairdressers' knowledge of clients' personal histories, knowing the names and circumstances of family and friends, was an important component of practice. The fourth salon was in a provincial town in a rural region that was enduring a three-year drought. The goals here included providing good value to maintain the clientele and managing the difficult balance between eliciting additional service (colours and perms) yet not causing clients to choose between the cost of a hair treatment and groceries for home.

The factors that constitute the work practice within each of the salons were identifiable by and may be explained through their activity systems (Leonteyev, 1987; Engeström, 1993) that include the division of labour, rules and norms, relationships with the client community and degree of internal cohesion. Each site had particular goals associated with the division of labour. For example, one salon had a division of labour based around the principle that hairdressers should engage in tasks whose complexity was most consistent with their level of skills, as the hairdressers became available on completing a work task. This was part of the particular work practice insisted upon by the owner-manager and resulted in clients frequently being attended to by a posse of different hairdressers during a treatment. In this hairdressing salon, there was a need for each hairdresser to monitor the progress and requirements of all of the clients in the salon, and work collaboratively with the other hairdressers. While at the salon in the low socio-economic suburb, disagreements among the staff about their conception of hairdressing were subordinated by common concerns about the 'awkward' clients and security of employment.

Indeed, how these common views were negotiated also differed across the social practices. For example, in the trendy salon there were common values about hairdressing that were different from the almost familial atmosphere of another salon, which had its own distinctive mores and values. In a third, there was a rigid form of internal press associated with the authority and presence of the owner-manager. For instance, the hairdressers operated under the owner's rule of 'no-yappers'—the hairdressing was to proceed in silence unless clients initiated conversations. The hairdressers in this salon, the one in which hairdressers frequently swapped in dealing with clients, developed a set of signals by which they communicated non-verbally. These mores led to particular work strategies being developed and practised in this salon, some primarily associated with responding to the idiosyncratic demands of the owner. The work in this salon progressed in comparative silence compared with the exchanges that occurred in the other salons and were almost in contradiction to the hairdressers' work requirements in the salon that catered to elderly women. In these ways, local negotiations (Suchman, 1996) determined the goals for and practices of the particular workplace (see also Chapter 8).

Similar situation-specific notions of practice requirements were observable in open-cut coalmines (Billett, 1994). Even across mines owned by the same company, some of them on adjacent leases, there were different requirements for performance. These were premised on the history of ownership, different demarcations of work, historically entrenched work practices, the mine's age and the mine's location in the coal-bearing basin. Consequently, conceptions of expert performance are not uniform across workplaces, with the differences being accounted for by the activity systems of the communities of work practice.

But more than stipulating the requirements for work, the workplace norms and practices also shape the workplace's participatory practices: that is what and how individuals are invited to participate in and how they elect to engage (Billett, 2002a; Billett et al., 2004). The work practice in each hairdressing salon afforded quite different access to novices and experienced hairdressers alike and made different demands, with different consequences, for what they learnt. One variable was size. In smaller salons, the apprentices had responsibility for a wider range of activities earlier than in the larger ones. Another was the culture of practice (Brown, Collins and Duguid,

1989), manifested as the division of labour. In the trendy salon, each hairdresser worked on their own clients from greeting them at the door to getting them coffee, washing their hair, negotiating with them about and styling their hair. So it was incumbent on the apprentice in this salon to take sole responsibility for clients as soon as possible. In another salon, key work tasks were divided among the hairdressers, and the apprentices were more focused on support and preparatory activities until their final year. There was also a privileging of particular knowledge amongst settings (Goodnow, 1990), some of which remained the sole domain of principal participants. For example, two owner-managers maintained control over the ordering and management of stock. Therefore, in these salons, even senior hairdressers were denied this experience. Yet, at another salon, the apprentice's role included checking and ordering stock. Consequently, although engaged in a common sociocultural practice, the salons not only had quite different requirements for expertise, but how they afforded participation to workers also differed.

Similarly, for medical practice, the location (e.g. rural town, inner-city suburb, retirement community, remote Aboriginal community), its objects (e.g. characteristics of patients in terms of health, age, dispositions), how the practice is organised (e.g. shared practice, community-based, availability of doctors in rural settings), and its location are all likely to shape how the medical practice is enacted, and, therefore its requirements for and means of enactment. Hence, culturally derived vocational practice only finds tangible form when enacted in particular workplaces. Being competent or a vocational expert, it follows, is linked to the ability to perform effectively in a particular instance of work practice and at a particular point in time.

Yet, more than the situational factors that shape the historically-derived norms and practices, it is through individuals engaging in work that work-place requirements are performed, refined and: remade. While there may exist social suggestions and press, manifested as particular practice (i.e. the culture of practice), it is an individual's understanding, appraisal and enactment of those tasks that constitutes how work is performed. So what constitutes situational factors are not solely the product of local social factors and forms. They also include individuals' subjective experiences of what they encounter, how they negotiate that and elect to participate in the work practice. In different ways, these experiences contribute to the situated practice, as exercise of personal preferences, capacities and agency, also shapes the work practice, hence the requirements for performance and its remaking.

In keeping with the concept of microgenetic development—moment by moment learning (Rogoff, 1990), the remaking and transformation of the practice occurs through these practitioners' participation in and construction

of their work. Both individual learning and the remaking and transformation
of the particular practice occur through the process of individuals engaging
in work tasks. For instance, it was found that a grief counsellor was able to
transform the practice at his workplace to include a personal preference for
face-to-face counselling, instead of phone counselling (Billett et al., 2004).
Similarly, it has been identified that other workers across diverse forms
of work have been able to shape their workplace practices in particular
ways (Billett et al., 2005). Consequently, it is important to understand the
intersection between the socially suggested requirements for work and the
engagement of individuals taking up of that work, through which they learn
and develop ontogentically and remake their work, through microgenetic
processes.

2.4   Microgenetic and ontogenetic development

Individuals' experience of engagement in work and their re-making of
it comprise inter-psychological processes that are socially sourced and
negotiated. They arise in situated practice from moment by moment
engagement or microgenetic development (Rogoff, 1990). These collectively
contribute to individuals' capacities and attributes over time: their ontogenetic development. More than performing work tasks, individuals acquire
a legacy in the form of cognitive and affective change referred to as intra-
psychological outcomes. That is, beyond deploying cognitive resources in
thinking and acting, their enactment also shapes and changes individuals'
capacities and ways of knowing (i.e. cognitive experience). A midwife
practising in a birth centre reports that through working closely with birthing
mothers over time, she developed a nuanced understanding of their progress in
the birthing process (Billett, 1999). She claims her understanding and ways of
knowing are quite distinct from gynecologists who are less engaged in the
entire birthing process, and are often most focused on difficult births. Such
experiences also shape how individuals engage in work and working life. Yet,
the construals comprising interactions between social and individual agency
will be based on individuals' cognitive experience, constituting earlier experiences. These experiences and the construal of subsequent experiences are
unlikely to be uniform. Each individual's construal of the concepts and
procedures associated with work and work practices is a product of their
personal histories and is particular in some ways (Billett, 2003b). Moreover,
some groups of individuals might construe what they experience based on the
way they or their cohort is treated. Disabled workers, for instance, face distinct
challenges in engaging in and maintaining their capacity to participate in work
effectively (Church, 2004), including at times needing to remain invisible and

not making too many demands lest they be characterised as liabilities in the workplace.

In this way, the requirements for work performance are generated historically, culturally and situationally, yet are negotiated, deployed and remade through the interaction between what is provided by society's gifts (Archer, 2000) and individuals' agency and subjectivity. Therefore, understanding the requirements for work and their transformation is not a product of just the immediate social circumstances (i.e. the workplace), and cultural needs and practices (i.e. the occupation), but a rich interplay between personal histories and situational factors.

In sum, the specific meaning of work is located in its embedded form: the particular instance of work practice. Disembedded concepts and generalisable procedures of an occupation exist and play important and necessary roles that are not wholly constrained by particular work situations. While the historically and culturally derived concepts and procedures of occupations are necessary components for performance in the workplace, on their own they are not sufficient to describe and elaborate the requirements for actual performance and their transformation. Instead, the applicability of these historically and culturally derived concepts and procedures, judgments about their worth, the classification of expertise, the pathways towards expertise and performance itself are manifested in and need to be understood in a particular workplace setting or work practice. Barley and Orr (1997: 15) come to a similar conclusion: "Because the clusters of attributes that define technical work depend on doing of the work, we think the most appropriate strategy is to study its practice."

Barley and Orr (1997) emphasise the enactment of work within an observable and enacted instance of practice. Similarly, Garfinkel (1990:77) observes that the localised and enacted qualities of practice stand as key bases for understanding phenomena such as the requirements for work performance: "Every topic of logic, order, reason, meaning, and method is to be discovered and is discoverable, and is re-specified and re-specifiable only as *locally produced* naturally accountable phenomena of order." Therefore, although a work practice at the situational level (Lave and Wenger, 1991) stands as a likely basis for analysis, there is also a need to consider individuals' contributions to that setting or practice: how they construe, engage in and reshape the practice. Such a basis needs to take into account the distinct activities that might be encountered in a work setting where quite different goals, practices and rules might apply (e.g. between design, production and administrative areas) and how individuals engage in and contribute to those settings (Billett and Somerville, 2004), as elaborated above.

3.   PERSPECTIVES OF UNDERSTANDING WORK PERFORMANCE

The discussions above lead to a consideration of the kinds of conceptual frameworks needed for understanding the experience of work and what constitutes competent performance at work. Much emphasis has been given to the social origins of knowledge and their manifestation in particular workplace settings. But equally, it is necessary to be clear about the requirements that individuals need in order for them to be competent in workplace settings. This competence is often referred to in the cognitive literature as 'expertise' (Ericsson and Lehmann, 1996). Significant work has been done within cognitive science to identify differences between the capacities of experts and novices within many fields of human activity. Through understanding these differences, it is possible to organise learning arrangements to assist individuals move from being novices to experts. As well as being useful for this purpose, (which is important to the overall focus of this book), it also provides a basis to understand what constitutes effective work performance. However, the cognitive literature tends to focus upon the cognitive qualities of individuals as either novices or experts to the detriment or exclusion of social factors and circumstances that shape effective practice in a particular setting. Therefore, in the following sections, the contributions of cognitive psychology into what constitutes expert performance are not only advanced, but also critiqued and augmented by views from social and cultural perspectives of competence. Together, these disciplines provide a framework for understanding the capacities that competent workers need to demonstrate, and also the premises upon which those capacities will be judged as being appropriate in any given work situation.

3.1   The cognitive perspective of work performance

Much work within cognitive science over the last thirty years has focused on understanding what comprises expertise in order to consider how best to develop this attribute. Through this research, the efficacy of experts' responses to work tasks has been identified as being premised on their ability to categorise these tasks by their means of solution. The breadth and organisation of experts' knowledge and experiences permits this categorisation (Gott, 1989) and enables them to engage with workplace tasks in ways quite different from novices who simply lack this knowledge (Charness, 1989) and may, therefore, respond only to the task's surface features (Sweller, 1989). Active monitoring assists the solution-based categorisation of tasks by experts; involving testing and refining selected responses to a problem—an approach that is simply unavailable to novices (Alexander and Judy, 1988). The rich repertoire of domain-specific experiences furnishes understandings that permit monitoring and informs experts as to whether the tasks are being completed as anticipated. This monitoring is guided by a rich knowledge base, which enables the progressive evaluation of responses to problems, and promotes evaluation of alternative strategies for securing solutions (Glaser, 1990). Judgements about the difficulty of the task, how to apportion time, assess progress and predict outcomes as the task progresses are enabled by monitoring and categorisation (Chi, Glaser and Rees, 1982). So, these conceptions privilege individuals' contribution to thinking and acting (i.e. cognition).

Because of their rich domain-specific knowledge bases, experts are also able to apply cognitive processes seemingly instantaneously thereby accomplishing routine tasks apparently automatically (Ericsson and Simon, 1984). Previous compilation and chunking of domain-specific knowledge reduces the cognitive load, freeing up the working memory to concentrate on unfamiliar components of their tasks. The breadth and organisation of their domain-specific knowledge permit experts to close gaps in the available information, consistently producing more useful solutions than novices. They are also more efficient with their search for solution options (Anderson, 1982). Further, as a product of extensive experiences within a domain of activity, experts' knowledge has become 'de-bugged' through numerous opportunities for learning through trialling and evaluating responses (Glaser, 1990; Gott, 1989). This permits quicker access to the knowledge required for both routine (regular) and non-routine (new) tasks in the workplace. It seems that when faced with non-routine problems, as might be expected, novices fare worse than experts because of experts' ability to deploy a systematic and conscious solution search (Glaser, 1990). These capacities are underpinned by three kinds of knowledge: (i) propositional and (ii) procedural knowledge and (iii) dispositions. It is these that shape individuals' experiencing, participating and remaking of work.

3.2   Propositional knowledge

References to the kinds of knowledge that underpin human performance within the cognitive literature encompass conceptual and procedural representations of knowledge and their dispositional underpinning. It is these representations of knowledge that individuals hold in memory and are deployed in thinking and acting in the workplace. This knowledge furnishes the basis for performance within a domain of knowledge (e.g. an occupation or vocation). Propositional knowledge comprises facts, information, assertions, concepts and propositions, and is differentiated by levels of stateable facts or concepts of increasing complexity (Evans, 1991). It ranges from simple factual knowledge (e.g. names of things) through to deeper or more complex levels of conceptual knowledge, such as understanding about workings of complex systems (law, the human body or a piece of equipment whose operating basis is hidden). Depth of understanding within cognitive psychology is premised upon the strength of relationships amongst concepts (Groen and Patel, 1988), emphasising its interconnectedness and causal relationships. That is, deep understanding is based on linkages, associations and an appreciation of the causal links in those associations, not on ponderous deliberations or quantum of knowledge.

3.3   Procedural knowledge

The knowledge that enables individuals to achieve goals such as being skilful is referred to as procedural knowledge (Anderson, 1982), comprising procedures used in thinking and acting. Whenever we humans are thinking or acting we are deploying procedures. In reading text individuals are applying a set of procedures that are associated with word and letter recognition (specific procedures) as well as procedures that are monitoring and interrogating the text. Consequently, to delineate these functions, procedural knowledge has been further classified into levels or orders of procedures to understand the different roles that procedures play. Following Evans (1991) and Scandura (1980), Stevenson (1991) proposes three levels of procedures. First order or specific procedures are employed to achieve specific goals. Being specific only to routine tasks, these procedures are not effective when non-routine or ill-defined tasks are encountered. Hence, when monitoring, evaluation and strategy selection are required second-order procedures are invoked. This order includes breaking the task up into a series of sub-goals so individuals can achieve the task (Greeno and Simon, 1988). First and second orders are managed by forms of third or higher-order procedural knowledge, which act upon lower orders of knowledge by monitoring and organising activities, and by switching between orders, when necessary.

Because procedures are deployed in ways not always observable, this leads to the modification of an earlier view that provided a conceptual distinction between cognitive and psychomotor activities. Indeed, propositional and procedural forms of knowledge are interdependent. Propositional knowledge cannot be engaged without enacting procedures. Yet, procedures are unlikely to be deployed without being directed towards particular goals.

3.4   Dispositions

Further enmeshing these types of knowledge are their dispositional underpinnings, comprising attitudes, values, affect, interests and identities (Prawat, 1989). Perkins, Jay and Tishman (1993a; 1993b) view dispositions as individuals' tendencies to put their capabilities into action, for example, how individuals conceptualise tasks and the values they place on the deployment of procedures. These dispositions are what motivate and initiate human cognitive processes and the direction and intensity of their application. So while there are cultural values and norms that shape activities and judgements in social practices such as workplaces, there are beliefs and values that shape and direct human performance.

In these ways, the cognitive perspective identifies the breadth and organisation of the kinds of knowledge required to perform non-routine (i.e. new or novel to them) tasks as well as completing regular tasks almost unconsciously. The significance of the cognitive perspective for this chapter is that it identifies the importance of domain-specific knowledge as well as the forms of knowledge that are required for expertise within that domain. The organisation of experts' knowledge around salient domain-based principles maximises the prospect for problem solving and transfer (Groen and Patel, 1988). Indeed, it is the existence and organisation of their knowledge rather than their ability to process that knowledge which sets experts apart from others (Sweller, 1989). Therefore, cognitive constructivism holds that the ability to perform effectively is premised on having domain-specific knowledge comprising both factual and deep knowledge, specific and higher order procedures underpinned by values and attitudes required for performance in the workplace. In particular, deep conceptual and higher order procedures permit performance with new tasks and allow transfer to other circumstances. These are key requirements of effective work performance.

3.5   Domain specificity of work knowledge

The qualities of expertise advanced in the cognitive literature are not held to be universally applicable. Instead, they are held to reside within particular domains of knowledge. Two issues emerge here. First, the organisation of experts' domain-specific knowledge sets them apart from novices who lack both the organisation and breadth of knowledge. However, novices are not necessarily weaker at processing information and may be expert in other domains. The hallmark of expertise in this perspective is the ability to resolve non-routine (novel) problems within a particular domain of knowledge. So performance focuses on domains of knowledge comprising some definable category of knowledge, such as an academic discipline or an occupation, or perhaps the actual circumstances in which they have engaged and constructed a personal domain of knowledge.

Secondly, the cognitive perspective also defines its potency in terms of domains of knowledge that tend to be disembedded. It frequently refers to disciplines or occupational knowledge in a general way, rather than their application to particular situations. In the sociocultural perspective outlined below, the concept of domains specifically accounts for these circumstances. Consistent with Stasz's (1997) critique of generic competencies, accounts from cognitive psychology fail to fully acknowledge the particular requirements of the workplace (Billett, 2001b), for example, that organisational norms and values are likely to differ across workplaces. The goals for performance in each enterprise are also likely to differ because what comprises domain-specific knowledge in one setting may not correspond with what is required in another. This is particularly the case when the view of domains is abstracted from, rather than embedded in particular practice. So, for instance, an understanding about the vocation of hairdressing may not take into account what it means to be a hairdresser in a particular salon. That is, what is taken as expertise in one work setting (e.g. hairdressing salon) may not be so in another, even when the same vocational activity is enacted (Billett, 2001b). These are not just cognitive phenomena. Also, the cognitive conceptualisation of expertise does not fully account for the circumstances in which knowledge is deployed. Its conception of domains is abstracted rather than being seen as embedded in particular work practice. With its focus on the internal processes of the mind, cognitive psychology alone is not able to furnish a comprehensive conception of expertise with all its social and cultural dimensions.

In summary, the cognitive perspective provides many useful contributions to understanding the knowledge experienced and required for participation in work. Central to these is the importance of goal directed activities as the means by which cognitive functions are deployed and through which skilfulness or expertise is developed. Moreover, as well as monitoring the enactment of processes and learning through practice, the cognitive view reinforces the importance of learning through everyday thinking and acting: the deployment of individuals' cognitive functions. Yet this deployment is shaped by the activities and interactions in which they are engaged. Domains of activities are shaped by historical and cultural factors. However, it is within the enactment of a particular instance of a work practice that the domain is manifested. Further, the construction of the domain of knowledge by the individual is unlikely to be some uniform version of the activities encountered in a particular social circumstance. Instead, individuals' dispositional attributes and previous learning processes stand as the basis for shaping their learning, including the construction of their personal domain of work knowledge.

However, a key criticism of the cognitive approach is that it fails to account for the social sources of work activities and interactions through which individuals engage in and learn the knowledge required for work and reshaping it. Therefore, it is necessary to reconcile the cognitive perspective with sociocultural theory that furnishes an understanding about situations and circumstances.

3.6 Sociocultural perspective of work knowledge

In previous sections, understanding more fully how expertise is embedded in a particular practice has been emphasised. Consequently, it is important to be able to account for the work requirements of a particular workplace or work practice. Leonteyev's (1981) definition of an activity system as "the social system that shapes activity" provides a useful basis for elaborating the nature, organisation and goals of the work practice in which that activity is undertaken. Activities can be considered as the external embodiment or manifestation of the workplace's requirements. As such, they also shape what is required for work practice in particular circumstances. When delineating activity systems, it is also necessary to determine how the activity is specified and constrained, and by whom (Newman, Griffin and Cole, 1989). These activities can be used to identify the particular set of factors required for achieving performance in work practice. This can only be understood through a consideration of each workplace's goals, division of labour, culture of practice and so on.

In advancing a more socially situated view of expertise, Scribner (1985a) emphasises contextual factors and contributions. She claims that expert performance is characterised by flexibility in modes of solutions to identical problems, creative shortcuts to simplify and economise on mental and physical effort, finely tuned to the environment, and effective use of setting-specific knowledge. This view accentuates the specific factors that shape performance in each setting. For example, in the study of four hairdressing salons referred to above (Billett, 2001b; 2003b), what it meant to be an expert differed across the salons. In the trendy inner-city salon, giving contemporary and fashionable cuts and colours, conversing about style and holding a particular set of values was all-important. In the salon set in a low socio-economic area, managing difficult customers who made strong demands and were prone to complain quite vociferously and forcefully was a hallmark of expertise. In the salon set in a provincial centre that had endured years of a rural recession and drought, expertise was in being able to maintain the clientele. This included balancing the hairdressers' need to secure additional services from clients, with the risk of losing their clientele. In the fourth salon, in a town in the United Kingdom, expertise involved being familiar with the personal histories and backgrounds of the elderly clients who came for weekly treatments. In varying degrees and in different ways, there was a requirement for the hairdressers to be a friend and confidant to the elderly clients, because they were a key social contact. Moreover, there were identified differences in the activity system in each workplace, despite their sharing the same vocational practice.

Therefore, the domain of knowledge required to understand expert performance needs a situational dimension, one related to the circumstances of the deployment of knowledge. It requires being seen as more than a cognitive phenomenon. Taking the ideas from cognitive constructivism above, expertise is fashioned within particular domains of activities or occupational practice (i.e. sociocultural practice), yet manifested in a particular situation comprising a particular configuration of social forms and practices. This embeds the concept of expertise at the situational level. Lave and Wenger (1991) refer to this as full participation in a community of practice, rather than expertise. Their concept of full participation is that all practitioners are peripheral because the work practice itself is constantly evolving. They refer to becoming an expert as a pathway to full participation in the community. Hence, access to, and participation in, the workplace's activities are required to meet the performance requirements of the workplace. Full participation implies being capable with new activities, performing new tasks and comprehending new understandings, which is analogous to and reconcilable with the cognitive view. This supports the view proposed earlier that an embedded view of domain-specific knowledge is required to understand the performance requirements of particular workplaces. Such a view responds to the need for expertise to be adaptable and transferable. Therefore, to understand the requirements for work necessitates accommodating situational requirements and also some means by which individuals can come to develop their own domains of practice. Their relational, embedded, competent, reciprocal and pertinent characteristics are important.

Consequently, to understand what constitutes the experience of work, workplace requirements and their remaking, it is necessary to include the enactment of skills and judgements in terms of their utility within particular circumstances. The workplace's range of variables means that it will have unique qualities that will determine what constitutes expert responses to particular problems (Billett, 2001b, 2001c). Even the most apparently standardised work activities will have unique variables. For instance, the clientele and composition of staff in a particular fast food chain or bank branch will render the task of working in and managing that work practice in some way unique. Work performance requirements are the product of extensive social practice, with meaning about practice derived by becoming a full participant, over time, and with understanding shaped by participation in the activities and norms of that practice. Developing an understanding of the variables, goals and mechanism for success are likely to result from extended participation in the workplace. Expertise comprises competence in the community's discourse in routine and non-routine activities, mastery of new understanding, and the ability to perform and adapt existing skills. Taking the study of hairdressers referred to earlier, it is unlikely that placing an expert hairdresser from one salon in one of the others would result in their ability to perform expertly. The requirements, norms and discourses of each salon are quite different and are required to be learnt. No amount of transfer of skills will assist the hairdresser to learn about the personal histories of her clients, for instance. Again, and analogous to the cognitive perspective, understanding the particular mores of the workplace, knowing what is and was is not appropriate behaviour or outcomes, is a premise for performance in problem-solving. Expertise requires pertinence in the appropriateness of problem solutions, such as knowing what behaviours are acceptable and in what circumstances are also qualities of expertise. This quality reflects the values a workplace assigns to problems and the appropriate amount of effort and understanding of what knowledge is privileged. In sum, this view emphasises rich association between setting and expertise—what is required to be effective in particular workplaces.

4.   COMPLEMENTARITIES BETWEEN THE SOCIAL AND COGNITIVE CONTRIBUTIONS

There are both commonalities and complementarities across the cognitive and sociocultural perspectives that can assist in understanding the individual and social dimensions of work (Billett, 1996). From the individual and subjective view, the construction of domains of knowledge, repertoires of experiences and their organization, and the role of personal dispositions are cognitive legacies from engaging in socially-derived goal-directed activities. Their formation and sources are explained by sociocultural theory which also acknowledges the diversity of practice and why that has to be the case. In this way, together and when reconciled, the cognitive and sociocultural perspectives outlined above provide a basis to understand further the requirements for a skilled workforce (Billett, 1996). The sociocultural literature yields ways of accounting for the situational factors that make sense of both common attributes and domains of knowledge. By acknowledging the circumstantial factors involved in particular workplaces, the literature provides a basis to reconcile the three perspectives to advance a set of dimensions of work practice, which can be used to determine the requirements of a particular work practice. Moreover, it is these localised factors, plus those brought about by changing cultural practices and technologies that individuals engage with and through which their agency acts to remake the vocational practice.

The individual contributions identified through the cognitive literature can be seen as the 'cognitive experience' (Valsiner, 2000). This experience comprises the understandings and capacities, including their values and beliefs, referred to as dispositions within the cognitive literature, which individuals possess and which shapes how they come to construe and construct the 'social experience'—what they encounter in a particular workplace, and representing the legacy of historical, cultural and situational factors. This perspective is consistent with the idea that the domain of knowledge can be both culturally-derived and person-dependent. That is, that the individual's construal of their vocational practice represents an important manifestation of that practice and comprises part of the cognitive experience. Yet, from a different perspective, a contribution of the social experience is to suggest that the domains of the human activity are shaped by cultural and social factors. Moreover, the social factors that shape practice are prone to change because the sources of these factors are subject to constant transformation and subject to construal and constructions by the individuals who engage in work and remake those practices. This is an outcome of individuals' cognitive experience negotiating with the social experience—enactment of two distinct kinds of domains of knowledge.

5.   CULTURAL, SITUATIONAL AND INDIVIDUAL GENESES OF WORK LIFE

In conclusion, despite the social and cultural geneses of knowledge that have developed over time, the individual experience of engaging in work and realising workplace goals is central to work and conduct and remaking of work. Yet, simultaneous to that learning, the norms and practices that constitute the work practice itself are remade and transformed. The work to be done, its enactment and transformation can be seen as inter-psychological processes leading to intra-psychological outcomes—products of social contributions—that arise in situated practice from moment-by-moment engagement or microgenetic development (Rogoff, 1990). These then contribute to individuals' ontogenetic attributes or learning.

There is an identifiable legacy of hairdressers' participation in particular hairdressing practices (Billett, 2001a; 2003b), comprising individual learning and remaking of the hairdressing practice. However, this legacy or competence represents a negotiated outcome between the situated social suggestion and individuals' earlier experiences. Ontogenetically-derived preferences shape how the hairdressers engage in hairdressing tasks and construct their hairdressing knowledge, albeit through collective processes. These experiences also construe how individuals engage in work and working life. Therefore, more than understanding competence in terms of cultural and historical derived sociocultural practices, it is necessary to account for how vocational practice is constituted situationally and influences the activities in which participants engage in relationally and learn through their participation. This process has been labeled co-participation at work (Billett, 2001a, 2002a)—the duality between what the workplace affords individuals in terms of access to activities and interactions from which they learn, on the one hand, and the degree to which individuals elect to engage with what is afforded them, on the other. That is, individuals decide what constitutes the invitational quality of workplace affordances. Therefore, objective analyses of work activities and interactions need to be coupled with subjective experiences of work.

To return to Figure 2.1, the transformations in the socio-genesis of vocational knowledge comprising the social suggestion and their interplay with individuals' ontogeny depicted in the figure are held to be inter-dependent, not one subjugating the other (Billett, 2005). This interdependence is enacted between levels as cultural practices and localised requirements transform, and as individuals engage with the practices agentically and purposefully thereby reshaping that practice. So although individuals' intra-psychological outcomes likely have some situational legacy, it is not a mere replication of workplace suggestion; they represent individuals re-working and re-making what they experience (Billett, 2003b, Billett et al., 2005) and in this way transforming culturally-derived practices. This transformation may ultimately contribute to phylogenetic development through generating practices that operate across diverse cultures. Consequently, the remaking of cultural practices can be seen as having individual, situational and cultural bases albeit negotiated in ways that are interdependent.

It is at the situational level, where cultural practices are renegotiated as individuals construe, remake and subsequently deploy them. This remaking necessarily occurs through the everyday moment-by-moment or micro-genetic developmental processes through the exercise of conscious thought (Rogoff, 1990), which is intentional and directed (Berger and Luckman, 1966). So there is no separation between individual engagement and learning, and this remaking. Giddens (1984: 114) notes that social systems "do not reproduce themselves, they require that active production and reproduction of human subjects." As Scribner (1997) notes, thinking is fitted to the functional requirements of the particular tasks. Yet, such thinking is required to be adaptive:

> The notion of creativity stresses human production as something new. Yet thinking in the dairy was both adaptive and creative. Adaptation of thought to its functional requirements had an active, not passive character, and it proceeded on the basis of worker invention of new

solutions and strategies. Invention is a hallmark of creativity and it played a major role in all of the occupations studied in the dairy community. (Scribner, 1997: 378)

The immediate or situated social practice, with its cultural and historical geneses (Scribner, 1984; Cole, 1998) is therefore important in understanding the requirements for work performance (Billett, 2001b; Brown et al., 1989; Engeström and Middleton, 1996), within and across instances of work activities (i.e. for adaptability and transfer), for understanding acts of collectivity (i.e. shared processes of learning) and their contributions to social suggestion, learning and appropriation. This learning or appropriation bridges the historical heritage of human beings and each new generation's taking over that heritage (Leontyev, 1981). If, as Valsiner (1998: 114) claims the "active role of appropriation presents the learner as a constructor of new choices, not constrained to those in immediate circumstances", the processes of and goals for learning throughout working life, in part, can be understood by how individuals' capacities are exercised within the requirements of specific workplace situations, and their prospect for applications in those and other work settings.

Yet, situational specificity also illuminates the limits of theoretical constructs that privilege the social (e.g. activity systems, situated cognition, distributed theories of cognition, cultural-historical activity theory). These views tend to privilege knowledge structured through history, comprising both past and existing cultural need as well as situational demands, yet seek to embed individuals in those circumstances. However, viewing individuals as situationally embedded (Engeström, 1993), socially subjugated (Grey, 1994) or saturated (Gergen, 2000) fails to adequately account for individuals' role in the simultaneous processes of learning and cultural change. More than the immediate social suggestions, is the energy, creativity and adaptability of individuals who participate in and adapt that knowledge to new circumstances (Baldwin, 1898; Billett and Somerville, 2004; Valsiner, 2000). It is in situated practice where the two different continuities of the workplace and individuals coming together are intertwined, negotiated and enacted: i.e. the work practice and those of individuals become intertwined in ways that are interdependent in relational ways (Billett et al., 2004)

In sum, it has been proposed in this chapter that understanding what constitutes work activities as institutional facts (Searle, 1995) requires elaborating the genesis of knowledge and practices that constitute work and how they are transformed over time. Institutional facts have cultural, social and situational sources, and collectively contribute to the social experience and its enactment through the mediation of particular sets of localized

workplace factors. Individuals' cognitive experience shapes how they engage in and enact work with each remaking generating a legacy in terms of
both individual (i.e. ontogenetic development) and social practice (i.e.
remaking of the work practice). Workplace performance needs to account for
situational requirements for performance and the engagement of those
conducting that work, that is, both objective analysis of work and subjective
analyses of workers.

It is these issues that are taken up in the next chapter, which examines
the relational interdependence between social and individual factors that
constitute work, work performance and changing work.

Chapter 3

A RELATIONAL BASIS FOR UNDERSTANDING WORK LIFE

...personality becomes socially guided and individually constructed in the course of human life. People are born as potential persons, the process of becoming actual persons takes place through individual transformations of social experience. (Harré, 1995: 373)

1.   RELATIONAL INTERDEPENDENCE BETWEEN SOCIAL AND INDIVIDUAL AGENCY

The purpose of this book is to understand the experience of work and working life—work life. To comprehend this experience, a relational basis is proposed in this chapter for understanding the experience of work life, including the changing nature of work, changing patterns of participation in work and changing requirements for work performance. It also considers how the changing requirements of work are negotiated and constructed by individuals and in relation to the changing context of employment. This consideration necessarily engages both the social factors that bring about these changes and also workers' personal and subjective experience of these changes.

The key premise used to examine and appraise these changes and their impact is the interdependence between the social and individual contributions that constitute work and working life. This interdependence comprises a negotiated and relational process between and through these two contributions. Underpinning this interdependence is the claim that neither the social suggestion nor individuals' agency alone is sufficient to understand learning and the remaking of the cultural practices that constitute work (Billett, 2005).

One dimension of this duality, the social experience (Harré, 1995; Valsiner, 1998) or press, comprises the societal norms, practices and values, and their enactment. Together, as elaborated in Chapter 2 these constitute the requirements for work performance, albeit shaped by local factors in particular ways. However, the social suggestion encountered in workplaces is never complete or comprehensive enough to secure socialisation: the unquestioned and unquestionable transfer of knowledge from the social world to the individual. As Newman et al. (1989) propose, if the social world was able to extend its message unequivocally, there would be little need to communicate; because understanding would be implicit, not requiring further communication to be construed and comprehended. However, individuals have to engage with and make sense of what they encounter socially. As Berger and Luckman (1966) and others propose, the social suggestion cannot be projected in ways that lead to socialisation. Instead, individuals engage with what is suggested through norms and practices and interactions with greater or lesser levels of receptiveness. This occurs, if for no other reason, because of the limits of the social suggestion. Individuals are required to be agentic and active in the construction of meaning. What arises from the social world requires interpretation and construal in order to understand what is being suggested. Yet, even beyond simply attending to, engaging with and comprehending what is being suggested, importantly although people are similar in many ways, they are also different. So beyond the suggestion of the social, individuals will construct their views about work, workplace participation and requirements for performance. In this way, the impact of the dynamic world of work is one that is negotiated between the individual and that changing world. For instance, although there were procedures that were privileged in each of the hairdressing salons referred to in the previous chapter ("what we do here is..."), nevertheless, hairdressers, even apprentices, were able to exercise their preference for particular kinds of treatments (Billett, 2003b).

All of this is particularly salient for participating, performing and learning in the culturally derived practices that constitute paid work. Much of vocational knowledge has its origins in cultural practices and historical precedents (Scribner, 1985b). The need for and requirements of occupational activities arise from a cultural need that has been refined over time through its enactments, as elaborated in the last chapter. Consequently, to access this knowledge that has a historical and cultural legacy, requires engaging and negotiating with the social world, because it does not have its genesis from within the individual.

Moreover, when individuals engage with this culturally-derived knowledge and reconstruct it, they are also actively remaking the cultural practices that comprise paid work at a particular point in time, and in negotiation with particular kinds of social suggestion and different kinds of access to it (Billett and Somerville, 2004). The remaking of cultural practice and individual learning is, therefore, not through some faithful enactment of social suggestion that results in its reproduction. Instead, there is a remaking through individuals' engagement with and construction of those practices, albeit mediated by the exercise of social and cultural norms and practices whose needs have to be met at particular points in time in individuals' personal histories. So, beyond workplace norms, practices and interactions there is also a key role for the agency of the individual in engaging, negotiating and remaking the practice of work.

2.   RE-ENGAGING THE INDIVIDUAL

Given the privileging of the immediate social and cultural contributions in recent theoretical accounts, it seems necessary and timely to bring individual agency back to the forefront of discussions about work, working life and the impacts of work transitions. There are at least four bases for acknowledging the role of individual agency.

Firstly, the exercise of personal agency is essential in transforming the cultural practices that comprise paid work as new cultural needs arise, such as those brought about by changing times or technologies. Wertsch (1998) distinguishes between *mastery* (i.e. compliant learning), which is superficial and may well be the product of forceful or compelling social suggestion of the kind identified by Valsiner (1998), and *appropriation* (i.e. socially derived learning in which individuals engage willingly) resulting in a concurrence between what is experienced and the individual's values and beliefs. For instance, the ordered salutations of sales staff in shops and check out operators stand as an instance of mastery: procedures exercised without commitment, but which are necessary to maintain employment. Appropriation might be the more enthusiastic account of the Mike the mechanic as he works effortfully and intelligently to locate the annoying noise in a customer's car (Billett and Somerville, 2004). Given that richer or deeper kinds of participation are likely to require effortful engagement buoyed by interests and intentionality (Malle, Moses and Baldwin, 2001), this kind of participation, and hence learning, may arise more frequently when it engages an individual's interests and agentic action. This is what was evident in Mike's accounts of his participation in his work practice. So, the first key premise is that there is an inevitable and important interdependency between the agency of the social world in projecting its suggestion and the agency of the individual in making sense of what and how they experience work. Therefore, central to understanding changes in work and working life is an individual's agency and intentionality.

A second reason to bring individuals' agency to the forefront of considerations about individual participation and engagement in work, and the remaking of the cultural practice that it comprises, is that these processes are person-dependent to some degree. Individuals' construal of what they encounter is uniquely socially-shaped through an idiosyncratic set of negotiations with the social suggestion throughout their life history that comprises their ontogenetic development. This development is the product of myriad forms of encounters with social practices, norms and interactions that individuals engage in throughout their lives. These experiences microgenetically or moment-by-moment (Rogoff, 1990) contribute to individuals' processes of thinking and acting throughout their life history. From the earliest age, processes that Piaget (1968) refers to as securing equilibrium and more recently von Glasersfeld (1987) refers to as maintaining viability, encompass an enduring personal epistemological venture of making sense of what individuals experience in the social world. For instance, each of the hairdressers could identify particular sources that shaped their preference for particular treatments (Billett, 2003b). These included: the favouring of particular appearances; an engagement in colouring early in apprenticeship; mild colour blindness; experiences in a particular hairdressing salon; to the accidental inhaling of perming solution powder. These experiences shaped the hairdressers' subsequent preferences for treatments.

As well as confronting novel experiences, the constructive nature of human cognition is also premised on an expectation of variability and inconsistency in the response from the social world as opposed to certainty and consistency (Baldwin, 1894). This active or pro-active process of sensing and appraising the social suggestion elaborates the individualistic and potentially unique set of experiences arising from a history of relations with the social world through their ontogenetic development. Here, easy claims about mastery and appropriation (e.g. Wertsch, 1998) leading to particular and more or less valued kinds of learning need to be treated sceptically. Being confronted by something that is inconsistent with an individual's beliefs may indeed lead to rich learning, because that inconsistency with existing knowledge and/or beliefs may have to be addressed, reconciled or it may in turn transform the individual's existing knowledge. For instance, in one hairdressing salon there were 'awkward' customers who would return and complain about their hairstyles. So the hairdressers expected and attempted to guard against these eventualities, mindful that that the absent employer often accepted customers' word over theirs (Billett, 2001b). Conversely, appropriation might result in the uncritical acceptance of existing practice (e.g. the marginalisation of certain individuals or groups) in the workplace, because the individual elects not to contest the norms they encounter. So, in the studies of coal miners, there was an appropriation of the values and practices of the coal mining community, and the coal miners seemingly exercised these values and practices relatively unquestioningly. Consequently, appropriation might be analogous to Piaget's (1968) concept of assimilation—the social suggestion being integrated with what is already known—through the individual actively seeking to appropriate new social suggestion, whereas mastery might enact accommodation or change in knowledge. This is because individuals exercise intentionality in making sense of much of the social suggestion and in the construction of meaning.

It follows that the individual's ontogenetic development (such as that through working life) arises through a personally agentic epistemological process that is shaped through ongoing interactions with the social world they encounter in their work lives. In turn, this influences how individuals engage with new experiences. Mike, the mechanic's earlier experiences as a road-side mechanic led him to develop a view about customer service that was distinct from his co-workers who had only experienced mechanical work in automotive workshops (Billett and Pavlova, 2005). The construal of these experiences is likely to be in some ways unique to individuals, because of their distinct personal histories. Moreover, the experiences are generative of cognitive legacies in ways that Vygotskians describe as comprising inter-psychological processes that lead to intra-psychological attributes. These legacies comprise both personally distinct conceptions as well as areas of commonality or shared understanding with others. The shared and unique conceptions are exercised in individuals' process of knowledge construction and their remaking of cultural practices (Billett, 2003b; Billett et al., 2005).

So thirdly then, because of ontogenetic legacy and personal epistemology, consideration needs to be given to the individual's premediate experiences, that is, those experiences that occurred earlier and in turn shape subsequent construals. It is these construals that are held to shape the individual's conceptions and subjectivities—gaze, if you like. For instance, Lev the Russian émigré's previous work history in Russia as an electronics engineer motivated him to engage in the long struggle to reach the same status in his newly adopted country (Billett and Pavlova, 2005). These motivations shaped how he viewed the kinds of work he was initially able to secure in Australia, which to him were menial and below his professional status. Consequently, these experiences shape how individuals construe their experiences of work and initiate and sustain their intentionality and agency as they engage in work, and remake and transform the cultural practices that comprise paid work. Because these pre-mediate experiences are themselves shaped by, yet contribute to, unique personal epistemologies even the most apparently uniform social experience which affords its contributions seemingly equally to all will be subject to different interpretation, construal and construction. For instance, the hairdressers when presented with identical hairdressing problems to solve offered distinct responses, which were shaped by situational factors, but also their personal preferences and construals (Billett, 2003a, 2003b). This leads to particular and in some ways unique personal kinds of understanding about work and working life, albeit socially shaped. So life history or ontogenetic develop-ment, comprising individuals' prior social experiences, stands as an important premise as to how a person engages with the world, including their sense of self.

Finally, the relationship between individual and social agency is not mutual or reciprocal; it is relational. Just as the social suggestion can be either weaker or stronger, so too the individual's engagement with a particular social suggestion (e.g. situated practice, cultural norm, cultural practice) can be more or less intense, focused in particular ways and engaged with to different degrees of intentionality. We engage in social practices with different needs and intentionality. The purposes of our engagement in the service station or workplace canteen is fleeting, but to those who work within them there will be different bases, but even then played out with different levels of intensity between the part-time worker and the owner, for instance. The prospects for individual and social agency being enacted in equal parts or ways that are equally shared is quite remote. The very interactive processes arising will be individually unique in some ways. As well, individuals may be selective in their reading of a particular social suggestion or simply be unaware of it, thereby not explicitly engaging with it (Billett, 2005). Therefore, central to the interdependence between social and individual agency, is that it is rendered relational as individuals encounter social experiences projected in multitudinous and diverse forms and construct meaning from ontogenetically diverse bases.

3.   NEGOTIATING BETWEEN OBJECTIVE AND SUBJECTIVE ACCOUNTS

A way to understand the negotiation between the objective and subjective phenomena that have been referred to above is through a consideration of personal agency and social structures and forms. The objective social world is held to be that comprising the institutional facts that cannot be wished away by individuals. It exists as a reality that is objective in so far as it can be understood through the exercise of social structures and forms. Some literature emphasises the social world in terms of social structures as being all embracing and rendering the individual as very much in a subordinate role (Ratner, 2000; Mansfield, 2000), a mere placeholder, subject to changes in the social world but not able to change that world. As such, when it is argued that the social world is creating anxiety, inevitably changing for the worse the individual's work and reducing their prospects and benefits, these facts are seen to be potent and overwhelming. For instance, Lev the electronics engineer perceived that his workplace was not acknowledging, respectful or utilising his full capacities (Billett and Pavlova, 2005). This was important to him as he was attempting to re-establish an identity as an electronics engineer. However, if these institutional facts are held to be subject to negotiation, interpretation and even rejection, there can be less certainty about the degree by which the facts and their consequences for individuals are as potent as is claimed. For instance, the bases for engaging in restaurant management work by two part-owners was distinct because one was experienced and was looking to expand his work away from restaurants, whereas the other was having his first experience of restaurant ownership (Billett et al., 2005). However, their bases of interest and engagement were quite distinct from that of the part-time waitress who was working to support her university studies. Consequently, the degree to which individuals are able to see these facts as suggestions that have greater or lesser potency and, indeed, can be interpreted, ignored or rebuffed, suggests that the role of individual agency needs to be accounted for more fully than in some current conceptions. The more the case can be made that individuals play a significant role in the process of meaning making, exercising their sense of self, then the greater the need to consider more subjective accounts of the experience of work and working. These issues have long been discussed within the major disciplines of psychology, sociology and philosophy, which are helpful in elaborating those premises.

3.1 Accounts of agency and structure within psychology

Some psychological accounts take the individual as the starting and focal point for considering how humans make sense of and engage in activities such as work and in workplaces, as noted in the previous chapter. Accounts of social practices (such as workplaces) are seen as contexts in which individuals participate to achieve their work goals and to learn. Certainly, theoretical movements such as cognitive psychology and the information processing perspective of this movement emphasise individuals and their capacity to manipulate their own cognitive structures (Chi, Glaser and Rees,

1982; Glaser, 1990) when engaging in activities such as paid work. Indeed, the cognitive account of expertise tends to emphasise individuals' capacity to manipulate this knowledge as the epitome of cleverness (Ericsson and Lehmann, 1996). Nevertheless, in its origins and even at its strongest, the cognitive revolution downplays the contributions of thinking and acting from the social world. These theories grant significant agency to the individual, but in a very internal way. Such views are aligned with earlier educational goals associated with a belief in general thinking capacities that are not dependent upon any situation. Both Bartlett (1958) and Bruner (1966) propose that the aim of education is to free the individual from the constraints of a particular time and place. The legacy of such views is to focus on the development of intelligence and general thinking processes that are held to be applicable to any situation (Brown et al., 1989). One of the most recent manifestations of these accounts is the core or generic competency movement that identifies and claims to offer generic skills, which if ac-quired, can be applicable to any employment situation, regardless of context. However, studies focusing on these kinds of abilities and capacity for adaptability or transfer have shown the limitations of individual cognitive capacity and experience (Beven, 1997).

Other psychological theories emphasise the social and cultural contributions to individuals' thinking and acting. In a response to the individual focus within much or the psychology literature, the last decade and a half have seen a strong emphasis being given to the cultural and social contributions to human cognition (e.g. cultural historical activity theory, activity systems, communities of practice, distributed cognition). Approaches such as activity theory (Cole, 1998; Leonteyev, 1981; Scribner, 1985a; 1985b) provide a means to understand the social geneses of work and the knowledge required for performance in work activities and workplaces. In some, perhaps more extreme instances, these accounts have suggested that individuals play a limited role in their cognition (i.e. thinking, acting and learning), but rather such cognitive activities are directed by social factors (Gergen, 2000; Pea, 1993). As noted earlier, these social and cultural per-spectives have tended to predominate in recent times, claiming in particular that there are strong associations between an individual's thinking and acting and the circumstances in which they are situated (e.g. Wenger, 1998; Engetrom, 1993; Collins, Brown and Newman, 1989). Some of these accounts infer situational determinism—that is the situation directs the thinking and acting of the individual (Pea, 1993). These perspectives are, in many ways, analogous to structural accounts from within sociology. That is, social factors and forms shape or determine cognition. Certainly, these perspectives grant considerable agency to social forms and structures. An inherent quality of these accounts is that the knowledge individuals learn has cultural and social geneses: its source is elsewhere and in the past as discussed in the previous chapter. This socially-derived knowledge is, however, manifested in a particular social practice (e.g. the workplace, home, community organisations, shops etc). Together, this social and historical sourcing can be seen as a great strength, as it reflects proven practices that have evolved over time as new demands emerge and technologies change. It is the application to the particular setting that underpins the remaking of the knowledge and practice. Such historically derived knowledge constitutes much of the occupational knowledge that is exercised through work. However, this socially sourced knowledge needs to be engaged with by individuals for their contributions to be exercised.

Such theoretical explorations and positions are understandable corrections to the earlier individual-focussed perspectives within psychology (Bruner, 2001). However, they may have limitations in assumptions about how the social contributions will be engaged with by individuals. Moreover, their capacity to address new situations or circumstances, or even explain the nature and context of working life, is questionable. Cole (2002), a principal advocate of cultural historical activity theory, which emphasises the historical and cultural genesis of knowledge and its social transition, suggests that individual agency stands as a necessary prerequisite for the successful deployment of historically-derived knowledge particularly to novel circumstances. He claims being unable to advise his teacher education students on how they might best survive and practice teaching in contemporary American high schools. In doing so, Cole (2002) concedes that the historically derived and culturally constituted classroom practices that might be expected to underpin a teacher's work performance would fail these novice teachers when faced with problems beyond those previously experienced and codified in their teaching practice. Instead, teachers' personal agency and capacities will largely determine their success in developing and negotiating classroom practices; thereby remaking what constitutes teaching practice. In this way, Cole (2002) proposes an interplay between the social practice and an individual's intentional task formation. But perhaps more importantly, instead of being subservient to historically and culturally derived experiences, individual agency is central to the remaking of the practices. Moreover, conceptions of self as an effective teacher may well be more dependent upon the individual teacher's perceptions of their success in the classroom, than adherence to precepts that were established elsewhere and in an earlier time. So the continuity of teachers' work and its valuing are not wholly premised in social, cultural and historical precepts. It is also shaped by the individual's experience and agency, and expectations.

From this example, the psychological contribution to understanding what constitutes changes to work, working life and how individuals respond to these changes suggests that there are important contributions to be made by both the individual and the social world. The social world provides much of the knowledge about what constitutes work, its valuing and purposes as well as its tried and tested practices. The individual contribution is to engage with, make sense of and enact the socially derived knowledge about work, including its values, at a particular moment in time and in a particular work situation. Moreover and perhaps of particular importance here, it is the individual's agency and their intentionality that is central to the process of experiencing and remaking the cultural practices comprising paid work.

3.2 Accounts of structure and agency in philosophy and sociology

Within sociology and philosophy, the relations between structure and agency are exercised with greater maturity than in psychology. Both of these disciplines offer accounts that emphasise the key role of social structures in which individual agency and autonomy is seen as illusory (e.g. Foucault, 1979; Bourdieu, 1991), accounts that grant individual autonomy (e.g. Goffman, 1990; Rousseau, 1968) and those that acknowledge interaction between the two (e.g. Giddens, 1991; Bhaskar, 1998; Berger and Luckman, 1966). Highly structured views, such as Foucault's earlier work, render individuals as mere placeholders in social networks (Mansfield, 2000) because they are so enmeshed in the social structures in ways that diminish their personal autonomy. Such views see individuals as being driven before the demands of changing work, or at best being only reactive to these changes. For instance, Bourdieu (1991) refers to the socially constraining nature of individual action, citing how social practice determines dialects. That is, the social is so pervasive as to determine the patterns and enunciation of an individual's speech. Similarly, Foucault (1979) suggests individuals are subject to pervasive social press and 'placed under' or subjected to the influence of the norms and practices encountered earlier within their life histories.

In these views, individuals' socially derived subjectivities determine their behaviour and cognition (Davies, 2000). It is possible to identify situations that begin to replicate the extent of social suggestion that is proposed in these accounts. For instance, studies of coalminers who lived in coalmining communities, that are often isolated or at least solely concerned with coalmining, have demonstrated how the exercise of a potent social press can be quite pervasive in shaping their work and work habits. Somerville (2003) notes how work practices in mine sites are shaped by the masculine culture of the workplace and mining community that often manifests itself in dangerous and unsafe practices in the exercise of that masculinity. Such is the pervasiveness of the mining culture that miners' subjectivities appear captured by the social suggestion of the community in which they live and work. Somerville found that it is only when significant events (e.g. severe accidents, severe ill-health) occur in coalminers' lives do they question the purpose and wisdom of the hegemonic masculine culture of the mine sites. When affected by an accident, miners who question the culture stand astonished at their lack of capacity to influence other miners' behaviours and practices. This is despite the obvious and visible evidence they present. The miners' circumstances where social factors operate in a highly deterministic way in work related activities are similar to those described by Lave (1990) in her study of learning tailoring which occurred in a physical and social environment (i.e. a street full of tailors shops in which the apprentices lived and worked) that comprised a powerful social press.

Yet, other commentators see the concept of structure as being more personally enabling. For instance, Giddens (1984) proposes a key role for human agency in the social structuring of knowledge through his concept of structuration. Through acknowledging intersections and interactions (interdependence) between social structures he links the individual's intentionality and their subjectivity. In ways analogous to the Piagetian concept of disequilibrium, Giddens (1991) later suggests the problem for the self is in maintaining its security in a culture that threatens its stability and the reference points for its stability. Yet, as Fenwick (1998) proposes, while permitting a role for individuals, this view positions them as anxiety ridden and their agency restricted to reflexive relations with culture. Instead, she holds them as being more agentic. Certainly, there seems to be scope to propose a significant role for individuals within socially structured circumstances, even those that are highly structured.

In both the coalmining study and the aged care sector that Somerville (2003) investigated, there was significant evidence of individuals electing to exercise autonomy in the face of social subjugation. Similar to the coalminers, some aged care workers were also able to challenge and change practices in aged care facilities that they felt were inappropriate. Equally, other studies of learning through work provide instances where workers acting outside prescribed workplace practices are evident, even in closely socially monitored circumstances (e.g. hairdressing salons). Clearly, this was easier for some workers than others. For instance, owners and managers of hairdressing salons seemed more able and likely to offer treatments that were outside of those normally provided by the salon than were apprentices and junior hairdressers who were not permitted such discretion (Billett, 2001b). However, this is not to suggest that these workers did not hold views and preferences that were different to those privileged in these workplaces. Indeed, they practised them in ways in which they had control and discretion. But in the public space of a hairdressing salon, there were constraints on how overt distinctive practices could be enacted. Analogously, small business operators were often less constrained by workplace norms and practices, because they were quite likely to be those who established and monitored the work practices within the small businesses.

3.3   Individual agency regulating meaning and purposes

It follows that some workplace situations will grant a greater space for individuals than others. Yet, regardless, there are also opportunities for individuals to create spaces for themselves in workplaces. That is, they are not so constrained as to be unable to exercise their agency and intentionality (Billett and Pavlova, 2005; Billett et al., 2005). This view finds support within the later work of Foucault (1986). He proposes that, despite being constrained and under surveillance individuals will not be so fettered as to be without personal beliefs and values that remain central to them and that no amount of constraint and surveillance will be able to expunge. He refers to desire. Other kinds of locus for human agency and intentionality also exist. Returning to Bourdieu's (1991) claim about language—yes, individuals' accents might well be shaped by the social circumstances in which language is used and practised. Indeed, such is the engraining and potency of this socially derived learning that ridding oneself of an accent is difficult and requires extensive conscious effort over time. However, the ideas and beliefs that sit behind the language, albeit articulated through the socially derived accent, are less likely to be so constrained (Billett, 2003a).

Indeed, others suggest that ultimately individuals are less or even not constrained by these structures (e.g. Rousseau, 1968). However, this position is strongly refuted by structuralists (e.g. Ratner, 2000), who claim that individuals are unable to separate themselves from the social world. Yet, again, it is possible to identify instances of work where this occurs. Apart from those who are self-employed and work in relative isolation (Fenwick, 2002), there are examples of individuals who deliberately work outside of or in contravention to social mores and practices. For instance, comedians and satirists, although using social structures and ideas, do so in a way that subverts, contradicts and confronts the social suggestion. Valsiner (1998) claims that humans have to rebuff the majority of social suggestion otherwise they would be overwhelmed, or what Gergen (2000) refers to as socially-saturated. Of course, the criticism here is that this work is still constrained by social structures and values. A key premise advanced is that paid work arises from a cultural need, and as such is a social and historical product. Individuals are unique social products arising from their engagement in different and overlapping social practices throughout their life history (Harré, 1995; Valsiner, 1998). So, this distinctiveness suggests that although shaped by social forms, there is separation between the social and the individual, and that this can serve to manifest itself in different kinds and levels of separation from social suggestion.

Central to considerations of the extent and kind of separation and the role of human agency are an individual's intentions when engaging with the social world. Baldwin (1894) proposed that individuals learn from an early age that they have to make sense of the social world and it cannot be relied upon to be consistent in its responses. Consequently, throughout their life histories, individuals make sense of the world in particular ways depending upon their interpretations of the socially derived experiences that they encounter. That is, they actively engage in making sense of the world rather than being merely subject to it. Here, the kinds of experience that comprise an individual's personal history provide a platform for their coming to know and making sense of what is encountered in workplaces, how work is valued and engaged with and the role that their subjectivity, intentionality and agency play in this activity. That is, what might be exercised as a social preference may not be favoured by individuals. In this way, accounts claiming general anxiety and disempowerment might not be so universal nor so universally compelling. Indeed, as argued in Chapter 4, what constitutes 'good work' for individuals might not be consistent with assumed social worth such as objective measures about levels of pay, security or opportunity. A more personally relative approach might be required, rather than one which accepts the universalistic approach.

Each of the theoretical orientations outlined above provides contributions that are distinct conceptually in their advocacy of the relative strength of individual or social agency. Moreover, each orientation might serve to explain particular workplace circumstances. The fact that it is possible to locate illustrative examples of these orientations suggests this might be the case of particular sets of work and workplace conditions, and variations within them.

However, a clear understanding of the changing requirements of work, how individuals engage in it, how they respond to its changing form throughout their working lives and realise their own career trajectories, is probably best served by a greater integration of conceptualisations that hold work, work practice and careers as both social institutions and as personal practices whose enactment is premised in relationships between the two. This is because accounts of work as an expression of the exercise of socially structured institutions remain incomplete without understanding how individuals engage with what these structures do for them (and, therefore, how they constitute their practices), as well as personal goals, practices and subjectivities. Conversely, without understanding these relations, the individual is potentially left isolated, dis-identified and without context. It is through a consideration of relationships between the two that rich conceptualisations of work, working life and identity are located.

In the next section, discussions about the relationship between individual and social agency are further elaborated and contextualised to provide a way of considering how individuals engage in work and working life, including inevitable changes which emerge both in workplaces and throughout the individuals' work life histories.

4.   WORKPLACE PARTICIPATORY PRACTICES

Workplace participatory practices constitute a basis to understand an individual's participation in the workplace, and its consequences for their capacity to engage in work activities and secure their personal and vocational outcomes (Billett, 2002a). This participation is an exemplification of negotiation between the individual and the social, and is conceptualised as a duality between the affordance of the workplace and the individual's engagement with what they are afforded. These two concepts and their interdependence are elaborated in turn.

4.1   Workplace affordances

The kinds of activities individuals are offered (afforded) are the product of workplaces' micro-social processes (Engeström and Middleton, 1996), that is, the exercise of their norms and practices. The knowledge to be constructed for effective work performance, the kinds of problems to be solved and what constitutes an acceptable solution are shaped by situational factors and local negotiations (Engeström and Middleton, 1996; Suchman, 1996; Wenger, 1998), as elaborated in the previous chapter. These also shape the workplace's participatory practices: in what ways individuals are invited to participate in workplace activities (Billett, 2002a). When individuals engage in workplace activities, they are invited and expected to engage in and practice tasks that contribute to the workplace's continuity. This participation is likely to be centrally directed towards sustaining or improving levels of the enterprise's profitability or service. Yet, they also include maintaining or improving the standing and employment of individuals or cohorts of individuals in the workplace. Consequently, opportunities are afforded in ways to sustain the work practice and/or particular interests in the workplace. As noted, the standing and well-being of particular affiliates (Bernhardt, 1999; Darrah, 1996) or workplace cliques might determine the ways individuals are permitted to participate in and learn from their work. For instance, in studies of coalmines it was unlikely that an experienced worker would assist the development of a worker who was not aligned or affiliated to their trade union (Billett, 1994). To do so would be to violate the basis of workplace affiliations and demarcations, including the standing of the particular union.

Given the presence of these interests in workplaces, which stand to distribute opportunities for engagement, participation and advancement, workplace practices and affiliations can lead to contestation over the distribution of work activities and support for participation and, hence, learning. Because workplaces are often contested (e.g. Darrah, 1996; Hull, 1997), the distribution of workplace affordances is far from benign. Instead, the distribution of these affordances is shaped by workplace hierarchies, group affiliations, personal relations, workplace cliques and cultural practices, which allocate opportunities to act and interact in workplaces (Billett, 2001a, 2004). Put baldly, opportunities to participate in and access support and guidance are distributed in ways that reflect workplace political and power relationships (Solomon, 1999; Beriema, 2001). For instance, Bernhardt (1999) identified how, in order to safeguard their own employment, full-time retail workers in pharmacy chain stores restricted the activities and learning of part-time employees. Then there are the inevitable tensions between labour and management about the division of labour particularly those centred on management's control over the workplace (Danford, 1998). Similarly, workplace support in the form of training and development opportunities for workers may be distributed to management's advantage. As discussed in Chapter 6 opportunities are distributed selectively to workers. Studies from countries with both regulated and relatively unregulated policies indicate that employers are more likely to provide opportunities and expend funds on younger and well educated workers than those who are older and less educated (Bishop, 1997). They are also more likely to support those who are white than of colour (e.g. McBrier and Wilson, 2004).

These tensions are constituted by and played out in workplace settings. It follows from the discussion above that the kinds of participation individuals are permitted and, in turn, elect to engage in, are central to understanding the learning that arise from their participation in workplaces. Individuals denied support may have more limited learning opportunities and outcomes than those participating in new activities supported by experienced co-workers. Yet, there may be other consequences. For instance, these individuals may well learn that workplaces are not to be trusted, not equitable, or they may learn the importance of acting in ways that align themselves to powerful individuals in order to protect themselves, their standing or those interests with whom they are affiliated. Many women commence their own small businesses after repeated frustration with gaining promotion within large workplaces (Kempenich, Butler and Billett, 1999). However, whether these affordances are developmental, helpful or not is, in part, a product of negotiation between the individuals and the workplace's affordances.

Nevertheless, these affordances are dynamic. The situational factors and local negotiations that constitute the social practices of workplaces and their enactment are in constant transformation. Workplace affordances are subject to constant change, in terms of tasks, goals, interactions, participants and relations. This dynamic quality reinforces the salience of understanding the ongoing negotiated relations between individuals and the social practice. These negotiations constitute workplace participatory practices, as both the bases for the workplace's continuity and the individual's goals are negotiated and transformed. Importantly for learning and remaking of work practice, more than being once-off sources of knowledge that result in some fixed cognitive legacy, inter-psychological processes (Vygotsky, 1978) are necessarily ongoing.

Moreover, beyond workplace affordances, individuals' activities and interactions in workplaces do much to change and remake the practices that constitute transformation to workplace requirements. It is their construction and the deployment of their vocational practice that is the making and transformation of paid work.

4.2   Individual engagement

Individuals' engagement in the workplace is the other element of workplace participatory practices (Billett, 2002a) which comprise the duality between the social and individual contributions to work, its engagement and outcomes. Despite the goal-directed activities and interactions that comprise the observable elements of work and their distribution being shaped by social norms and practices, individuals also exercise their agency in determining how they construe, construct and engage in work. This agentic action and its exercise are shaped by individuals' personal histories or ontogenies and are constituted in the form of subjectivities and identities (Somerville and Bernoth, 2001). Individuals participate simultaneously in a number of social practices (Lave and Wenger, 1991). However, the quality of their engagement in these practices will not be uniform. Full-bodied participation in one social practice can be contrasted by reluctance in another. The degree to which the individual's engagement is full bodied is influenced by their values, beliefs and sociocultural background. Workers of a South Vietnamese heritage rejected teamwork in an American manufacturing plant, believing this work practice reflected the very communal, indeed communistic, values and practices they had fled Vietnam to avoid (Darrah, 1996).

Central to these local negotiations and participatory practices are individuals' agency that shapes how they engage with what is afforded them albeit culturally derived. Personal agency is, as advanced above, guided by the learners' identities and subjectivities, which are themselves socially-derived through personal histories. Therefore, the individual's participation in social practice and the processes underpinning learning are interdependent. Learning through engagement in social practices such as workplaces is not a unidirectional process of socialisation or enculturation with the outcome being the mere reproduction of situational values and practices (e.g. Giddens, 1984). Instead, individuals' subjectivities have social geneses that are shaped through participation in different social practices throughout their life history or ontogeny. This positions the social as much an individual as a collective phenomenon. Each individual is uniquely social in some way. This is because individuals' interpretation of and engagement in social practices and the learning that occurs through that participation will always be unique in some ways to their personal history and subjectivities (e.g. Billett, 1997; Valsiner and van de Veer, 2000). So there is interdependence between what is afforded individuals by social practice and how they elect to engage with and construct what is afforded them by that social practice.

The process of individual engagement within workplaces is premised on a relational interdependence between the individual and the social world, as proposed in Chapter 2. Dewey (1887 cited in Valsiner and van de Veer, 2000) proposes an individual's experience is the product of their intellect engaging with sensations, those arising through the social world as well as through the brute world. However, this definition of experience as intentional and active engagement may exclude the subtle yet ubiquitous social suggestions that are encountered almost unconsciously in the conduct of daily life. These are analogous to what Bourdieu (1991) refers to as habitus: the battery of clues, cues and models that suggest and guide conduct. Bloomer and Hodkinson (2000) propose a habitus as enacting a legacy in terms of personal dispositions that shape how individuals engage with the social world and with what intent. Yet, there are different relations between individuals and the social world. This battery of social suggestion is experienced in different ways and/or construed differently by different individuals (Newman et al., 1989). Foucault (1979) suggests that individuals become subjected to the social world through the discourses and discursive practices of the social, primarily through language. In this way, the stories workers tell about their work and learning reveals the storylines through which their subjectivities are constituted in the workplace. The worker subjectivities have a particular relationship to learning.

The subjectivity of coal miners, for instance, was found to be constituted within a strong hegemonic masculine culture of aggression, competitiveness and risk-taking which was at odds with the company's new training in safe work practices (Somerville, 2002). The culture of mine work is handed down inter-generationally in mining communities. The mines as workplaces are described as 'closed communities' where workplace practices are highly regulated by the social pressure of subjugation. Mine workers tell stories of consistent harassment of other workers, especially bosses, or those who are different and they link these practices to the stress of a dangerous environment; "I guess it's a bit of a release and a relief from the, the pressure and the other, the other stresses that just come with being underground, being in a, it's a hostile environment."(Somerville, 2002: 152)

A culture of masculine competitiveness has been characteristically cultivated in mining workplaces because of its relationship to production (Somerville, 2002). The mineworkers described competitiveness among workers as the basis of the mining industry and many of those interviewed referred to what might be described as the intersection of discourses of competitiveness and production and the conflict between production and safety that is played out in the bodies of the workers. It is these bodies that take the brunt of physical and sometimes dangerous work. As one worker put it, "To be competitive, that's the system we use. If we're not competitive, the mines closed and that's where it is." Older workers, in particular, are portrayed as being steeped in a culture of production where the workers cut corners instead of being safe. While there appears to have been a marked change in the relationship between production and safety promoted by the company, participants suggested that many workers still cut corners to save time and energy. Younger participants continue to maintain that saving hours by cutting corners and lifting things that are too heavy is justified even though they add that "it might go against them later" in terms of chronic back injury (Billett and Somerville, 2004).

According to most of the participants in the coal mines, young workers regard themselves as invincible, believing they "can lift anything, do anything, carry anything" without damage to their bodies. These younger workers themselves admit that, "there is stuff where you can lift it but you probably shouldn't be. Well there's a lot, there's heaps of that." They reported that older workers, on the other hand, want to prove that they are still as strong as they were when young, "blokes go and lift things they shouldn't because they want to show themselves they can still do it." Masculine peer pressure supports unsafe work behaviours, preventing workers from expressing problems and admitting mistakes or weakness.

Another less spectacular, but even more pervasive, aspect of risk taking behaviour is the attitude to wearing protective gear. Yet, some mine workers do not like wearing protective gear because it is seen as a sign of feminine weakness: "A lot of people won't wear gloves even like—you tart, y'know to protect their fingers." A similar response is reported when a worker is offered pink boots, and asks that they be thrown in the rubbish bin because of their connotation of femaleness and thus weakness. While the social press for mine workers was strongly supportive of hegemonic masculine work practices, there were nevertheless some mineworkers who persisted in asserting their difference, either through natural inclination or through a self-conscious process of transformation (Billet and Somerville, 2004).

Social interactions comprising the social press can be of the close interpersonal (or proximal) kind, such as in teaching or guided learning. This kind of interaction is often directed to secure intersubjectivity or shared understanding or the development of workplace procedures that cannot be learnt without interactions between a more experienced and less experienced social partner. On the other hand, pervasive forms of social suggestion that comprises social norms and practices that individuals are subjected to and represent potentially pervasive social press have been conceptualised as habitus (Bourdieu, 1991) or subjectification (Foucault, 1979). It is these forms of social suggestion that individuals elect to appropriate, transform or ignore. Linking this proposition to learning and remaking practice, it seems that both close guidance and the more distal forms of social suggestion do more than shape behaviour in the immediate circumstance. They also have a cognitive legacy in the form of permanent or semi-permanent change in individuals: that is, learning.

5. CONVERGENCE OF THINKING, LEARNING AND REMAKING PRACTICE

It follows, then that the processes of thinking, acting, and learning at work are simultaneous, (Lave, 1993; Rogoff, 1995) and include the formation of working identities or subjectivities (Lave and Wenger, 1991). Lave (1993) concludes that wherever you encounter practice, you also identify learning. Rogoff (1995) similarly emphasises the central role of participation in learning. Across these theories, and consistent with cognitive views (e.g. Anderson, 1993), the consequences of individuals' engagement in goal-directed activities is more than achieving those activities' goals. There is also a cognitive legacy: change that is shaped by this experience (Anzai and Simon, 1979; Newell and Simon, 1972). Vygotskian and Piagetian constructivist perspectives hold that in deploying our cognitive resources when engaging in tasks and interactions, cognitive change results (Billett, 1996). These, as well as cognitive theories, suggest the scope of change is likely to be influenced by the novelty of the activity to individuals and the degree of effort they elect to engage in when undertaking activity (Newell and Simon, 1972). So the kind of problem or impasse that constitutes the individual's responses shapes the kind and extent of cognitive change (Van Lehn, 1989).

In a range of industry sectors, where no college based preparation or ongoing professional development exists (i.e. coalmining, food processing) workers reported that they largely learnt their often quite skilful work through everyday work activity (Billett, 2001c). Detailed analyses of the micro-social processes that individuals engage in and the social sourcing of the knowledge in the workplace indicates how this learning occurs (Billett, 2003b). The conscious process of engaging in activities and interactions that secures knowledge is not separable from changes to their knowledge, that is, the process and outcome for individuals referred to as learning. This process is both shaped by, and in turn shapes, individual identities.

Few aged care workers, for example, choose aged care as a vocation before they begin to work in the industry (Somerville, 2003). They often commence work in aged care for pragmatic reasons (availability of work, local contacts); it is not an intrinsic part of their subjectivities. However, once they are working in aged care they experience a growing passion and commitment to their work that becomes part of their sense of self. This process through which doing the aged care work becomes part of the aged care workers' identity begins early in their careers, and was described by a trainee Assistant in Nursing as 'entwining'.

In these accounts there is little distinction between the engagement in thinking and acting and the process of cognitive change and trans-formation of subjectivity or identify. For instance, in different ways, the five individuals whose work life was monitored over a nine-month period, all engaged in activities that shaped or reinforced their work identities (Billett and Pavlova, 2005). Changes in legislation caused an insurance broker to concentrate on large accounts, which was consistent with his work life ambitions. The emphasis on electronics based security measures buttressed Ken's goals of secure employment that returned a significant super-annuation. Achieving and then struggles with his identity as an electronics engineer emphasised the central role of his identity as a professional worker. In this way, individual learning, which includes the construction of their identities, is ongoing in everyday conscious thought. This is not reserved for particular learning moments (i.e. significant events) or situations (i.e. those designated for intentional learning—schools). It is a product of everyday conscious thought, which is active in seeking to make sense of what is encountered, as constructivist theories hold. Giddens (1991) refers to individuals seeking to balance what they encounter with their own goals and interests. Importantly, this drive to secure the self energises and directs individual learning.

So, there exists a close, interdependent relationship between the individual worker's sense of self and identity and their engagement in work. From that engagement emerge two kinds of legacies: individual change and the re-making of the cultural practices that constitute work. Given that individuals play an active role in constructing meaning from what they encounter, this suggests that a focus on learning for change, working life, and participation in the workplace need to account for the individual's sense of self and identity, which are both shaped by and shape their agency and intentionality.

6.   SALIENCE OF THE SELF

Individuals' identity and subjectivities shape the agentic action and intentionality that constitute the self. There is a person-dependence to how individuals engage with what they encounter and learning from it, because of the uniqueness of each individual's cognitive (pre-mediate) experience (Valsiner, 2000). This uniqueness arises from the distinct and individual pathway that constitutes individuals' ontogenies or personal histories. So an individual's construction of self and how they construe work is person-dependent, as individual ontogenies and ontogenetic development are unique—any one person's prior experience is not and cannot be the same as others as it is individually negotiated through a lifetime of interactions with the social world. Moreover, the means of social suggestion are never complete (Berger and Luckman, 1966) nor the social suggestion capable of a uniform effect (Valsiner, 1998). Instead, individuals responding to the same policy documents on learning societies engage in re-contextualising and re-negotiating meaning (Edwards and Boreham, 2003), thereby reflecting localised and individualised imperatives. Harré (1995: 373) suggests that the development of personality is socially guided and individually constructed in the course of human life: "People are born as potential persons, the process of becoming actual persons takes place through individual transformations of social experience."

The diversity of individuals' personal histories and vocational pathways and the process of negotiation they comprise was well illustrated in a recent study (Billett and Somerville, 2004). For example, during an interview about his working life, Jim reflected upon both his and his subordinates' approaches to work as motor mechanics. It was a conversation that emphasised the fluctuating relationships among identity, engagement in work and learning. He referred to the initial enthusiasm of school students' engagement in work experience programs at the garage, and their enjoyment at being allowed to undertake authentic work activities. He also noted how first-year apprentices initially were keen to work after normal working hours, putting cars away each evening and so on. They received overtime for this and were initially grateful for both the responsibility and the extra pay. Initially, they also accepted being responsible for tidying up the workshop at the end of each day. However, as they progressed through their apprenticeship they came to resent these menial tasks and the amount of overtime paid for the additional duties. Yet, they were enthusiastic about being given more complex and responsible tasks, such as conducting routine services on new vehicles, albeit under supervision. Later, they were eager to be offered tasks that were more complex than servicing new vehicles or those that comprised just the replacement of parts. As they progressed towards the completion of their apprenticeship, Jim noted that apprentices were often disrespectful towards and dismissive of more experienced mechanics, and were quick to leave at the end of the working day. He put this down to them being ready to move on to another workplace, where they could practice in a work environment different from where they had learnt their trade.

Then, he noted a time when after qualifying to become a mechanic he questioned whether this was what he wanted to do for the rest of his life. For instance, just a year prior to the interview, Jim had decided never to work as a mechanic again. Yet, having tried a few other jobs, he had returned to work as a supervisor of a large motor workshop. He worked long hours, many of which were voluntary, derived much personal satisfaction and immensely enjoyed his job that included hands-on mechanical work. He referred to a number of other mechanics who had also questioned whether they would continue on as mechanics. Some mechanics currently in his workshop had been through this experience and had now reconciled themselves to continuing their working life as a mechanic, though this was not always seen as a compromise. This negotiation of individuals' sense of identity is analogous to the stages of personality development that Erikson (1982) proposed, although not as linear. In ways analogous to his own commitment, Jim noted the older mechanics were more likely to be concerned to complete a job before leaving work. It was they, rather than the younger mechanics, who would request overtime in order to complete a job and be concerned about precision and thoroughness in their work (Billett and Somerville, 2004).

From this example, the knowledge encountered through engagement with the social world, such as in workplaces, and the energy or agency an individual deploys when interacting with that knowledge is likely to be central to what they learn, that is, in the way they constitute the concepts and practices they encounter. Different bases exist for these encounters and what individuals construct. Therefore, how individuals engage in workplace tasks is central to the learning that occurs. This engagement is, at least, in part shaped by individuals' identities. Jim, the workshop supervisor, referred to the wavering and changing engagement of apprentices during their indenture and work beyond their apprenticeships. Similarly, hairdressers were found to be quite strategic about selecting the kind of salons that they wished to work in (Billett, 2003b). This was associated with their identity as a hairdresser and desire to practice in circumstances that reflected their self-construction of that identity. These instances provide different accounts of relationships between identity and learning. The mechanics engage in tasks enthusiastically that reflect their evolving identity as mechanics from work experience, through apprenticeship and in their post trade development. The aged care workers embrace their role, building upon care giving within the family or connections with the community and gaining passion and interest in their work as they came to know the people that they cared for (Somerville, 2003).

So, rather than the abstract concept of occupation, it was the reality of their role that forged their identity with their practice. That is, the sense of self as a particular kind of worker and how they work. The coal workers engage in their work in ways validated by their community and under the direct tutelage of more experience workers. Given the potential dangers of their work, the need to work together and be trusted and reliable in their responses may be used as justification for these values. The engagement and learning of these workers is therefore associated with securing, developing and fulfilling work identities associated with difficult, tough and potentially dangerous work. That is, they actively participate in and appropriate core values and practices associated with their work.

However, despite this, their engagement and learning is not a process inevitably leading to unquestioned appropriation or socialisation. Indeed quite the opposite can happen, for instance dis-identification and rejection of the social sources and suggestions (Hodges, 1998). So, there is a relational basis for their engagement and learning, because the individual and social world can never come together in uniform or reciprocal ways. This relationship is founded upon the intensity of individual agency (e.g. the interests and dispositions), on the one hand, and the intensity of the social agency (i.e. the kind of affordances that are provided) on the other. These forms of agency are exercised and engaged in constructing the self and learning through work. Yet, in exercising their agency, individuals' actions also work to remake cultural practices.

7.   WORKPLACE TRANSFORMATIONS

A central issue for the cultural practices that constitute paid work, is their transmission and remaking over time. This process is achieved not through some uniform wave of change that propels each new generation of practitioners. Instead, it is a process where individuals actively play a role in remaking and refining the cultural practices as they confront particular problems and adopt new technologies in addressing those problems. So, cultural heritage is remade incrementally, individually and yet in ways that constitute a pattern of change. At the heart of this process are changing environments, requirements and technologies that are products of evolving history. Structuralist views suggest that these social factors and forms determine change and represent the locus of new learning or change (e.g. Ratner, 2000).

However, other views suggest that it is individuals actions that trans-forms cultural practice (Leontyev, 1981; Rogoff, 1990; Valsiner, 1998), such as work. For instance, the dramatic experience of an aged care nurse through a workplace injury, led to her focus upon improving work practices in the industry (Somerville, 2003). She exercised energy and intentionality in her efforts to improve (transform) practice. In the same sector, the appro-priateness of behaviour in dealing with the deceased was transformed by the agentic action of one worker, who raised issues of sensitivity that had not been adopted as practice in the aged care setting. In a mortuary that performs coronial autopsies, one counsellor succeeded in changing the processes of counselling the next of kin which transformed the operation and practice not only of the counsellors, but also other workers in the facility (Billett et al., 2004). That individual's belief about appropriate counselling, the opportunity to advance his view, and an invitational environment in which he was afforded professional standing all contributed to his transforming the counselling activity. These instances of changing practices illuminate the possibilities for individuals to make significant changes to the conduct of their work, and the requirements for work performance. For instance as Scribner (1997: 381) identified:

> Because adaptation is a concept that emphasizes the fit of human thought and behaviour to an existing environment, describing thinking at work as adaptive would seem to preclude its characterisation as creative. The notion of creativity stresses the human production as something new. Yet thinking in the diary was both adaptive and creative. Adaptation of thought to its functional requirements had an active, not passive character, and it proceeded on the basis of worker invention of new solutions and strategies. Invention is a hallmark of creativity and it

played a major role in all of the occupations studied in the dairy community.

The enactment of work, the act of negotiating the kind of crises of identity that Jim the mechanic referred to, as well as through everyday events as part of working life, is likely to be salient for an individual's learning and their engagement in events that transform work. The self both energises and directs the intentionality required for robust learning from events individuals encounter, yet the self can be transformed by these very events. As Fenwick (1998) proposes, the self is not just reflexive of socially-derived subjectivities and practices, it has intentionality that is personally directive. So individuals' identity can play more than a reflexive role in responses to these events (i.e. what is learnt) and in turn can be reshaped by particularly traumatic events.

Coal miners also witness or experience events that cause them to question work practices and, hence, their worker subjectivities (Billett and Somerville, 2004; Somerville, 2002). One mineworker described how he decided to become a supervisor, placing him in a contested relationship with much of the workplace practices and community values with which he had previously identified. Others have had particular kinds of experiences that led to questioning these practices. These events were not some inevitable and unfolding stage in the individual's life history, nor were the outcomes predictable. However, they did cause transformation in individuals' identities and their focus upon and approach to work. They also disrupted one set of subjectivities allowing others to play a role. Yet, the action and changes that transpired was, at least in part, a product of the individuals' intentionality and agency, not just the press of the immediate social suggestion. The disruption to the subjectivities, led to a transformation of identity and the appropriation of new kinds of subjectivities (e.g. safer working practices, more ethical approaches to work, a healthier lifestyle).

In the case of two coal workers, this transformation illuminates the powerful role of subjectivity on learning (Somerville, 2002). One had been seriously injured in a mine site accident. The other had experienced a life-threatening health problem due to mine workers' lifestyle (i.e. heavy consumption of alcohol and unhealthy diet). In both cases, these events lead to a reappraisal of the subjectivities that had directed their behaviour and work practices, eventually leading to both disassociating with these subjectivities. However, both experienced frustration and rebuttals as they attempted to get others to question their practices and lifestyle. In contrast, other miners having experienced similar traumatic events were still uncritically subject to those practices. So the process of dis-identification (Hodges, 1998) which these two miners had encountered differed from the continuing identification with the mining work practices of other workers. While the same barrage of social press existed, these workers construed it differently. Moreover, the change of identity was reinforced by the realisation of their incapacity to disrupt others' subjection to the set of social suggestions that they had rejected. So, in seeking to understand how individuals engage with, ignore or embrace change in their working lives at a time of frequent and sometimes significant change in the requirements of work and work practices, it is important to understand the relationships between an individual's identity, subjectivity and intentionality and how they engage in responding to changes in the workplace, themselves change through that engagement, and how factors outside of the workplace act to shape that identity and subjectivity.

Against what is often reported in the literature about the de-skilling, marginalisation and alienation of contemporary working life brought about by such changes, each of these individuals benefited from the changes. In four of the five instances, the changes were actually consistent with and buttressed the individuals' career trajectories. That is, the changes provided the vehicle by which they could enact their preferences, gain greater security in their work, practice fulfilling and personally rewarding work and direct energies into projects that were closely associated with their identity and values. Of course, others associated with these participants were identified as not faring so well. However, these changes provided the context for individuals to play a constructive role in changing practice. Leontyev (1981: 195) identified this process of remaking culture as being a product of an individual's active engagement in and appropriation of particular cultural practices and values: "…through activity, human beings change the environment, and through that change they build their own novel psychological functions."

Similarly, small business operators' efforts to learn about the new goods and service tax, was the key basis for directing their learning. It shaped who they consulted with and how and the degree of effort sustained in learning about the new initiative was dependent upon their identity and intentionality (Billett et al., 2003). The response to the uniform initiative was diverse in its scope, attention and enactment. Even when compelled to conform to particular practices, individuals decided how they would respond, including how they constructed the initiative.

8. A RELATIONAL WAY OF UNDERSTANDING WORK

In conclusion, that rather than being wholly subject to change, individuals are actively engaged in remaking cultural practices, such as those required for effective work practice. The change or learning that arises from everyday and novel events is associated with how individuals direct their intentionalities and agency when engaging with what they experience through these events in ways that can be seen as a relational interdependence. Individual experiences in social practices, such as workplaces, will incrementally, contribute to transformation changes in their ways of knowing and sense of self. Individual subjectivity both shapes the kind of changes that occur and is shaped by events, particularly singularly dramatic events, because it shapes response to those events. Perhaps as Rogoff (1990) suggests, it is the engagement of individuals in solving novel problems, generated by culturally and historically derived knowledge confronting new circumstances, through which culture and cultural practices are remade.

The interplay between the social and individual is not restricted to norms and workplace practices. It also shapes the basis for both human and social agency associated with work and the worth of work. The key arguments in this chapter are that what constitutes work is negotiated between institutional facts (Searle, 1995) and other social forms (Valsiner, 1998) that constitute the social experience (Harré, 1995) on the one hand, and individuals' 'cognitive experience' on the other. Given this, it is necessary to identify elaborate bases for these negotiations in their role in what constitute work and its remaking. These processes are held to be interdependent: each requiring the other. However, rather than mutual or equally exercised, the relationship is relational, with different emphases and contributions being afforded in different ways by the exercise of individual and social agency.

In the next chapter, these conceptual platforms are engaged to elaborate conceptions of the worth of work, including those that have a social basis as well as those denying the subjective experience of individuals. More so, it extends these ideas to explain the distinct ways the worth of work is viewed. Such worth is central to the how individuals and other experience work, participate in and remake it.

Chapter 4

THE WORTH OF WORK

For most employees, work has a generally unpleasant quality. If there is little Calvinist compulsion to work among property-less factory workers or clerks, there is also little Renaissance exuberance in the work of the insurance clerk, freight handler, or department store saleslady. (Wright Mills, 1973: 3)

Changes in the kinds of work available have different consequences for individuals and communities. For some individuals, opportunities for paid work and continuing personal careers have become enhanced while for others, the opportunities have been reduced. As well, the prospects and purposes of some communities and those who live and work in them have been reshaped by such changes. As personal and work identities are closely linked, these changes can have significant impacts for communities and individuals. These include affirming the worth of an occupational identity and a community's continuity, or challenging or transforming both. Similarly, changes in how individuals participate in work can also transform the nature of work, again with implications for those who participate in and seek to develop and maintain a sense of self associated with their work activities. Consequently, these changes can reshape the worth of work to individuals and their communities. Together, these sets of concerns draw attention to the bases by which the worth of work is understood and transformed. In this chapter, bases for considering the worth of work are categorised and discussed.

Consistent with the case developed throughout this book judgements about the worth of work, and how these are negotiated between societal and values-based views of work and what that work means to individuals and their sense of self have been provided. This chapter firstly discusses how the concept of work quality can be understood. Parameters are established for making judgements about the worth of work premised on a consideration of both an objective account of work and its worth and also what work means to individuals. Following this, four perspectives on the valuing of work are elaborated. These comprise: (i) socially sanctioned views of occupations; (ii) values-based judgements of occupations; (iii) material rewards and benefits of occupations; and (iv) the worth of occupations to individuals.

1.   WORK QUALITY OR QUALITY WORK?

Discussions about the experiences of work, the availability of different kinds of work and changes to how people participate in work, inevitably become linked to questions about the quality of that work for those who engage with it.

One approach to judging the worth of work is to acknowledge that society views some kinds of work as being more well-regarded than others. There are often very good reasons for such judgements based upon the depth or complexity of skill required for the work or its crucial nature. Another approach is to identify material qualities of work as well as likely benefits, such as hours worked, levels of pay, superannuation, extent of paid leave and so on. This then provides a platform to make judgements about the kinds of demands that jobs make upon individuals and the benefits that might accrue to them. So, for instance, because teachers often receive extended periods of paid leave teaching might be seen as attractive work. Similarly, work that attracts very high salaries might also be considered attractive. This provides a vehicle to make comparisons across different kinds of occupations. Highly paid work that is dirty and potentially dangerous (e.g. coalmining, commercial trawling) might be compared against that which is conducted in offices and without obvious inherent personal, legal or financial risk (e.g. professionals' work). Yet, even this more objective approach is laden with complexities, particularly when comparisons at a much broader level need to be made. Benefits, such as health insurance, paid for by the employer have quite a different meaning and significance in Australia than America, for instance, where only limited public health care is available.

However, even where objective measures are applied, there is still debate about what constitutes the bases for worthwhile work. For instance, McGovern et al., (2004) referred to distinct views between those who claimed that non-standard forms of work (i.e. flexible working hours or part-time work) provide time for work, leisure and also family life thereby making for a more fulfilling involvement in public and private life. Handy (1994) and Bolle (2001) are seen as advocates of this kind of view. Certainly, there is evidence of many individuals seeking to balance their life in and outside of the workplace (e.g. Billett and Pavlova, 2005). Some part-time workers do so voluntarily to secure an effective balance between a working life required to sustain their economic needs, and time to dedicate to family and community (Bolle, 2001; Noon and Blyton, 1997; Tam, 1997).

In contrast, according to McGovern et al. (2004), the likes of Beck (1992) and Gorz (1990) claim that new kinds of non-standard work merely represent the next stage in the commodification of labour that goes beyond distinctions between white and blue collar workers and erodes the standard concept of full-time employment as an acceptable norm. For many contemporary workers, retrenchment from a permanent job and subsequent employment in a job that is part-time and offers lower benefits can have significant impacts upon their material and psychological well-being (Van Horn, 1996). However, while useful in many ways, for purposes of comparison within and across occupations and across countries, objective measures such as benefits, hours of work and even societal standing fail to account for the degree to which workers find their work personally satisfying, on the one hand, or are held in high esteem within their community, on the other.

To propose that worthwhile work is confined to that which is highly paid, and/or of presumed social benefit, may render the majority of workers as engaging in worthless pursuits. Yet, across different kinds of work, individuals want to be seen as performing effectively, often gaining a sense of identity and self through their work and its relationship to their lives in the community outside of the workplace (Billett, 2001c). Somerville (2002) illuminates the powerful links between community norms and practices and individuals' identities in the aged care and coal mining sectors. This link extends to individuals sustaining and accepting injury as part of the interplay between individual and community identity (i.e. all aged care workers have bad backs, coal miners carry work-related injuries with pride).

These examples provide instances of work that may be held in low regard within the community generally; yet, within coal mining communities, coal mining work, is of high standing, and is often very well remunerated. So, while not enjoying high status within the broader community, coal miners' work is central to the coal mining community's very existence and continuity. Equally, the work is important to the individual's sense of self and identity, not only as a worker, but also as a community member. It may not be surprising then that young men in coal mining communities state a preference for this kind of work from an early age. However, it is probably more surprising for a young person to suggest that they want to work in aged care. Somerville (2003) notes that aged care is considered low status work, even within nursing. She reports an incident of a lecture room full of nurse undergraduates being asked about their preferences for nursing specialisations. When the topic of aged care was mentioned, there was general laughter within the lecture theatre, which was shared by the lecturer. However, in their collective humouring of this nursing option, they failed to observe the single student whose arm was raised. It seems that many aged care workers engage in this work because of convenience, rather than a commitment to caring for the aged (Somerville, 2003). However, once engaged in the work, they can develop the identity of the aged care worker, which includes carrying with pride injuries that come from lifting elderly patients in and out of beds. Indeed, the emblematic quality of a bad back is held to stand in the way of securing more safety conscious working practices, as it does for coalminers. In this way, work that is lowly regarded in the general community, despite its obvious important public purpose, becomes important to individuals' sense of self and identity when they work within that sector or community. That is, there is a different, perhaps more embedded, relationship between a broadly societal view of work, and one premised on benefits and issues of worth and identity of the individuals engaged in particular kinds of work.

Yet, even beyond these accounts, where individuals' sense of worth and identity are at least embedded in communities or a particular occupational practice, there is also evidence that valuing occupations is more individually focused (Billett et al., 2003; Billett and Pavlova, 2005; Somerville, 2002). That is, while often associated with societal roles and expectations, studies of the working lives of individuals have demonstrated that work activities and work identity have particular meaning to individuals that are derived through their personal histories. Moreover, perhaps as with many of the aged care workers, there is an active process of interdependence between an individual trajectory and the workplace which can lead to the buttressing, reshaping or transforming of the individual's sense of self. However, this sense of self is not solely a product of the immediate social experience encountered in communities or workplaces. Individuals also play a role in terms of what they value, why it is valued and how this relates to their sense of self at a particular point in time in their personal history. For instance, the satisfaction that individuals might gain from employment, how it com-plements their sense of self, is an important dimension that is not wholly addressed in many of the sociological accounts of work. Of course, the emphasis of local and individual valuing of work is not without problems. Some social theories would portray workers who are engaged in work of low status and with low remuneration yet who gain a sense of self through their work as a product of the development of a false consciousness (Ratner, 2000). That is, these workers have been duped into believing the worth of their work in ways that are ultimately self-exploitative. There are however instances where individuals' sense of self is supported in ways that are less easily dismissed than this. For instance, while for many individuals part-time work is involuntary and has undesirable consequences, for others it provides a more effective balance between work and family life, than full-time employment would (Bolle, 2001; Tam, 1997).

McGovern et al. (2004) suggest that the distinct positions outlined above have quite different conceptual premises. Moreover, they suggest that the reliance of leading European sociologists such as Beck (1992), Bauman (2003) and Giddens (1991) on theoretical assertions, rather than empirical analysis of evidence based in practice stands to make any reconciliation between these perspectives problematic. In this way, their views might be seen as no more than a refined articulation of the kind of societal and values-driven perspectives that consider particular kinds of work as more or less well regarded. That is, they use a particular conceptual lens to make judgements about the worth of work as an objective fact premised within a set of values. Yet, as illustrated, beyond these socially derived perspectives, there are also more individually derived constructions about the worth of paid work, albeit set within a socially derived milieu or setting.

So, how do we understand the worth of work to individuals, communities and societies? In the next section, four perspectives of the valuing of work are proposed.

2.   PERSPECTIVES ON THE VALUING OF WORK

In considering how work might be valued, approaches can be described as being either principally objective or principally subjective. The objective approaches comprise those relating to: (i) socially sanctioned work in terms of its status and remuneration; (ii) values-based judgements about work; and (iii) the material rewards and benefits afforded to different kinds of work. Subjective accounts involve (iv) the meaning that work has for individuals and their sense of self. Although not wholly distinct as a set of categories, they provide a way of considering how different kinds of work are valued and how those values must change over time. These four categories are now discussed in turn.

2.1   Socially sanctioned views of occupations

Well-regarded work is often shaped by socially sanctioned views about occupations that might exist generally across society and within particular communities. The major professions of law, medicine and accountancy with their high levels of pay and discretionary capacities, for instance, are often seen at the top of such hierarchies. These occupations are perceived to enjoy autonomy of practice and are proposed as being enacted with a negation of self-interest that may be evident in other kinds of work that are more about trading time for remuneration. Similarly, professional work is often seen as clean work not involving dirt or physical labour. Playing out here is the distinction between mental and manual work. In Western societies, there has been a long tradition of dualism which has sought to separate the mind from activity, the head from the hand and theoretical culture from utility, and in the context of work, superior from inferior occupations (Skilbeck, Connell, Lowe and Tait, 1994). Distinctions of what comprise worthwhile occupations and how they might be differentiated are articulated through such traditions. For instance, occupations that comprise more or less amounts of physical activity can be categorised such that the latter are often perceived as more prestigious. That is, working with the head constitutes a more dignified and worthwhile form of work than using the body; hence, the longstanding distinction between white- and blue-collar work. Such sentiments are quite powerful, yet abstracted. As noted elsewhere, the efforts by Korean governments to encourage young people to go into manufacturing work is being resisted by both teachers and parents who claim that such work is low status and dirty (Cho and Apple, 1998). They advise, respectively, their students and children not to heed the government requests to consider manufacturing as a worthwhile form of work. Instead, clean professional and administrative work is seen to be desirable and in keeping with Korean societal values.

Oaths or codes of practice are more likely to govern professional work, than close supervision. Self-regulation may be proposed as more appropriate for the professions, than external regulation, since it is considered that professional conduct is of its very nature in the general interest. Medical and law professions have their own professional bodies that monitor and regulate professional practice and can apply sanctions to members whose practice is deemed inappropriate or unprofessional. The status of these well-regarded forms of work is underpinned by competitive entry, rigid requirements for qualifications and professional bodies to maintain the standing of their practices, and also regulate the flow of new entrants. Some would argue that this regulation ensures levels of relative scarcity that serve the profession's interests.

Of course, such societal views are also sanctioned by beliefs about the complexity, significance and crucial character of these professions' practices, including the level of responsibility that such works carries (e.g. individuals' health, companies' operations and the administration of justice). However, such distinctions imply that other forms of vocations lack profound bodies of knowledge and are more likely to be practiced in ways characterised by self-interest, thereby demanding external regulation of practice. No such professional body exists for the trades and regulation of their practice is more likely managed by a government agency, not by the practitioners themselves. There are exceptions, however. For instance in Germany trade guilds play a role nationally and locally play a key role in regulating the practice of skilled work. However, in this country skilled trades work is valued in ways that is distinct from many other countries.

Yet, it is unclear how useful these distinctions about professional practice are given that they are premised on occupational classifications and assumptions about practice. It is reasonable to ask in what ways is the ability not to act in self-interest or to profess confined to lawyers, accountants and medical doctors and not to those in other kinds of occupational practice? Also, some professions involve physical work and long hours that may be associated with lower levels of work, thereby challenging the distinction between mental and manual work. Similarly, not all work activities with minimal manual components are highly prized (e.g. clerical work). Therefore, it is necessary to consider the values that are used to form assumptions about categories of human activities that seek to differentiate them in particular ways. Certainly, many of the attributes ascribed to professions are desirable in and practised across many forms of vocational activities. That is, they can be seen as attributes of performance, rather than categories of occupations and are not constrained to those occupational categories defined as professional.

There are also likely to be more localised sanctioned views about occupations that exist within particular communities or groups of interest. However, these views may arise from societal norms that may not reflect the complexity and value of the occupational tasks. For example, Lewis (2005) notes how the work of truck drivers has become increasingly complex as their work demands not only fuel efficiency and delivery of goods at specified times, even through unpredictable traffic conditions, but also management of the increasingly complex technology of a contemporary truck. Such work includes managing the load, fuel efficiency, emissions and wear and tear on the vehicle. So, beyond understanding how to drive the vehicle effectively and knowing the routes along which to travel, the truck driver has also to manage the effective use of an expensive asset. Moreover, if the truck driver also owns the vehicle, they are engaged in managing a small business. Such requirements are not restricted to truck driving, of course. However, to those outside of the road transport industry, the conceptions of truck driving are probably quite remote from the complexities of contemporary truck driving practice. Yet, these views are likely to be inconsistent with societal views about truck driving as a form of well-regarded work, despite it being essential for people to having available the food stuffs they wish to eat. Instead, and inflating societal prejudices, sociologists, such as Rifkin (1995) and Wright Mills (1973), claim that few workers are engaged in worthwhile work, thereby supporting contemporary commentators views that service work, such as call centre work, is inherently without worth. Such work can be complex, varied, skilled and subject to worker discretion with the operators working in a collaborative way (Billett, 2002b). The work has many qualities that elsewhere (in professional high discretionary work) enjoy high status. So valuing work by its extrinsic qualities alone is precarious.

Yet, salary levels and status do not assure social worth, nor do socially derived values. While there may be socially sanctioned views about what constitutes well-regarded work, and the level of societal endorsement distributed to different kinds of work, there is also likely to be localised views about what constitutes desirable work that may be inconsistent with the broader societal view. Certainly, as Darrah (1996) suggests, the complexity of paid work is only partially revealed through the objective analyses of work. In examining the work undertaken in various kinds of occupations this sentiment seems to be quite true.

However, what constitutes well-regarded work within a society or culture is not fixed, it can be subject to change, with consequences for those engaged in that kind of work. In 1994, at a conference in Moscow, hosted by the Russian Academy of Education, a senior professor who chaired that Academy referred to the significant transformations occurring in Russia as the state led command-economy transformed into a more mixed and, in some ways, free market economy. He noted that emerging entrepreneurial and service occupations were trammelling the previously prestigious occupations of science, academic work and the arts. Senior scientists' salaries, including his own, were now a fraction of those paid to individuals securing lucrative service and entrepreneurial work. Lifetimes of career development in previously prestigious forms of work were being summarily undercut by transforming cultural values that were manifest in forms of work quite distinct from those previously well-regarded. He scoffed at the idea of room attendants in Moscow luxury hotels being paid a higher salary than his own (which they were).

Similarly, after the attacks upon New York in September 2001, it appears that the status of fire fighters has been elevated. Fire fighters in Australia report people waving to them in the street when responding to emergency calls and their sense of being highly valued in the community is endorsed through interactions with community members (Billett et al., 2005). One fire fighter happily reported fire fighters' standing as being far higher than that of police and ambulance workers and being invited to join social circles that had previously excluded him. In a recent visit to North America, I witnessed a similar phenomenon as people waved to and cheered a fire truck with the

fire fighters nonchalantly waving back to those on the street. The irony here
is that the fire fighters in our study also report that fighting fires is becoming
a decreasing and small part of their work since fire prevention and control
strategies are more becoming more effective, and buildings are being built
to resist fire. Consequently, their work now comprises dealing with emergency incidents involving motor vehicle accidents and other kinds of rescue.
However, despite these changes in work allocations, the workers still
strongly identify as fighters of fires. This story depicts the transformations of
work: change in societal or cultural requirements for particular kinds of
work.

Yet, how particular kinds of work are regarded in society is not the only
basis for making judgements about the worth of work. Although doctors,
lawyers, accountants and, now, fire fighters are seen as desirable occupations
with potentially positive social purposes, they are not immune from bad
practice and exercise of self-interest. Also, even within the professions, some
forms of work and individuals engagement in them is more or less highly
regarded. Cosmetic surgeons may, for instance, have lower standing than
those who assist burns victims, even though they both have similar focuses.
The appointee to a judicial position through having associations with a
current government may well struggle to secure the same professional
standing as those who are seen to have secured their promotion through
effort, diligence and good practice (i.e. merit). Furthermore, to judge the
worth of individuals' work on the basis of a hierarchy of socially regarded
occupations stands to render the majority of workers as engaged in unworthy
work. Such a hierarchy will position the majority of workers in an inferior
relationship to the relative few who are engaged in high status professional
work. So, beyond broad categories of the regard for different kinds of work,
there will need also to be values-based and relational judgements about
occupations.

2.2   Values-based judgements of occupations

There are sets of values within the community and society that will be
used to make value judgements about the worth of particular kinds of work.
For instance, the social worth of work in performing a social good might be
applied. So, for instance, nurses and teachers might be viewed as engaging in
work that is inherently more worthwhile than those who buy and sell houses
and cars. Thus, from a values perspective, it might be claimed that because
the work of auditors is non-emancipatory, preparation for this work is not
worthy of being conducted in universities. This view proposes the value of a
person's work should be appraised by some objective measure associated
with particular sets of values. In this case, that auditing does not constitute

emancipatory work. This suggests that individuals' work can be valued on objectified measures of its emancipatory worth. From this perspective, work nominated as being for the social good (e.g. teaching, nursing, social work) will be seen as most valuable. Presumably, from this perspective other forms of work such as business and commerce might not be deemed so worthwhile. Moreover, the standing of occupations under this value system would be such that only worthy forms of work would warrant preparation in universities, and be publicly funded. So for instance, nursing is now held to be worthy of university-based preparation. Yet, is nursing so very different in its requirements from other occupations (e.g. trade work in electronics) that are not deemed worthy of a university-based preparation in many countries? Clearly, there are values based judgements as well as societal sentiments about occupations that carry through into decisions about the worth, standing and level of required preparation of that occupation.

However, continuing with the auditor example from above exposes some of the limits of solely classifying work in this way. For instance, to somebody from a low socio-economic background or who achieved poorly at school, becoming an auditor might be taken as being personally or socially emancipatory. Furthermore, auditors' work might be used to expose corruption or to assist with the work of charities and aid agencies—the outcomes of such work could also be seen as emancipatory. Thus, applying such a measure to a classification of occupation, without knowing to what purposes that occupational activity is to be directed is problematic. Also, obviously, socially sanctioned and privileged knowledge is not restricted to work which is labelled as emancipatory.

A values based approach to understanding the worth of work is also prone to contestation within a community because different values and perspectives exist. In contrast to countries such as Australia, Britain and America where call centre work is seen to be low status work, in India it is highly sought after with well-educated young people in India competing to secure employment in the growing call centre sector. The work is relatively well-paid, conditions are relatively good and corporations take care of their employees in ways that are more common of those in Western countries. Moreover, the concentration of these call or service centres creates environments where young educated Indian men and women and their lifestyle that may be different from what is available elsewhere in India. Yet, often the parents of these workers advise them not to engage in this kind of work because they see it as being antithetical to Indian cultural values and practices (personal communication). That is, the work can include working through traditional Indian holidays, getting holidays in line with those in the countries they service and engaging in shift work. As well, the work is seen as antifamily, with younger men and women working together in ways that confront traditional values, and exposing them to unacceptable aspects of westernisation. So, there can be contradictions between two value systems about what constitutes worthwhile work.

This balancing of preference and benefits is consistent with another perspective about how work should be valued, and that is the benefits that it accrues to individuals. So, a values based approach to considering the worth of occupations stands as an important and relations basis to make judgements about how work might be judged and valued.

2.3   Material rewards and benefits of occupations

The rewards and benefits of work are also a compelling and important basis by which the worth of paid work might be valued. Given that a fundamental purpose of engaging in paid work is an exchange of labour and time for remuneration, the level of direct remuneration and associated benefits that particular work attracts stand as a basis by which work can be valued and appraised in both societal and individual terms. The benefits of good jobs, those offering opportunities for and the prospects of promotion and substantial increases in pay, security and social status, stand as a consideration for what constitutes worthwhile work. Levels of remuneration are contested and hard-fought for bases to order the returns to individuals and the cost to employers for paid work. It is these and other conditions and benefits of work that have been the substance of the long-running contestation between organised labour and capital. Moreover, the capacity to secure a liveable remuneration and to secure a high material quality of life probably stands as a major motivator form most workers. Yet, there are benefits beyond levels of immediate remuneration. McGovern et al. (2004) propose that opportunities for personal promotion are central to the definition of what constitutes good or bad work. Consideration of a broad range of work benefits including levels of pay, opportunities for promotion, and non salary benefits such as pensions and health care, offer a more comprehensive set of factors through which to make judgements about the worth of work. For instance, Kalleberg, Reskin and Hudson's (2000) analysis of 'bad jobs' in America, characterised such jobs as those with low pay and without access to health insurance and pension benefits. They found that approximately one in seven jobs in America are 'bad' on these dimensions. Interestingly, their study concluded that, economic returns to work tended to reflect the kinds of societal judgements discussed above about well-regarded work. That is, bad jobs are those that are low paid, have few benefits and lead nowhere: dead-end jobs. McGovern et al. (2004: 235), claim that between "one quarter and a half of the working population in Britain are in jobs that have at least one bad characteristic. Over a quarter of

all employees (29%) are low paid, just over one third have no pension
(37%), a similar proportion have no sick pay (36%) and half are in jobs that
do not have recognised opportunities for promotion (51%)". Aggregating
these data, McGovern et al. (2004) claim that about 10% of workers are in
employment that is bad on all four dimensions, yet only a little over a quarter
(28%) of the labour force are in jobs that are not bad in any respect. They
conclude that their analysis also supports the popular societal conception of
Mac jobs " ...in that they tend to be held by young people, with few
qualifications and possibly a history of unemployment, require little skill, are
poorly paid, have few fringe benefits and little prospect of upward mobility"
(p. 241).

In this way, these authors provide evidence to support the case made by
Beck (1992), Baumann (1998) and Rifkin (1995) that many new forms of
work, in terms of material and financial benefits, are not as worthy as those
from an earlier era, and that the new forms of workplace participation serve
to disempower those who participate in them.

Consequently, a consideration of rewards and benefits arising from
particular kinds of paid employment provides an important perspective on
the worth of work, that is, the extent of benefits that accrue to those
individuals or groups of individuals who participate in particular kinds of
work. The extent to which some individuals are more able than others to
negotiate effective benefits for themselves stands as a key premise upon
which the worth of work may be considered. Taking a relative rather than
absolutist view, which perhaps Wright-Mills (1973) does, is to suggest that
there should be benefits of particular standards that warrant work being
tagged as 'worthwhile'. If a ranked analysis is conducted based on societal
status of work, this then would suggest that only those at the top of the
benefit hierarchy are engaged in worthwhile work. Such an analysis still fails
to account for relative times and different needs, perspectives and personal
trajectories. The level of benefits and salary alone is not sufficient to fully
account for the kinds of work that people are drawn towards and in
which they willingly engage. For instance, on the basis of benefits and
remuneration alone many, perhaps even the majority of workers are engaging in unworthy work. Yet, the kinds of rewards that individuals are
interested in securing and willing to make sacrifices to secure are likely to be
uniform. For instance, Grey (1994) notes how individuals are willing to
present themselves as something other than they are (i.e. the entrepreneurial
self (Rose, 1990)) in order to secure permanency and promotion. However,
this is merely a facade that they are projecting to secure benefits and
rewards. For others, the direct financial benefits are offset by goals associated with position and status. For instance, many politicians are paid a
fraction of the levels paid to key positions with industry. Perhaps for these

individuals, the capacity to make laws, make change, and advance particular set of values and beliefs stands as a significant benefit and motivation to engage in public life. The point is that financial benefits and even rewards such as public standing and the capacity to exercise power will not be uniformly welcomed or embraced by individuals. So what constitutes benefits and rewards remains in some ways relational. Using the example of paid part-time work it is possible to identify the relational process enacted. As Bolle (2001: 307) suggests of part-time work:

> If it is freely chosen and protected by law, part-time employment no doubt offers workers a good way of striking a balance between the time they must spend earning a living and the time they wish to devote to other activities.

This consideration of a relational view of benefits leads to consideration of another perspective on the worth of work. That is, what that work means to individuals.

2.4 Worth of occupations to individuals

Work is often important to the individuals who participate in it (e.g. Noon and Blyton, 1997; Pusey, 2003) in ways beyond or in addition to the necessary financial remuneration it provides, and its societal standing. There is an economic necessity to work, but also intrinsic rewards (e.g. enjoyment, creativity, personal fulfilment). As Noon and Blyton (1997) propose, the majority of people in all categories of jobs would continue to work even if there was no financial need. That is, work also has salience for individuals in terms of exercising their capacities as humans and contributors to their workplaces and communities (e.g. Pusey, 2003). Barley and Orr (1997: 2) also acknowledge the important personal dimension of work and its worth to those individuals who enact it: "...the evolving goals and nature of work must be seen within the context of human existence itself. For work is the purposeful *human* activity directed towards the satisfaction of human needs and desires."

Here, the notion of engaging in useful work is consistent with their preferred life trajectory: their vocation. While the term 'vocation' is used commonly to describe paid work, often in association with employment activities that have strong trade or manual components, it can have specific meanings for individuals. Dewey (1916) referred to vocation as a calling that is central to an individual's identity or key purpose in life. He argued that for individuals to spend their life in a vocation (i.e. occupation) to which they were not suited and did not exercise their full capacities was a significant waste of human intelligence and energy. The proposal of an individual basis to consider the concept of vocations is consistent with a more person-dependent and identity based conception of the worth of paid work:

> A vocation means nothing but such direction in life activities as to render them perceptibly significant to a person, because of the consequences they accomplish, and are also useful to his [sic] associates. ...Occupation is a concrete term for continuity. It includes the development of artistic capacity of any kind, of special scientific ability, of effective citizenship, as well as professional and business occupations, to say nothing of mechanical labor or engagement in gainful pursuits. (Dewey, 1916: 307)

Associated with this sense of vocation is the importance of an individual's sense of self and how this can be realised through their paid work and how that paid work contributes to their identity. Dewey's proposal that it is the significance of the vocational activity to the individual that is paramount subsumes the societal view of the worthiness of a particular form of work. Not only does Dewey suggests that the significance of the in-dividual is important, but also the individual's continuity. So, rather than being either highly individual or socially sanctioned, it constitutes something which is interwoven with the individuals' continuity and life direction.

These perspectives also acknowledge that, ultimately, it is how individuals direct their energies and capacities in their conduct of work that is central to workplace performance. Engagement in paid work is not a process of unthinking and disengaged deployment of individuals' capacities. Instead, individuals and work interact in ways shaped by their understandings, capacities and values, as discussed in previous chapters. Therefore, the individual perspective's contribution to work and its changing character should not be downplayed. For instance, the degree of discretion (in terms of the scope of their work, the level and intensity of their engagement and the extent to which is consistent with their personal goals) which an individual's work affords might also be seen as a measure of its worth. This discretion is often qualitatively associated with high status professional work, as noted above.

Although the degree of discretion workers are permitted is typically seen as highly desirable it too can be a perilous measure. In a recent study, (Billett et al., 2004) a health-based worker granted high levels of discretion in work, which closely aligned to her personal goals and values, was exploited by the breadth and discretion her work practice afforded her. Even though her work was of social worth, being directed to social justice, it made almost intolerable demands upon her. Essentially, it was the independent and highly discretionary nature of the work that was making unrealistic demands on her time and health. Depending upon the perspective, the individual is either exercising their agency to the fullest or is being subjugated by a usurious employment arrangement.

Some views suggest that changes to work in the post-industrial era are not considerate of these kinds of individual goals. For these perspectives, changes to work are about disempowerment and de-skilling (Bauman, 1998; Beck, 1992; Rifkin, 1995), thereby potentially violating this important facet of work for individuals' sense of self. Indeed, taking technology itself as a case, the very technology that Barley and Orr (1997) discuss is held by some as playing a key role in disempowerment and de-skilling, while others propose a less deterministic account of technology and changes to work. Best (1992:2) suggests that while technology may transform the nature of work, it is not the sole determinant of our futures:

> While technology may decide the inertia, constraints and opportunities work is still a human activity, and it will be the actions stemming from our individual and aggregate human needs which ultimately determine the use of technology and the future of work.

One way to address, although not resolve, this conundrum is to consider how individuals think about and participate in their paid work. In research that sought to understand learning in workplace settings, individuals were identified as engaging in a highly committed manner in work that many would view as being low status or lowly paid (e.g. coal production workers, process workers, call centre workers) (Billett, 2002b). While these workers often reported dissatisfaction with their workplace affordances (e.g. conditions and the actions of fellow workers and employers), they also claimed and demonstrated high levels of commitment to and interest in their work. These were workers who took their work seriously, wanted to do a good job and be accepted by their peers as good performers. That is, they engaged in this work in ways that exercised their agency, yet directed to their subjectivities (e.g. approval of peers) and identity (e.g. being seen as a good team worker). Does the notion of socialisation of false consciousness play out here? Are these individuals merely cultural dopes, who have been duped into self-exploitation and false consciousness as structural accounts (Ratner, 2000) would suggest? Or are they intentionally exercising agency consistent with their identities and subjectivities? If the former view is taken, it suggests that we should only value an individual's vocational practice and engagement in terms of its extrinsic worth (e.g. its status, standing, purposes). "In the future, personal stability will have to come from the meaning and values that workers construct subjectively for themselves, not received objectivity from their occupational titles" (Savickas, 1999: 54).

Consequently, the processes of valuing a particular vocational practice over others are dynamic, relational and also person-dependent. It seems no more problematic to value work for its worth to individuals' identity and subjectivities than to more socially objectified and commodified purposes. Such a view is consistent with that advanced by Dewey (1916) who proposed vocations as directions in life, a personal journey linked to individuals' goals and interests. He proposed that all kinds of human activity should be seen as equally valid vocations, from the practice of professionals, to the trades, to the act of parenting. Their validity resides in what they mean to and how they suit the individuals engaged in them. For Dewey, as Quickie (1999) notes, the opposite of vocation is not leisure, but activity that is aimless, capricious and involves dependence on others, rather than cumulative achievements for the individual. To engage in paid pursuits that individuals were not suited to or interested in was a waste of human potential and akin to slavery. In this view, individuals' subjective experiences stand as being central to understanding the worth of work. Bases of these subjective perceptions might include: (i) appraisal of current circumstance against previous experience; (ii) and reflective appraisal—not premised on actual experience (e.g. heightened concerns about job security during times of relatively high employment); (iii) societal press or suggestion by accepting lower or higher expectations of career progression and upward or downward expectations of salary growth; and (iv) these factors are relational (Handel, 2005). So, individual's construal and construction of work stands alongside societal views of the worth of work, albeit mediating those views in particular and differentiated ways.

However, and importantly advancing individual agency as a means through which individuals can be fulfilled, is not to absolve social problems such as inequity, nor is it about creating a false sense of equity, democracy and fulfilment and denying alienation, as some claim (e.g. Ratner, 2000). It is about humanising social relations and social structures, and locating a legitimate and appropriate role for individuals in directing their cognition, learning and remaking of culture (Billett 2005).

3.   WORTHY WORK

In conclusion, there are different perspectives to understand what constitutes worthwhile work, how we should think and make judgements about this work, and what changes in the available work and transformations in occupations mean for those engaged in that work. These dimensions include: (i) socially sanctioned views of occupations; (ii) values based judgements of occupations; (iii) material benefits of occupations; and (iv) the worth of occupations to individuals. The first three largely represent examples of institutional facts, that is how social factors have come to influence the standing, worth and rewards associated with particular kinds of work. The fourth factor represents as individual and subjective perspective on work. There is a rich interplay among these perspectives of work. Yet, to consider the impact of changes in work from just one perspective is to, on the one hand, overly privilege the contribution of the social world to individuals' autonomy and sense of self as workers, while on the other hand, positions individuals as mere cultural dopes, who are duped into engaging in work without considering its standing, status and benefits. In their discussion on lifelong learning, Borgir and Peltzer (1999) provide a useful way of considering the interplay between these conceptions of valuing work. They suggest that rather than assuming economic goals and goals that are central to individuals' identity and sense of self as separate, they may play out in rich and intertwined ways.

> To many, lifelong learning is a goal in itself, a crucial basis for the personal fulfillment of the individual. Lifelong learning is essential to get a job, to keep a job, and to develop a job. It must also contribute to enabling working people to cope with periods of unemployment, and early retirement and to access and re-access work opportunities. Lifelong learning is at the same time fundamental for society as a means to promote democracy and human rights to prevent social exclusion, and to foster solidarity and international awareness. (Borgir and Peltzer, 1999: 54)

From these perspectives, and as Dewey (1916) suggests, we should perhaps begin to think of the worth of work in the broader and inclusive rather than the narrower sense. Just as being a hairdresser is a vocation, so is being a parent; so too being a doctor, teacher or a classical scholar. Beyond the economic necessity to work there are also important intrinsic qualities (e.g. enjoyment, creativity) that motivate individuals to work and seek fulfilment in their work life. Such a claim suggests that vocational goals are not easily separable from personal goals and aspirations. Curiously, given his dismissal of some kinds of work as being inherently less worthy (see opening quote), Wright Mills (1973) agrees. He refers to the ideal of the craft worker, noting that what is necessary for work as craftsmanship is the tie between the product and the producer.

> Even if the producer does not legally own the product he [sic] must own it psychologically in the sense that he knows what goes into it by way of skill, sweat, and material and that his own skill and sweat are visible to him. (p. 11)

He continues:

> In the craftsmen [sic] pattern there is no split of work and play, of work
> and culture. If play is supposed to be an activity, exercised for its own
> sake having no aim other than gratifying the actor, then work is supposed
> to be an activity performed to create economic value or for some ulterior
> result. Play is something you do to be happily occupied, but if work
> occupies you happily, it is also play, although it is serious just as play is
> to a child. (p. 12)

In this view, work and culture are not separate; the craftsperson's work is
the central guiding force and brings the values and qualities developed and
employed in his working time to non-paid work activities. "His idle
conversation is shop talk; his friends follow the same lines of work; and
share a kinship of feeling and thought" (Wright Mills, 1973:12). This view
enhances the centrality of subjectivity to individuals' development, rather
than it being seen as wholly subordinate to economic goals. Moreover, it
says much about those whose work is not fulfilling or are without work.

In sum, it has been argued in this chapter that, given the social forms and
institutional facts that comprise paid work, are exercised and afforded in
different ways, individuals valuing of them will be central to how they
construe, construct and engage in particular ways. Individuals valuing of
work will likely shape how their work is conducted, the valuing of work
being undertaken and its remaking. Four perspectives of the worth of work
are offered to elaborate discussion beyond those that are privileged widely
and socially. It would seem that the worth of work is inherently intertwined
among the social standing of the work at a cultural or local level, the
particular sets of values that it articulates and how these have meaning for
individuals who participate in that work and also in the ways the work
supports, develops and even transforms the individuals' vocation. In
different ways, this intertwining between individual and social forms will
have different meanings for particular cohorts of individuals, particular
individuals, and at particular times in their working life history. There will
be relationships of different kinds and orders between factors which are seen
to be socially subjective, objective and individually subjective.

It is these ideas which are now explored in the next chapters that
comprise the second section of this book which examines the changing
nature of work that is available, changing work practices, changes in
individuals participating in work and the changing requirements of the work.

SECTION 3: CHANGING CONCEPTS AND REQUIREMENTS OF WORK

The third section of this book, *Changing concepts and requirement of work,* begins with Chapter 5—Changes in available work—which argues that the kinds of work available in Western-style economies are changing, and these changes will have impacts of different kinds across workforces. Drawing upon studies of workforce participation from Australia, the United States and the United Kingdom, a case is made about the transforming nature of work, and its consequences for individuals' working lives and the communities in which they live. It is argued that the very bases for categorising work and its standing in the community are also transforming. The consequences of these transformations are discussed in terms of their impact upon workplaces, communities and individuals, using examples from Australia, the United States and the United Kingdom. The purpose here is to identify not only the changes in the kinds of work being undertaken but also what this means for individuals' working lives, career trajectories and occupational identities. These changes are posited as having relational consequences for those who engage in work, who seek to develop or sustain their occupational identity, as in learning throughout working life, and for those who are required to locate new occupations and new identities as the work available is transformed. The means by which we should come to make judgements about work: what constitutes, worthwhile or well-regarded work are also considered.

Chapter 6—Changing participation in work—proposes that beyond the kinds and requirements of work, a salient feature of contemporary work is the diverse and growing bases for participation in work and working life. That is, how people are engaging in work is being transformed with these changes have considerable impact upon workers' identities, their loyalties and their vocational aspirations, as well as the enterprises that employ them. Despite strong economies and prospering enterprises in economies such as the United States, the United Kingdom and Australia, the contingent workforce has persisted and grown. These workers are not restricted to low skill and menial tasks as institutions such as universities, banks and government departments have workforces comprising high percentages of contingent employees.

Then, there is also the outsourcing of work conducted by contractors or individuals. Added to this are a growing percentage of workers who are based away from the workplace, at home, or are remote from the workplace.

These kinds of workers may have divided loyalties across a number of workplaces and between their work and other demands, such as the home life of parenting responsibilities. So for many workers the traditional relationship between individual and the workplace is made tenuous, anxiety ridden and/or peripheral—in short unsatisfactory—by the current kinds of participation in paid work they are able to access or wish to engage in. These emerging forms of participation have consequences for individuals, their work and workplaces. They may render improbable the individual's desire for a positive and sustained work identity. Work and work practices may become differentiated for those who are full-time and permanent and those who are contingent. Therefore, the processes associated with maintaining workplace competence need to account for diversity in the ways in which individuals engage in workplaces and the different degrees of support for learning they will receive in workplace settings.

Chapter 7—Changing composition of paid workforces—identifies, elaborates and discusses changes in those individuals participating in work and some consequences of the participation and how they work. In particular, it notes the significant increase in the number of women participating in paid work and how this has impacted upon the workforce and the standing of the work in which women are participating. It also identifies the conesquences of changing patterns of participation for disadvantaged workers and older workers, who are seen as being increasing components of the emerging workforce. The case made is that despite participation by women, older workers and the otherwise disadvantaged, there can be no guarantee that their engagement, participation and advancement will be commensurate with their level of participation.

Chapter 8—Changing requirements for work performance—proposes that along with changes to the kinds of work being conducted, there are also quite diverse and highly situational changes in what constitutes work and, therefore, the requirements to be effective in work. How occupational practices are enacted in specific workplaces suggests that even what might be taken as common forms of work (i.e. as an occupation) are manifest in particular ways in each workplace. Nevertheless, it is possible to suggest that there are technical (e.g. Barley and Orr, 1997; Cook-Gumperez and Hanna, 1997), organisational (Berryman, 1993; Hughes and Bernhardt, 1999) and interactional (McGovern, 1996) dimensions to the changing requirements for work, and these have consequences for the capacities that individuals need to develop, maintain and adapt to new requirements.

Without an understanding of these kinds of requirements, efforts to develop the skills needed initially, or continue to develop them throughout an individual's working life may be ill directed. In particular, forms of knowledge that are opaque, conceptually dense and multifaceted are the kind that requires particular attention for their development. Drawing upon a wide disciplinary base these requirements are elaborated. Moreover, as a means of understanding what constitutes the requirements for work a scheme comprising categories of activities and interactions is proposed as a means to both describe and illuminate the changing requirements for work. Issues associated with the initial development and ongoing learning from working life are then elaborated and discussed.

Chapter 5

CHANGES IN AVAILABLE WORK

The greatest number of new jobs will be in conventional low-skilled positions such as retail salesperson, cashier, office clerk and truck driver. This version of the argument that the economy will continue to need garbage men is also consistent with that both upskilling (creating new jobs with greater skill demands) and deskilling (creating jobs of lower skill level) are taking place simultaneously; it is consistent with evidence of increasing inequality in the distribution of earnings. (Grubb, 1996: 231)

Drawing upon studies of workforce participation, mainly from Australia, the United States and the United Kingdom, this chapter seeks to identify and discuss key trends in the transformation of the kinds of work available. It then discusses the consequences of these changes for individuals' work and the communities in which they live. It acknowledges that changes in work are inevitable, because work arises from social and cultural need and innovations in technology that are inherently dynamic. Further, these can comprise either incremental changes required for the continuity of a particular form of occupation or significant change that can ultimately see that kind of work transformed, disappear or become far scarcer, perhaps being restricted to specific locations. Among these changes are also the bases for categorising paid work, occupations, and their standing.

In order to make sense of the impact upon individuals, some initial consideration is given to how work might be valued both within the community and by those who participate in it. As proposed in the previous chapter, the bases by which work is to be valued goes beyond objective measures, such as quantifiable benefits and the societal standing of work, to include what it means subjectively to individuals. Consideration of both objective and subjective perspectives offers a more comprehensive and inclusive set of bases to make judgements about the impact of work upon individuals and their communities.

As foreshadowed in Chapter 1, some views propose that changes to work inevitably lead to the disempowerment and marginalisation of those affected by the changes. However, while evidence suggests that there are changes to workers' satisfaction and levels of engagement in workplaces, these may be as much about remaking relations between workers and their work as inevitable disempowerment. These changes are posited as having relational consequences for those who engage in work (and who seek to develop or sustain their occupational identity by learning throughout their working life); and for those who are required to find and become competent in new occupations, or form new work identities, as the kinds of work available become transformed.

1.   CHANGING WORK AND WORKING LIVES

To understand individuals' experience of work it is necessary to understand the realities of the labour market in terms of the available work. There are at least four reasons that this is the case.

Firstly, understanding the kinds of work that are available, provides some bases to predict the skill and occupational requirements in national workforces and attempt to align the development of the skills for work with those requirements. Governments wishing to align workforces and educational efforts with emerging forms of work express this concern. Here, the key concern is often to sustain or improve the national economic prospects, through having a workforce capable of being both import-competing and producing exportable goods and services. A related priority for governments is to assist individuals develop skills that they will be able to practise over a significant part of their working life, certainly much longer than that period of time taken to develop skills in the first place. Also, for governments there is a concern for workers to have the kind of skills that will resist their becoming redundant.

Secondly, given the duration of working lives and claims about individuals needing to engage in different kinds of careers throughout their working life, it is important to understand the prospects for occupations that they may wish to engage in over an extended period of time. Clearly, some kinds of work are more prone than others to the fragilities of the labour market and level of economic activity (e.g. food service workers would fall into this category). The ability to advise individuals about likely work skill requirements is useful in making decisions about further skill development and education. For instance, in the American context, Skinner (2004) suggests that urban dwellers with less than a college education are increasingly unlikely to secure well-paid and continuous work.

Thirdly, given the importance of work to many individuals' sense of self and identity, the prospects for continuity in that occupation, and the degree and frequency of change experienced by that occupation are likely to influence their well-being and capacities to adapt to constant change. Therefore, information about the prospects for their preferred occupation might be of significant value to some individuals.

Fourthly, there are likely to be particular and significant problems for employees who are dislocated in dynamic economies. This is true particularly for those with specific skills of low marketability and low levels of educational success (Merrifield, 1997). It also may apply to older workers, firstly because of a societal preference for youth as evidenced by how enterprises distribute their support for their employees' development (e.g. Brunello and Medio, 2001) and secondly by their relative difficulty in being able to relocate to pursue work options. For these reasons, it is important to gauge the extent and scope of changes to work.

1.1 Changes in the kinds of work available

Changes to paid work have been particularly turbulent in the last quarter of the 20th century and extending into this century (Handel, 2005). The source of the scope and intensity of the changes is at least twofold. Firstly, significant adjustments in the global economy and, secondly, structural reforms implemented by governments in response to the changing global economy and its threats to national sustainability and economic well-being (Pusey, 2003). Some of these changes are consistent with what governments claim is important to maintain economic activity and existing social welfare provisions. Other changes, however, reflect the turbulent times and increasingly competitive and globalised forms of employment that now comprise an increasing number of occupations. In Western economies, such as America, changes to the kinds of work engaged in include a move to those required to increasingly produce high value-added goods (e.g. aeroplanes, high technology products) a shift towards service industries (e.g. food preparation and service), and an ability to work with high technology support systems (e.g. software systems in banking and insurance) (Appelbaum, 1993; Barley and Batt, 1995). Typically, such goals are buoyed by the claims of a movement from an 'industrial society' that predominantly concentrated on the manufacture of goods and products, to an 'information society' that adds value by turning information into knowledge and services. These views are supported by some evidence and predictions about changing patterns of employment.

Historical labour market data and predictions for the future, consistently propose a significant reduction in the demand for 'semi-skilled' and 'unskilled' work and an increase in the demand for management, professional and administrative staff (e.g. Noon and Blyton, 1997). Others paint a slightly different picture. Skinner (2004), McBrier and Wilson (2004) and McNair et al. (2004) identify a polarisation and dualism in the American labour market based on skill and wages, with a hollowing out of the mid-skill labour market. Sassen (1991) proposes that causes for this polarisation include: (i) industrial employment shifts from manufacturing to service work; (ii) the technological destruction of middle-income jobs; and (iii) a rising demand for labour-intensive, low skilled services among the high income urban gentry. The shift from manufacturing to service work and the deployment of technology to undertake middle skill work has led to the decrease of the middle skill component of the American labour market in urban centres (Skinner, 2004). This polarisation between high skilled, high paid workers and low skilled, low paid workers also points to the two areas where job growth is occurring.

1.2   Changes to the American workforce

Data on categories of occupations as a component of the workforce are available for both the United States and Australia. These data reiterate much of what has been foreshadowed above. In Table 5.1, Barely and Orr (1997) present American data on occupational categories as a percentage of the national labour force over a 40 year period from 1950 to 1991. The left hand column lists the occupational categories used by the US Department of Labor to delineate the kinds of work comprising the national labour force. The five columns in the middle depict the percentage of workers who are assigned to each of the categories. The far right column indicates the net change between 1950 to 1991 for each category of employment over that 40 year period. The data indicate that, as components of the workforce, some occupations have experienced a significant decline when compared with others.

Those experiencing the greatest decline include Farm workers, Craft and kindred and, in particular, Operatives and Laborers. Occupations that have experienced a relative increase as components of the American workforce through this period of time include Professional/Technical, Sales workers and Managerial/Administrative forms of work. Nearly all of these trends are unidirectional, rather than representing fluctuations in the need for particular kinds of work. Some reflect greater transformation in the percentage of the overall labour force than others. For instance, the decline in farm work to a quarter of its earlier proportion of the American workforce is quite dramatic. Contrasting this is the strong growth of professional and technical work that has doubled in the same period of time. However, none on its own increases to the same degree as the decline in percentage of workers categorised as Operatives and Laborers.

Table 5-1. Occupational categories as a percentage of the labor force in US 1950-1991 adapted from Barley and Orr, 1997)

	1950	1960	1970	1980	1991	Net Change
Farm workers	12	6	3	3	3	- 9
Professional/ Technical	8	10	14	15	17	+ 9
Craft and kindred	14	14	14	12	11	- 3
Operatives/ Laborers	26	24	23	18	15	- 11
Clerical and kindred	12	15	18	17	16	+ 4
Service	11	12	13	13	14	+ 3
Managerial/ Administrative	9	8	8	10	13	+ 4
Sales workers	7	7	7	11	12	+ 5

A feature of this data is that it contradicts the claim that it is only in the last quarter of the twentieth century that significant turbulence and restructuring has occurred in advanced Western-style economies. The percentage of individuals employed in farm work is presented as being halved between 1950 and 1960. Since the 1970s the percentage of the workforce reporting as farm workers has remained quite constant. This period is often portrayed as a time of unbridled prosperity and optimism in countries such as America, Australia and Britain. Perhaps it was the introduction of technology in the immediate post-war period that precipitated this decline. However, whatever the cause, even during a period of economic growth and development, there existed significant change in rural employment, and, doubtless rural communities. Only one sector indicates a significant decline after the mid-seventies: Operatives/Labourers.

These trends are also reflected in the data provided by the Educational Policy Foundation (2003). They report that in America over the 60 year period from 1940 to 2002 there has been a significant shift from production and manufacturing work to management and service-orientated occupations. In 1940, American managers and professionals were only 18% of the non-farm labour force, yet by 2002 this category increased to 32% of that labour force. Through the same period, production employment shrank from 48% of the workforce in 1940 to 28% by 2002. It is also claimed that:

> Of the 37.4 million full-time year-round private sector jobs created between 1970 and 2002, 45% of the jobs—16.8 million positions—were administrative, managerial, professional or technical in nature. Only 26.4% of new jobs were created in transportation, production or service occupations. (Educational Policy Foundation, 2003: 3)

Skinner (2004) also notes the decline in the share of mid-skilled administrative support and precision production, craft and repair occupations and the growth in high skilled managerial and professional occupations, again suggesting skill and wage polarisation. Predictions for the future reflect similar trends with new jobs increasingly falling into the managerial, professional or technical occupational categories (Employment Policy Foundation, 2003 US Department of Labor, 2005). Similarly, Barley and Orr (1997) claim the number of professional and technical jobs in America have grown more than 300% since 1950. These authors hold that even sales work (at 248%) and managerial work (at 182%) are dwarfed by the growth in professional and technical jobs and along with the Department of Labor claim that these occupations comprise 17% of the workforce. They claim similar trends for Canada (18%) and the UK (20%). Moreover, they propose these estimates may well be conservative, because "numerous occupations that the government currently allocates to other categories also have strong technical components" (Barley and Orr, 1997: 5).

Technology also impacts upon other categories of work. Skinner (2004) claims that new information-based technologies in banking, legal services, telecommunications and some durable goods manufacturing have destroyed large numbers of mid-skilled administrative support and production jobs in the United States, thereby creating workforces that are increasingly polarised by skill level. Similarly, Budd and McCall (2001) claim that technological change in the grocery store industry, including introduction of scanners and increased use of pre-packaged meats, between 1984 and 1994 has reduced the skills required of both sales clerks and meat cutters.

1.3   Changes in the Australian workforce

Similar patterns of change are also evident in the occupational categories comprising the Australian workforce. Over a shorter period of time and using different bases for categorisation, similar patterns of change are evident in Australia. Table 5.2 presents changes in occupational categories as part of the workforce between 1983 and 1998 in the Australian workforce. These data also indicate unidirectional declines in some occupations (i.e.

Manufacturing, Agriculture, Transport) with increases in others (i.e. Finance, property and business services, Construction, and Retail). Consistent with those in America, some changes are quite significant such as the decline in agricultural work and increases in Finance, property and business through this period.

Table 5-2. Occupational categories as percentage of the workforce–Australia, 1983-1997/8 (Source: ABS)

	1983	1988	1993	1997/98	Change
Agriculture, forestry, fishing and hunting	6.6	5.8	5.3	4.9	- 1.7
Mining	1.5	1.3	1.2	1.0	- 0.5
Manufacturing	18.1	16.4	14.1	12.8	- 5.3
Electricity, gas and water	2.2	1.5	1.2	0.8	- 1.4
Construction	6.2	7.2	7.3	7.2	+ 1.0
Wholesale and retail trade	19.5	20.4	20.9	20.7	+ 1.2
Transport and storage	5.9	5.2	4.8	4.6	- 1.3
Communications	2.2	1.8	1.5	1.7	- 0.5
Finance, property and business services	9.2	11.0	11.2	14.6	+ 5.4
Public administration and defence	5.0	4.4	5.1	3.9#	- 1.1
Community services	17.3	17.8	19.4	16.7	- 0.5
Recreation, personal and other services	6.3	7.2	8.0	6.2	- 0.1
Total	100	100	100	100	
National Labour force (1000)	6,241.1	7,353.4	7,621.0	8,555.0	

Note # - defence forces not included in this estimate

Using similar data, Pusey (2003) similarly concluded that in the period from 1985 to 2000, there were significant changes in the Australian labour market. Although, those employed in manufacturing declined as a proportion of total labour force from 17% to 13%, greater declines were experienced elsewhere. For instance, those employed as public sector employees through this same period experienced a drop from 31% to 20%. Commensurate with this change was the increase in private sector employees as a proportion of all wage and salary earners from 69% to 80%. These two figures together indicate an 11-point increase in private sector employment through this 15-year period. This indicates a significant shift in the forms and terms of employment for a large number of Australian workers in the shift from the public to the private sector. Also, the kinds and characteristics of work and work life available in the public sector have transformed through the period, as the priorities and focuses of government have changed. Indeed, although the Australian Bureau of Statistics changed its system of categorization after 1998, making a continuation of the comparison in Table 5.2 problematic, the trends identified above continued from 2000 to 2005 (ABS 2005). In particular the employment in the Agricultural category declined in three of the five year periods, as did Manufacturing. Communication Service also suffered three periods of decline in employment growth, although these followed a period of spectacular growth (14% between August 1999 and 2000). Through this period employment in Mining grew significantly as the demand for this sector's product were high.

The Australian figures also show a steady increase in the numbers of workers participating in paid work; so the dynamic nature of work has been able to accommodate the growing number of Australians seeking paid work. Yet even industries that have a high profile and enjoy high investment interest do not necessarily increase in employment levels (e.g. Communications). This re-emphasizes the point that high-profile occupations do not necessarily make significant contributions to the quantum of available work and may instead indicate a hollowing out of the labour market.

The figures from both the US and Australia indicate the decline in manual work and a strong growth in areas of professional and service work. However, the increase in these sectors might in fact be lower than it is represented. In Australia and the United States, as in other Western countries, many manufacturing jobs, for example in the clothing and footwear industry have been removed from the domestic labour markets through their export to other low labour cost countries. Therefore, as components of the labour force disappear, the overall percentages of the current occupational categories in all remaining kinds of work are likely to appear stronger as a proportion of the workforce. In summary, there has been a fundamental shift in the kinds of occupations that are available to be employed in. Hence, what remain are those occupational areas for individuals to participate in and to build and/or maintain careers and work identity.

To make this point more strongly, the data on changes in workers' occupations in Korea presents an interesting comparison to those of America and Australia mentioned above. Like many Western countries, the proportion of Korean workers in agricultural, forestry and fishing jobs declined significantly in the period between 1970 and 1993. Similarly, through the same period, Professional, Technical and Administrative jobs, Service and Clerical jobs have also increased significantly, while Sales jobs have enjoyed modest increases. Yet, in contrast to the countries listed above, Production jobs have experienced strong growth and constitute the single largest portion (32%) of the Korean labour market (Korean Economic Planning Board, 2005). Presumably, this is a result of manufacturing being relocated to Korea from countries such as the USA and Australia. Indeed, the Korean government is having difficulty in encouraging enough Koreans to work in manufacturing.

As a consequence, the government has had to establish programs in schools to promote manufacturing as a viable employment option (Cho and Apple, 1998).

Other comparisons indicate that even these patterns of change in occupations are not being enacted consistently across all countries. Unlike the more economically advanced countries discussed above, Vietnam saw little change in the patterns of employment across industry sectors between 1980 and 1990 (Table 5.3). In particular and in contrast to other countries, agricultural work remained overwhelmingly the most common form of work. This has lead to claims of stagnation and a lack of capacity to respond to the needs of a modern economy and globalized economic activity (Ronnas, 1992).

Table 5-3. Vietnam: Industrial structure of the labour force and its rate of growth (adapted from Ronnas, 1992)

Industry	1980	1988	1989	1990
Agriculture	70.7	73.0	71.2	71.6
Construction	4.7	3.0	2.7	2.7
Industry	10.4	10.9	11.2	11.2
Transport and Communications	1.7	1.6	2.0	1.7
Trade	5.0	4.6	5.5	5.6
Education	3.4	3.1	2.9	2.8
Health social services	1.0	1.1	1.0	1.0
Government and administration	1.2	0.9	1.1	1.5
Total	100	100	100	100
Total (1000)	21,639	28,477	28,940	30,286

Such changes were supposed to shift the Vietnamese workforce from a reliance upon overseas aid and state investment through 'doi moi' policies that arose through post-unification (Ronnas, 1992). These policies sought a balance between state control and free enterprise in generating an export-oriented economy. Yet, the stability of the occupational composition of the labour force was seen to inhibit achieving this goal. Two points are made here.

Firstly, whereas transformation in Western-style economies is often seen as leading to the dislocation of much of the existing work and implications for workers, the lack of change in the composition of the workforce has led to claims about stagnation and a decline in living standards for those within Vietnam. This suggests change per se is not the key concern; it is how those changes are managed and supported to achieve outcomes that secure both a viable economy and available work.

Secondly, this case reinforces the point that the kind of change that occurs in the labour force is likely to be shaped by national, local and individual agendas as much as those that are global. Moreover, because of these more localised factors, the nature, scope and character of the change of work and its availability need to be understood as localised, albeit shaped by global phenomena. Shifts in work that is available bring about or require changes in societal conditions and sentiments.

2.   WORK AND CHANGE: CONSEQUENCES IN OVERVIEW

As argued in Chapter 2, paid work arises from and is an expression of cultural need, which is subject to constant change. Transformations in cultural need albeit empowered by technological innovations, changing legislation, shifts in particular nations' productive capacities, demographic shifts, changing geopolitical structures and global events such as conflict, terrorism or climate change, all can potentially lead to changes in work. Indeed, the dynamic conception of work is reflected in the definition of occupation provided by Skinner (2004: 69) who proposes: "an occupation may be broadly defined as a set of activities, with individuals producing specific goods or services in a given society at a given historical period."

Furthermore, because these changes play out in different ways across workplaces within and across countries and at different times, their impacts upon nations, industries, communities and individuals are likely to be un-even. For instance, the increased developmental cost, technological require-ments and infrastructure support for aircraft manufacture means that this activity is now limited to a few countries or collaboration across countries. Aviation work in other countries is often limited to service and maintenance tasks. Hence, the availability of particular kinds of aviation work is distributed across countries and communities in very clearly delineated ways. Similarly, the advent of cheap telephone communication has seen the location of service centres shift to places where these services can be provided most cost effectively. This can include transferring jobs from metropolitan to provincial communities or, increasingly, from one continent to another, as in the growing call centre industry being established in the Indian subcontinent which provides a cost effective business service for customers in North America, Europe and Australasia.

Moreover, as the demands and requirements for goods and services fluctuate and transform, so do the skills associated with the goods and services to be provided. For instance, demographic changes and shifts in government policies in countries such as Australia and Canada have resulted in a growing requirement for private schooling, increased private aged care facilities and expertise in managing privately funded retirement. Another example is the reduced costs of electrical goods and electronic devices driving down the demand for repair work, but creating new roles for technical advice and support during installation and maintenance. These changes bring about demands for particular kinds of work.

At a more macro level, there will be different degrees of community tolerance to the exporting of jobs from one country to another and the service jobs that arise within highly liberalised labour markets. The acceptance of these practices is far from uniform. Carnoy (2001) notes how the American model of a liberalised economy has been resisted in its fullest form in many European countries because of a cultural valuing of social welfare provisions and a reluctance to embrace individualism to the extent it is acceptable in America. This means that the availability of particular kinds of work and forms of employment and the experience of work may be quite different across these countries.

Moreover, some forms of work are not for export and others not export-table. For instance, government subsidies might be used to secure high employment industries for their strategic or political reasons (Shah and Burke, 2003). Other activities are restricted by community sentiment (e.g. the placement of correctional facilities, the location of large supermarkets and noxious industries) or just practicalities such as immediacy and localised need. So although technology and global finances play key roles in facilitating the transformation of kinds of work, there are differences in what communities are willing to tolerate. Similarly, changes in the availability of natural resources and national concerns about the environment means that work associated with primary (e.g. mining) and secondary production (e.g. mineral processing, paper manufacturing) are likely to be distributed across nation states in different ways and locations. This distribution can have significant impacts upon the available kinds of employment. For instance, as easily exploitable coal seams move deeper underground, open cut coal mining gives way to underground coal mining that requires quite different skills, and has a different sense of values and community. Yet, as under-ground coal mining is more expensive than open cut coal mining there might be implications for the communities that go beyond a transformation from open cut to underground mining work. In the absence of an existing coal-mining community, employers might decide to operate employment on a 'fly in and fly out' basis that does little for the local community's development or availability of employment.

In their analysis of future Australian job growth, Shah and Burke (2003) identify forms of work that were more or less vulnerable to global competition and technological innovation. In their analysis they classified occupations into three kinds: (i) those advantaged by globalization and technology change; (ii) those relatively insulated; and (iii) those that are most vulnerable. So, in sum, changes to technology, demand from societal needs in different ways and combinations bring about requirements for changes in paid work.

2.1   Technological changes and work

Technological innovations also lead to the introduction of forms of work that did not exist before and can provide opportunities for different cohorts to participate as workers. For instance, access to low-cost tele-communications has led to the development of service centres that conduct service related activities, work that might previously have been conducted by people classified as clerks, bank tellers, travel agents, receptionists and so on. The development of remote call and business centres means that this work does not need to occur in places that provide the goods or services. They can be centralised elsewhere. In Canada, for instance, the provincial government of Newfoundland encouraged call centres to be established in areas with declining employment options and high unemployment by pro-viding less expensive operating costs and generous subsidies for businesses to shift their activities to the province. Church (2004) notes that as well as locating these workplaces in relatively low labour cost locations, their relocation also provide access to diverse kinds of workers. Among these are disabled workers, who are able to perform this kind of work effectively and do so away from the public gaze that might otherwise brand them as not competent to perform, for example, bank work such as the management of customers' finances.

Within a particular country, portability can see the concentration of work in particular locations where appropriately skilled and remunerated workers can be secured. In one large corporation, during a period of restructuring, the call centre functions of the food manufacturing companies in the corporation were centralised to a regional location in Australia (Billett and Boud, 2001). Set in a rural community, the call centre provided employment for female workers, some of whom had specialist skills in nutrition. However, in the same workplace, male workers engaged in manufacturing of food products and maintenance of plant and equipment were made redundant through the same period. This occurred through changes to and rationalisation of production, consumer preferences and technology. These changes were generative of quite different outcomes for workers in the same regional location.

However, like manufacturing work before it, increasingly, call centre work is also being exported to countries with lower wage levels and access to cohorts of highly skilled and motivated workers. India, for instance, is currently providing a growing range of call centre services for the customers of American, Australian and British banks. Moreover, rather than being seen as low status work, the work is highly prized with well-educated Indians competing for employment in the sector. As well as generating new forms of work technology is reshaping a range of occupations, by casting them generically as business service work. However, in other ways, technology has transformed work by making it highly portable through electronic communications.

Consequently, changes in the kinds of work available in particular communities are being transformed by changing need and technological innovation. The changes impact upon industry sectors, occupations, workers and communities in different ways, and at different times. Berryman (1993) claims that the shift to post-industrial forms of work requires workers to be flexible, adaptable and have a depth of understanding about their work that sets them apart from their predecessors. As the new forms of work are adopted by enterprises and industries, they will have their own impacts at particular moments in time. These kinds of work requirements are held to be more demanding, requiring higher levels of skills to perform and therefore, needing and deserving a thorough and exacting preparation.

2.2 Globally advantaged and disadvantaged work

Occupations that were categorizable as 'globally advantaged' included those grouped under the headings 'conceptual and technical' which include professionals and business-related occupations. For example, Hewlett Packard provide business services to more than 1 billion customers in 160 countries (Waight and Stewart, 2005) The occupations classified as being relatively insulated were those that comprise the 'in person service' professional occupations such as medical practitioners and schoolteachers, and "also some skilled and low skilled occupations for which overseas workers or products cannot be readily substituted" (Shah and Burke, 2003: iii). These include real estate workers, community service workers and police officers (categorised as skilled workers) and waiters, bus drivers, and elementary sales and service workers (categorised as low skill workers). Vulnerable occupations were those which were most susceptible to being produced either abroad or by new technology. This category included manufacturing workers and some clerical work.

Shah and Burke (2003: iii) estimate that most of the growth in employment opportunities would be within either the globally advantaged or relatively insulated occupations: "more than four out of every five jobs that are generated, because of growth in employment, are projected to be in the globally advantaged occupations or in the insulated occupations".

However, views of a workforce polarized between high and low skill occupations are evident here. The high rate of job turnover in the vulnerable occupations would also likely provide a substantial number of job openings for new entrants. Shah and Burke (2003) conclude that because these turnovers are likely entrances into the labour market, such forms of vulnerable employment are likely to be the focus of considerable training efforts. So although there is employment growth in the vulnerable occupations, the high level of turnover is predicted to provide options for employment.

Overall, the principle of 'in person' or face-to-face work seems to hold up. In Australia, there is a significant shortage of skilled trade workers, which is boosting their security and levels of remuneration. Employers and employer organizations are mobilizing government to assist overcome the problem, however, the demographics of an aging skilled workforce are intensifying the challenge. So, although the occupations may be categorised as vulnerable, the difficulty of replacing the workers with technology or overseas workers appears to be buttressing their prospects for quality work conditions and continuities. However, it is this very shortage that is now prompting employers to argue for importing skilled labour from overseas countries to engage in annual maintenance work and large-scale maintenance projects. Conversely, another example supporting Shah and Burke's (2003) proposals is the security in employment currently being experienced by coal and metal ore miners. In the mid-2000s the worldwide demand for coal and metal is boosting the profits of these mining operations as well as the salaries and job security of the miners.

However, predictions that refer to occupational groups in general such as these may fail to capture the changes that occur within sectors. Different patterns of employment and scopes of tasks are evident in the retail sector, for instance. It has been shown that quite different labour segmentation and levels of skilfulness are evident and characterise distinct strategies (Bernhardt, 1999). In a high-end retail store and a hardware chain, retail staff are required to be knowledgeable and also develop relationships with clients. There, retail workers enjoy wider autonomy, above award wages, and are typically employed in full-time positions with benefits. However, in other types of chains (fast food, discounters), providing fast service for people who know what they want at competitive prices is the strategy. In these workplaces, jobs are low wage, dead-end, with limited pay and have constantly changing work schedules (Bernhardt, 1999). So there can be significant differences within the kinds of occupational categories that have been used above. However, as the retail industry shifts from small independently owned stores to large corporately owned units, even retail jobs that are high status and secure may fail to deliver relatively high pay and conditions to those who work in them in the future.

3.   AVAILABILITY OF WORK

As foreshadowed above, the distribution of changes in the demand for work is unlikely to be distributed uniformly or equitably across countries, regions or communities. The growth of professional and technical occupations may have provided a strong impetus for job growth in cities and urbanised centres (Skinner, 2004), while call centre work has shifted to rural and provincial areas, or to overseas countries, which offer lower cost labour. Some communities may prosper, other communities may falter. For instance, it is commonly reported that the decline in agricultural employment also leads to a decline in the availability of professional, clerical and technical work in rural communities, ultimately rendering these communities unsustainable.

While much of the discussion so far has focused on non-professional work, it would be wrong to see engagement in the arguably more prestigious work conducted by professionals as being immune from similar changes. For example, in the United States in the 1980s and 1990s, there was a downturn in the demand for some managerial and administrative occupations. The cause was a recession that saw job displacement less concentrated in blue-collar work but rather shared across all sectors, with greater concentration on administrative, professional and technical work. McBrier and Wilson (2004) suggest this led to a hollowing out of work in these occupational categories. While the impact of economic restructuring went beyond blue-collar workers at the time, its effects were still unevenly distributed across communities as it seemed to have greater impact upon African-American workers than their white counterparts. This was particularly ill-timed for many African-Americans who, at that time, were attempting to use education as a means to secure economic mobility into administrative and professional work. Yet, it seems some of these efforts were rebuffed by a down-turn in these kinds of work which impacted heavily upon them and, indeed African-Americans' downward mobility was in greater numbers and further than their white counterparts (McBrier and Wilson, 2004).

There are also long-term consequences for particular cohorts, individuals, communities and countries which can arise from changes in the need for particular kinds of work. Take the skilled labour required for manufacturing, for instance. The decline of manufacturing industries in the United Kingdom during the 1980s and the concurrent decline in apprenticeships has arguably led to the reduction in that country's ability to sustain a strong manufacturing base. Similarly, in Australia, the emerging skill shortage in the traditional craft trades is, in part, a product of an ageing workforce, but also in part a product of a reduced emphasis on genuine apprenticeship training. Therefore, in both countries, opportunities to value-add in manufacturing are limited by a lack of skilled labour. In the United Kingdom, this has led to an emphasis on assembly and warehousing for goods manufactured elsewhere (Carnoy, 1999)—an employment option that has expanded because of the absence of highly skilled manufacturing workers, coupled with comparatively low levels of wages. However, the question remains whether this kind of employment is in the country's strategic interest.

Quite a different situation currently exists in Germany, for instance. There, industry and training systems have continued to produce highly skilled workers, but now, there are not always jobs for them. So, the problem here is less one of a lack of skills, but an oversupply of skilled workers whose practice will become redundant without opportunities to work. Consequently, the personal and societal investment in their preparation stands to be squandered, unless they are able to engage in the skilled occupation for which they are trained. However, if the economic activities of countries like Germany continue to change, quite different skill bases may be required. This may lead to widespread redundancy of existing skills, as in the Landers (i.e. German federal states) comprising former Eastern Germany. The difference between a temporary increase in demand for skills is quite distinct from their displacement from the economy. Each country may well engage in a different kind of cycle of work availability and at a different time than others as its economy is restructured.

Some claim that in well-regulated Western-style economies, the overall pattern of the availability of employment is now far more stable than in earlier times. They suggest that the periodic booms and decline in economic activity that caused employment hiatuses, such as in the Great Depression, are now a thing of the past. It is held that structural changes in Western-style economies prevent the level of unemployment experienced in those earlier times and that even in times of relatively low economic activity, jobs are now more readily available for those in the labour force. The Employment Policy Foundation (2003) claims that in America, in comparison with the 1930s when the unemployment rate averaged over 18.4%, during recent economic downturns unemployment levels of only around 6% were the highest experienced. The relative robustness of gross employment levels is held to be a result of structural changes in and the better management of national economies. However, these structural changes can bring about significant change and dislocation within the workforce itself. These will play out in particular ways, such as the claimed hollowing out of the mid-skill and middle paid workers in the workforce (e.g. McBrier and Wilson, 2004).

Overall, and given the increase in gross employment that has accommodated newcomers to the labour market, the level of employment in Western-style economies is claimed to be far more stable. While this may be so, the issue of how changes in economic activity play out in different regions and communities and for individuals and cohorts of particular kinds of workers (i.e. high skilled, low skilled, highly educated, men, women, migrant, indigenous, handicapped workers) becomes important. Also, perceptions of availability have an impact upon individuals' concerns about employment. For instance, during the recession of the 1980s, American data report a significant drop in work satisfaction, which has been aligned to concerns about employment security (Handel, 2005). Yet Handel (2005) also notes that anxiety about being displaced from work can be ill-founded. Perceptions of low availability of work exist even in times of relatively high levels of employment. So an individual's concerns about the self can lead to differences between the so-called realities of labour markets and their impact upon those engaged in paid work.

In these ways, issues associated with changes in the work that is available need to go beyond discussions about work capacities and include a consideration of issues of individuals' identities and sense of self, as well as the communities and countries they live in. The next section attempts to provide an overview of the scope and extent of these changes.

4. CHANGES TO OCCUPATIONAL CATEGORIES

Changes to work activities and technology have also lead to questioning the bases for categorizing occupations. The categories are based on historically derived sets of tasks, yet their alignments may not be effective in describing and categorizing more recently developed characteristics of the occupations they classify. For instance, accountants are labelled as managers, computer operators are classified as clerical and kindred workers; but these descriptors may not reflect accurate categorisations or groups that are cognate. Barley and Orr (1997) claim that the enhanced use of technology in workplaces has increased the numbers of workers who could rightly be classified as technical workers, yet are currently classified as clerical, craft or production workers. They propose that the current occupational categories understate the percentage of workers categorised as technicians, drawing on examples of individuals who repair and maintain computers as being categorised as crafts persons. However, in doing so, this claim suggests a narrow view of technology, one solely associated with electronic computing, rather than embracing the wide range of technologies used by individuals who are classified as crafts persons. They understandably struggle to offer a clear definition of how technicians' work is distinct from other kinds, such as craftwork. This suggests some reconfiguration of existing categories of work arising from technological transformations might be required.

Some also claim that data on the decline of particular kinds of work might not accurately reflect shifts of employment within the same industry sector. For instance, agricultural lobby groups claim that agricultural employment is still the highest single base of employment in America. They note that there has been a decline in farm work per se, such as farm labouring. However, the number of workers who are now employed in the distribution and transportation of food has offset the overall impact of this shift within the sector. Because of the concentration of food production in, for instance California, the foods that Americans consume have to travel further, requiring significant employment in food transportation, warehousing and distribution. That is, the range of work associated with getting food from the 'gate to the plate' has increased proportionally to the number of workers displaced from direct agricultural work. There are also other examples of shifts within categories of work. Hughes and Bernhardt (1999) claim that the availability of much bank work has changed, with fewer people employed in 'backroom jobs' and with 'front room jobs' transformed. They refer to banks making salespersons out of tellers—workers who are now required to have greater and different transactional and organizational skills than were required of the tellers of an earlier era.

These kinds of claims warrant a critical appraisal of the kinds of data presented in Table 5.1 and 5.2. Also, such claims about shifts in emphasis say little about the impact upon individuals and communities. In particular, they say little about whether the forms of work that individuals are increasingly participating in (such as the growing service sector) really offer worthwhile alternatives to traditional manufacturing in terms of wages, benefits and working conditions (Merrifield, 1997). For instance, as elaborated in Chapter 7, women largely dominate some forms of administrative work. However, it has been noted that when they begin to populate senior management positions, in some instances the status and remuneration of these positions appears to decline. So, while the work remains the same, access to high status work becomes less available.

These examples indicate how changes to work brought about by technology and change in demand play out for different cohorts of workers, that is, the consequences are different for different kinds of workers. What constitutes an opportunity for the handicapped worker in provincial locations might come at the cost of an urban employee. Similarly, the personal and financial benefits arising for a call centre worker in India come at the cost of their counterparts in other countries. Or, the removal of mundane monitoring tasks by nurses, can lead to the intensification of other aspects of their work and an increased reliance on patients recuperating by themselves, and in locations outside the hospitals where most nurses are employed. The call centre work moved to the rural community might provide employment for some in that area, yet deny others a kind of masculine work that is part of their identity and is now required less in farms and in manufacturing work. These sorts of considerations about changes in the work available and individuals' capacity to engage in work lead to the consideration of the value of work for individuals, and perhaps more fundamentally how the quality of work is to be appraised and judged.

All this indicates that the requirements for work, its changing nature and what it means for individuals cannot be satisfactorily understood through an analysis of occupations and universal patterns of change within and across labour market. Instead, there is a need to account for the overall changes to work and how these play out in particular countries and communities, and for particular individuals. However, to make some sense of how we should think about the available work, categorise it or make judgements about its qualities, we need to identify and consider some premises for its conduct.

5.   CHANGING WORK

It follows from the above that the growth, decline or restructuring of industries arising from technological and global factors has led to changes to the quantum and focus of available work (Skinner, 2004). Sometimes, even where an industry has been restructured and largely exported, the remaining work becomes quite specialised or addresses local needs. For instance, the remnants of the steel industry in Pittsburgh (USA) and Newcastle (Australia) engage in boutique type steel production. These changes can have particular consequences for communities where options for employment develop, decline or have been transformed by the changes. Over the last two decades communities in the United States, Australia and the United Kingdom have been affected by the decline of steel, automotive and textile production. Some communities have experienced new forms of work, as service work is relocated in centralised units away from relatively more expensive facilities and labour in cities.

Yet, these new forms of work do not always adequately replace the kinds of jobs that have been lost, and while providing work for some kinds of community members, fail to meet the needs of others. For instance, the shift from underground to open cut coal mining and back again can lead to the need for quite different skill requirements and shifts in entire mining communities as has happened with Australia. In modernising industries in Germany's East, there is a pattern of creating high skilled jobs; yet these skills may not be possessed by the existing workforce and in far fewer numbers than those jobs they replace. Further, it is claimed that about a thousand skilled jobs a week are being exported, as German companies establish manufacturing facilities in Turkey, and countries in Central Asia. Not only does such a move either create or fail to address growing unemployment in Germany, it can lead to a denuding of its workers' skills and the capacity to locally manufacture automobiles and machinery. So not only are occupations being transformed, but the local and global distribution of those occupations is also changing, making them available in different ways across different communities.

These changes may differ across industry sectors. Some sectors of service industries could be affected by globalisation of the economy in ways that are similar to manufacturing. For instance, as noted earlier, both manufacturing and service centre work has been exported from countries like Australia, America, Canada and United Kingdom. However, some face-to-face or 'in person' service work is not judged as being so 'footloose' (Shah and Burke, 2003; Herzenberg, Alic and Wial, 1998). Bank tellers, room cleaners, teachers, nurses, doctors, secretaries, childcare workers and management staff must work locally; their work cannot easily be shipped overseas or transferred to low cost labour areas elsewhere within a country (Bernhardt, 1999). However, even this work will not remain wholly immune from globalised changes as it will be transformed by technology, changing cultural requirements and demographics. For example, while much of teachers' work remains relatively continuous, their way of working may change as students, schools and colleges change. So, while motor vehicle, textile and garment manufacturing, and coalmining have largely vanished from the place of my childhood, Lancashire, teachers still work in the school I attended over forty years ago and doctors and nurses still practice in the hospital that treated my childhood misadventures. With the closure of car manufacturer British Leyland automobile company, coalmines, textile mills and garment manufacturing factories, some forms of work no longer exist, whereas teaching, doctoring, hairdressing and nursing work are still available.

Moreover, management decision-making within individual enterprises has played a significant role in how tasks have been allocated across low skilled workers or high school graduates, and college graduates. Skinner (2004), for instance, refers to a number of studies that emphasise managerial discretion in deploying technology and organising work systems to create different skill demands across workplaces. Thus localised factors may shape how global and cultural changes are manifested in terms of workplace transformation.

So, changes to work may have different impacts upon individuals as workers or prospective workers, depending upon their choice of occupations, their skills, their locations and their employer's decision about how work is to be conducted. The range of available options for work can render a community as being highly robust or fragile (if the work is of a certain kind and prone to export) and dependent (if the work is of just of one kind that is so prone). In these ways, the availability of and securing of employment has consequences beyond securing a desirable level of income. For many and perhaps most workers, their work identity is either part of or central to their personal identity, and the capacity to practice their skills is a component of their self in action. Moreover, these changes might have quite different impacts upon different groups in each community. Changes in access to available work may impact harder on older workers who are less mobile and less attractive to employers than younger workers (see Chapter Seven). So, just as there are inevitable changes to the kinds of work to be undertaken, there is also a range of consequences that impact upon individuals and communities. In this way, there are profound implications for an individual's sense of self which result from changes in the forms of work that are available within communities and for individuals.

6. CHANGE IN AVAILABLE WORK

In sum, it has been argued in this chapter that work is changing both its form and availability. Despite the view that periods of rapid change in economic circumstances are aligned to cycles of boom and recession in Western style economies, it seems that there is a prospect of the kinds of change being experienced in contemporary working lives becoming a constant. Skilbeck et al. (1994) warn that with greater global economic competition, including that from countries seeking the same kinds of life chances and standards of living as Western countries, there will be an ongoing struggle by Western nations to maintain their standard of living. The capacities of individuals to extend and develop their working knowledge beyond that initially constructed during their initial vocational preparation will be central.

Also, the work that is available and accessible to individuals is changing. These changes cannot be wished away, and have particular impacts upon individuals and communities. There are patterns of change in the forms of and availability of work across nation states. These patterns are quite similar in some ways, but offer national variations (e.g. differences in the availability of manufacturing work). Some of the requirements are for more demanding forms of work, and possibly a lack of support. Moreover, what constitutes categories of occupational practice is being transformed by technology and changes in the workforce.

Chapter 6

CHANGING PARTICIPATION IN WORK

> In the high performance work organisations which are projected as the basis for our future prosperity, all workers are supposed to make decisions about their work, to think critically, to solve problems and work in teams rather than competing on piece rates. (Merrifield, 1997: 276)

A salient and changing feature of contemporary work and workers is the growing diversity in work participation factors, including in what ways individuals are participating and under what kind of conditions. While some workplaces are claimed to prize reciprocal roles and responsibilities and to offer high involvement forms of work practice (i.e. claims that employers and employees have never needed each other more), the evidence suggests that, in practice, this is not always, and perhaps rarely and selectively, the case. Also, whether it is the intentions or practices of management, or those of co-workers, workplaces can be highly contested environments. Participation is central to that contestation. This has implications for individuals' identities, loyalties and their vocational aspirations, as well as the enterprises that employ them, their family life and the communities in which they live. Taking up these themes, this chapter first discusses the central role of participation for work practice requirements as well as learning through work and throughout working life. The concept of workplace participatory practice (Billett, 2002a) is used to identify and discuss workers' participation in working life. As outlined in Chapter 3, this concept proposes a duality between, on the one hand, how individuals are permitted to participate in working life as shaped by the affordances or invitational qualities of the workplace (i.e. support, access to prized activities) and on the other hand, the degree to which individuals elect to participate with what they are afforded.

119

In considering changing ways of working, firstly it is proposed that the means of participation in work are being transformed with what is broadly referred to as 'non-standard' or 'contingent' work arrangements employing an increasing proportion of the workforce. This change appears to be coming more common in many Western countries, even those with highly performing economies and high levels of employment. Economic pressures in countries with traditionally stable work conditions, as in Japan, are now seeing changes to standard patterns of employment as the promise of lifetime employment within one enterprise is threatened by new economic times. Secondly, the frequency and scope of paid work being conducted in isolation from the physical place that employs the individual appears also to be increasing. New technologies are providing ways of working that permit physical separation from the workplace. This means of working appears to be on the increase in many countries and forms of work. In some ways, it offers greater flexibility for managing busy work and family lives. Yet, these arrangements can produce isolation, and separation from the workplace. Moreover, they further blur the distinction between the individual's work and their life outside work.

1.   CHANGING WAYS OF PARTICIPATING IN WORK

How individuals are invited to participate in work by their employers, other workers and workplaces norms and practices, and they, in turn, elect to engage with their work and the degree by which they exercise their full capacities in their paid work is salient. It is central to the continuity and viability of the enterprises that employ them. As well as participation, their learning and development are linked to how they are able to participate in work and in doing so remake work practice. Workplaces require the energy, commitment and intelligence of workers and, perhaps, never more so than in times of constant change that characterise the current era. Yet, individuals' learning and development throughout their working life is contingent upon the kind of experiences and interactions they can secure from their workplaces. So, there is some shared interest between enterprises and those they employ. This interdependence, although not always obvious, stands at the heart of the continuity and development of both enterprises and the individuals who work within them, as argued in Chapter 3. The workplace requires its employees to use their capacities in providing effective goods and services and, in turn, the employees require the workplace's affordances to assist them achieve their vocational goals. This is not to suggest that the enterprises' and individuals' goals for continuity and development are the same. For instance, the workplace might be seeking to reduce labour costs or restrict individuals' development and career trajectories in order to retain a viable workforce. It might, to that end, provide support for achieving its particular workplace goals (e.g. multi-skilling, introduction of labour-saving technology), yet may restrict the development of skills that are inconsistent with these goals. Workers' development, if seen as potentially leading to claims for additional pay or extending their control of the workplace's production of goods and services, may be inhibited. So while there will be particular purposes for the workplace's engagement with individuals, the workplace also will require the workers' engagement and agency to achieve many of its goals, particularly in times of change.

Conversely, individuals' goals may not always be consonant with those of the workplace in which they are employed. For instance, in Australia, most school age part-time workers are employed in retail and service roles that provide them with remuneration, but do not constitute their targeted career destinations (Fullarton, 1999). In this way, employment might be merely about securing paid work to meet personal and family needs, or a stepping-stone to another more desirable job. Yet, such workplaces potentially provide a setting for these young people to engage in developing their vocational practice and identity and achieve vocational goals that are central to their sense of self. This might occur coincidentally as they engage in forms of work that they have not specifically aspired to. For instance, Somerville (2002) notes that most workers in aged care facilities came to undertake that work because it was available locally and convenient. However, once engaged, many find that the work is important and meaningful to them and their professional identity.

Given the importance of individuals' paid work to their identity and sense of self, their engagement in work is also likely to have implications for individuals' working lives and lives outside of work. For instance, studies of participation in workplaces identified the capacity to fulfil both vocational and individual goals through work (Billett et al., 2004, Billett and Pavlova, 2005; Billett et al., 2005). Similarly, the purposes for students engaging in work experience programs and paid part-time work included a rich interweaving and irreducible relationship between individual and workplace goals that arose from:

- Part-time employment directed towards supporting living costs during university education;
- Securing paid part-time work that focused on individuals' career trajectories because it was linked to that career;
- Assisting the formation of a working life identity;
- Learning to be more effective in one's vocational practice; and
- Progressing on a career trajectory. (Billett and Ovens, 2005)

In these ways, the boundaries between work and personal goals are richly interwoven, albeit exercised through work.

As proposed in Chapters 2 and 3, the processes involved in work participation are directed towards the ongoing process of remaking cultural practice through individuals' engagement and learning in their work. The cognitive legacy arising from engagement in work for individuals is their learning (Billett, 2003b; Billett et al., 2005). For many, perhaps most workers, learning through work will perhaps be the most common source of learning throughout their working life. Such ongoing learning will likely become more and more important as work requirements change more frequently—for most individuals there will be an ongoing task of remaining competent throughout the working life. So, as individuals engage in work they are also remaking the cultural practices that constitute work. This process is necessary because the enactment of vocational practice is not some behavioural-like reproduction, but rather a process of actively cons-tructing meaning and the application of the individual's construction of the procedures required for work activity (Valsiner, 1998). The form and direction of this remaking is central to an enterprise's continuity and de-velopment. So, there are relationships between individuals and their work-places that are fundamental to both the workplace and individuals achieving their goals. For both, this need is perhaps no more important than in times of workplace change, because of the threat it represents to the continuity of both employment and the continuity of the enterprise.

2.   WORK AND WORKPLACE PARTICIPATION

Not surprisingly, there are distinct perspectives on the worth and role of relationship between individuals and their workplaces. For some com-mentators, the changing nature of work is held, more than ever before, to require a synergy between employers' and employees' interests (Davis, 1995). This kind of relationship is claimed by some enterprises that have sought to engage their employees more fully in workplace practices and decision-making. These enterprises are characterised by human resource development theorists as 'high involvement workplaces' that aim to use the involvement of workers to secure productivity and service gains. It is argued that such workplaces seek to shift power and control away from management in ways that best capitalises on workers' expertise, energy and agency. In doing so, the aim is to secure workers' enthusiasm, intelligence, skills and commitment to secure the enterprise's goals, and provide purposeful and secure employment. Given the constant battery of changes and challenges that are now confronting enterprises, in this vein, Carnevale (1995) proposes:

> Such richly engaged relationships require the removal of 'top-down' hierarchies and their replacement by approaches to work organisation that "drive autonomy, skill resources and new flexible technologies down the line towards the point of production, service delivery and interface with the customer." (p. 239)

Howard (1995) claims that enterprises and workers have never needed each other more in confronting constant change. That is, to best capture the agency, talents and resources of employees so that the enterprise will survive and prosper, employees need to be integrated with the organisation of and decision-making within the enterprise. In this way, employees' interests will become aligned with the enterprise's goals. This suggests a level of workplace engagement leading to a shared understanding and commitment that is perhaps best described as familial. Here, the engagement in and agency of workers is to be secured so that it is their commitment to the enterprise, rather than their remuneration, which directs the engagement of their agency and capacities. Rowden (1995; 1997) has identified analogous characteristics in successful small to medium sized enterprises. He claims those American small to medium sized enterprises that have remained viable over time have: (i) unique market niches supported by the development of the workforce's skills, knowledge and attitude; (ii) integrated employees into the enterprises' work practice; and (iii) enhanced the quality of working life. Such examples provide empirical evidence to argue for the importance of rich engagement, shared understandings and values, and specific capacities of workers as being important for an enterprise's survival and development, and for offering workers a rich engaged and fulfilling working life.

However, although fashionable and much vaunted, actions by enterprises to secure employees' attachment and shared goals through rich engagement between the enterprise and its employees, is not the reality in many, perhaps most contemporary workplaces. In 1993, Berryman claimed that only five per cent of American enterprises were adopting work practices that would be categorised as 'high involvement'. Moreover, the enactment of higher involvement in the workplace may be only partial or highly selective. In information technology enterprises and banks, it has been suggested that such high involvement strategies are reserved for workplace elites, and not the majority of workers (Bernhardt, 1999). Some, perhaps many, workplaces appear to be more concerned about violating rather than securing high levels of engagement. For instance, some service sectors, particularly retail and food service, appear to be directed towards marginalising and controlling employees' work (Hughes and Bernhardt, 1999). Others suggest that, even Japanese workplaces, such as automotive plants, allegedly modelled and operated on high involvement principles, are in fact quite rigid, prescriptive and top-down in their work organisation (Danford, 1998). Instead, in these Japanese enterprises it is more likely that the culturally derived work ethic and loyalty to the employer is what drives the workers to engage their intelligence, capacities and commitment to the fullest. For instance, while workers in most advanced economies have had their work hours steadily reduced over the last century, Maddison (1982) showed that those in Japan had remained high. According to these data (see Table 6.1), in 1979 a worker in Japan (2129 hours per annum) was possibly working almost half as much again as their counterpart in Sweden (1451 hours per annum). This suggests that more broadly based culturally-derived values are being exercised as much as goals developed in the workplace. Where there is evidence of high involvement work, this tends to be directed towards highly skilled and highly valued employees (e.g. Darrah, 1996; Hughes and Bernhardt, 1999), rather than a practice being deployed more broadly.

Forrester, Payne and Ward (1995) in noting the peripheral and precarious status of many workers, particularly those in the service sector, question the assertions of human resource development theorists about a move to high involvement workplaces. They see this contrasting state of affairs as the inevitable conflict between management and employees (i.e. capital and labour). The work process of and outcomes for these workers are the very antithesis of 'high involvement' work. Danford's (1998) investigation of management attempts to superimpose team working on a repetitive, low skill assembly line in chocolate manufacture provides another example of the conflicts and tensions in management and worker relations. These conflicts arose from an attempt to secure more disciplined work practice while exercising the rhetoric of participation and empowerment. Contradictions and tensions arose between management's desire to build worker commitment to the enterprise and the context of maintaining control of the production processes. Similarly Scott (1994) recounts how management disestablished autonomous work groups they had introduced when it was realised that these groups gave the workers greater control over the production processes, thereby weakening management's power. Further, Danford (1998) questions the claims made for the Japanese-style team work that were attempted to be introduced in many workplaces in the 1990s to improve workplace performance. He claims that through cost-squeezing exigencies of intensified market competition and new customer-supplier relations, management merely exploited the new labour flexibility imperatives for team working to disempower workers. That is, management imposed a mode of team organisation that dismantled workers' control over the regulation of their labour. His analysis contests easy assumptions about team workers becoming enriched in post-Taylorist workplaces.

Instead, Danford (1998) suggests that in low skill and repetitive work, shop floor tasks may become increasingly subject to work intensification and workplace subordination through a regime of direct management control. Engagement for these kinds of workers is characterised by changing patterns of participation (e.g. part-time work, split shifts) that may inhibit the development of individuals' skills as the workers become peripheral, and more readily substituted by other workers. Also, in direct contrast to high engagement work, it is claimed that management utilise 'control through ignorance'. Workers are discouraged from accessing either tools (e.g. engineering drawings) as supervisors believe this would lead to staff undertaking tasks beyond their competence, or gaining insights that they would take to another (i.e. competing) workplace. In addition, controlling labour costs are seen as a priority and crucial for an enterprise's continuity (Darrah, 1996). In times of deregulation and increasing liberalism, Leicht (1998) darkly predicts:

> Once global competition and union decline are in full stride, employers lose what little incentive they have to comply with statutory workplace rights and gain every incentive they have to violate these rights and wait for the snail paced courts to bring them into line. (p. 38)

Moreover, having flexible workplace employment arrangements, for instance, offers greater flexibility in responding to changing requirements in the market place and securing productivity gains. It is noted by Bolle (2001) that part-time work can also serve to lower the unemployment rates, thereby addressing desirable governmental goals of perceived high levels of employment.

2.1 Changing duration of work

However, there are other trends that offer different perspectives. For instance, the number of hours that workers work per year has reduced considerably in advanced economies during the last hundred years. Maddison (1982) claims that overall the hours individuals work in many advanced capitalist countries have been reduced significantly between 1870 and 1979. However, the rates of decreases in annual working hours claimed are not uniform. Noteworthy are the hours worked by Japanese workers that have reduced at a more modest rate than those in other countries. Again, this suggests that transformations occur in different ways in different countries, and for perhaps quite distinct reasons.

Table 6-1. annual hours worked per person, 1870-1979 (adapted from Maddison, 1982)

	1870	1913	1950	1979
Australia	2945	2588	1838	1619
Austria	2935	2580	1976	1660
Belgium	2964	2605	2283	1747
Canada	2964	2605	1967	1730
Denmark	2945	2588	2283	1721
Finland	2945	2588	2035	1790
France	2945	2588	1989	1727
Germany	2941	2584	2316	1719
Italy	2886	2536	1927	
Japan	2945	2588	2272	2129
Netherlands	2964	2605	2208	1679
Norway	2945	2588	2101	1559
Sweden	2945	2588	1951	1451
Switzerland	2984	2624	2144	1877
UK	2984	2624	1958	1617
USA	2964	2605	1867	1607

Bosch, Dawkins and Michan (1994) note that American workers are close in their potential lifelong working hours to Japanese workers, although the latter still work about 200 hours more per year (Carnoy, 2001). They also note distinctions in the hours worked across different industry sectors within the same country as well as differences across countries. For instance, it seems that sectors such as retail, banks and insurance are likely to have longer working hours within many countries, compared with manufacturing, construction and trade work. There are exceptions however, with Portugal and Ireland having workers in the blue-collar sectors working longer than their white-collar counterparts. As well, there are sometimes differences in the hours worked depending upon the size of enterprise across many countries (Bosch et al., 1994). The typical pattern is to expect to work longer hours when working in small enterprises.

So there are differences in the duration of working hours that are likely to have their origins in cultural and occupational factors, albeit within a trend that has seen the reduction in overall working hours throughout the last century. Nevertheless, there will be those who note that in recent times, with the intensification of economic activity and, as a result, more intense work lives, workers are now working longer in many developed economies (e.g. Pusey, 2003). Those longer hours might be performed by salaried workers, whose remuneration is not directly tied to hourly rates of pay, and through the increased overtime worked by those who are employed on hourly rates. So, while over the long term, there has been a reduction in working hours, even if they have plateaued or increased in recent times, there is the potential for these powers to increase or the characteristics of those hours to change in some ways. For instance, the general trend to reduce working hours is likely to have distinct impacts for workers and their employers. On the one hand, workers will have more time outside of work and possibly be less exhausted as a result of shorter working hours. On the other hand, shorter working hours may press enterprises to organise greater intensification of work and the need for securing increased productivity, that is, to maximize the time workers spend in the workplace. Hence, the common claim that the contemporary workplace is becoming increasingly intense and demanding (see Chapter 8).

2.2   Changes in workplace relations

Allied to the above concerns about contemporary work practices is the reported erosion in relationships between employers and employees. This change may be influenced by increasingly liberal labour regulations and moves to disempower trade unions. This erosion is evident in countries experiencing structural adjustments and the enactment of neo-liberal policies, such as individual work contracts, increasingly perilous work tenure and an emphasis on the individual to maintain their skilfulness and to resist unemployment throughout a working life (Organisation for Economic Cooperation and Development, 2000). It is also evident in the erosion of unionised workplaces in countries such as the United Kingdom, and the ongoing use of contingent employment conditions (see below). This disengagement takes different forms. As noted, in Japan for instance, the prospect of lifelong employment within large enterprises is now being eroded. In countries like Australia, that have a long tradition of collective industrial arrangements and bargaining, government is imposing requirements for individual contracts, rather than the standard award conditions. This concern is reflected in the growing percentage of workers who are employed in contingent employment arrangements, in both the public and private sector. These arrangements have persisted even in times of high economic activity. For many commentators, the prospect of secure employment is becoming increasingly selective and strategic rather than something desirable for and extended to all employees (Baumann, 1998; Beck, 1992; Rifkin, 1995). Yet, there are also other kinds of changes, which question or complicate these claims. For instance the shortage of labour in countries, such as those in the European Union and the opening up of their labour markets is seeing a migration of labour across borders and assumptions that this labour is for the convenience of both parties. In a large food-processing factory in North Wales there is a reliance upon contract workers from Poland, because these Polish workers are willing to engage in work and for wages which domestic workers are reluctant to embrace. So, in contrast to what the human resource development theorists advocate, for many workplaces and many workers there will be a less engaged relationship in future because of both workplace practices and changes in labour markets which create demand, and in some instances, liberalised migration arrangements which permit workers to engage in opportune working arrangements.

So as has been argued above, there are quite distinct views about the goals for, processes of and prospects of relations in the workplace that will effectively achieve the goals of both enterprises and individuals. Certainly, it is claimed throughout that workplace participatory practices are likely to often fall far short of the high involvement ideal of human resource management theorists. Yet, regardless of their intended purposes, there is interdependence between workers and workplaces that comprise these participatory practices that are central to the continuity and development of both the worker and workplace. These are manifested in: (i) workplace affordances and (ii) individual engagement, and (iii) the negotiations between them.

2.3   Changing workplace affordances

The enactment and distribution of workplace affordances stands as a key premise for individuals' participation in work. They also encompass the value placed upon support for workers, and how contested workplace relations play out for particular cohorts and individuals and do much to shape workers' participation in work, how that work is conducted and remade (Billett et al., 2005). In Australia, the shift from national industrial awards that stipulate pay and conditions to enterprise-based agreements, and now increasingly individual work contracts, negotiated under a far more restricted set of basic requirements has permitted employment conditions to become bereft of some commitments of the past (e.g. training) that were central to previous employment conditions. Yet the requirements of employers to support employees' development are seen in some countries (e.g. Holland) to wed the interests of employees and employer closer together, and for employers to consider how best to employ their workforce.

Where there is a requirement or expectation for training as part of the conditions of employment, enterprises are more likely to be concerned for that training to be purposeful and to be maximised to secure effective outcomes for the enterprise (Billett, 2000a). This is in contrast to the low-level attachment in employment arrangements in the United States that can lead to low skill, low paid forms of work. More elaborated and value-added forms of work result from employment conditions that emphasize retention, training and skill utilisation. Because enterprises in The Netherlands are required to provide extensive workplace support and generous conditions for their employees, they are more likely to be interested in maximising the full range of skills for employees. This suggests they are, of necessity, likely to engage in more value-added kinds of work, and a range of work activities that reflect the cost and obligation of employing staff. This practice can be contrasted to labour-hiring practices in the US where such obligations are minimal and where there may be less concern to utilise the resources and capacities of employees to the full, thereby promoting the use of low paid and low skill service work. So, it follows that the kinds of labour regulations enacted can potentially lead to particular kinds of economic activities (i.e. those focused more or less on value-adding), with direct consequences for the kinds of work activities available and the kinds of participation that are enabled.

Certainly, government initiatives to enhance the quality of workplace participation need careful consideration and planning, least they achieve the opposite effects to what they intend. For instance, although governments in Australia and France have introduced levies and countries in northern Europe are expected to support employee development, the Australian Labor Federal Government in the early 1990s tried to convince Australian enterprises, that as beneficiaries of their workers' skills they should contribute to their initial and ongoing development. They legislated to introduce a training levy based on a percentage of the wages paid by the enterprise. This has arguably had a number of effects. Firstly, equating training to investment positioned it as an economic variable, rather than a social good (Smith and Billett, 2003). Moreover, as it is far easier to calculate the cost of skill development than its benefits, it is easily identifiable as a cost to the enterprise. Therefore, as employers began to see training and development as a cost more than an inevitable investment in the enterprise's continuity, government efforts to enrich the quality of workplace participation arguably had the opposite effect.

Similarly, reduction in apprenticeship intakes by employers led to the Australian government establishing Group Apprenticeship Schemes to employ apprentices, thereby taking the burden from enterprises. These organisations lease apprentices on a day-by-day or week-by-week basis to enterprises, depending on the enterprises' need. This arrangement for structured entry-level training, which had its origins in a reciprocal commitment on the part of employer and employee (the apprentice), has evolved to become little more than a convenient way of hiring labour for an employer. Because of the ad hoc arrangements associated with diverse employer needs at a particular moment in time, there is a danger that the apprentice will not receive an organised, appropriately structured and sequenced, and monitored workplace learning experience. Arguably, this is the case in United Kingdom where comparatively ad hoc apprenticeship arrangements have done much to dilute the integration of both workplace and college-based experiences for apprentices (Fuller and Unwin, 2003). There, the unregulated approach to apprenticeship has largely meant that employers are reducing or negating their commitment to apprentices. Indeed, the availability of such schemes in Australia provided a vehicle for some enterprises to further divest themselves of their involvement for trade skill preparation, despite being aware of and often only too ready to complain about skill shortages (Billett, 2000b). In one regional area in Australia that has a contained and stable labour force, employers commented that the availability of these schemes, removed their need to employ apprentices, as they could hire apprentices on demand, rather than make a commitment to their development.

From the instances above, it is possible to suggest that there is a growing sentiment within enterprises that is the very opposite of what 'high involvement' workplaces entail. Rather than a long-term goal of maintaining their workforce through the training of skilled workers, some enterprises seem only too ready to rely on external sources and providers. In this way, they are selective and strategic in how they expend enterprise funds on the skill development of their employees. These kinds of practices are the opposite of what is advocated by human resource development theorists about high levels of engagement (Carnevale, 1995; Rowden, 1997) and what governments suggest enterprises should do to ensure a sufficient supply of highly and appropriately skilled workers. Without a sentiment or set of values within enterprises that is supportive of affording opportunities to workers to participate and opportunities for workers to realize their vocational goals, both workplace and individual goals for continuity might be imperiled (Smith and Billett, 2003).

In addition, workplaces are often contested environments that also make participation in work, activities and working life a varied experience across and within workplaces. Depending on the workplace, that contestation can be between: labour and management; workers and owners; 'new-comers' and 'old-timers'; part and full-time workers; English speaking and non-English speaking workers; different workplace cliques; male and female workers and/or union and non-union labour, or among different union affiliations. Conflicting workplace relations between and among individuals, teams and key interest groups cannot be reduced to a mere footnote. These relations pervade work, conceptions of performance and importantly influence how individuals are able to engage in work activities and the degree to which they are afforded opportunities to participate and, therefore, learn through work. In a study of working lives (Billett et al., 2004), a worker engaging in a highly demanding job to which her personal and professional capacities and values were well aligned, referred to the damaging toll of contested work. Although her work was central to her agency and sense of identity, it was contested workplace relations, rather than the demand of any workload, which would see her leave the employment.

Whether the contestation is between 'new-comers' or 'old-timers' (Lave and Wenger, 1991), full or part-time workers (Bernhardt, 1999); teams with different roles and standing in the workplace (Darrah, 1996, Hull, 1997); individuals' personal and vocational goals (Darrah, 1997) or among institutionalised arrangements such as those representing workers, supervisors or management (Danford, 1998), contestation is an enduring feature of work practice and influences the relations within workplace settings, and therefore, how individuals work, learn and deploy their capacities and energies in remaking the cultural practices that comprise their work activities. These contestations can inhibit how individuals participate in, advance and learn through their work. For instance, part-time workers may struggle to engage in the worthwhile tasks prized by full-time workers. Similarly, there are issues about women's participation in work and that of older workers. Workers who sit outside the workplace clique may be ostracized and not supported in their endeavours whereas those within the clique will be strongly supported and promoted.

2.4   Ways of individual engagement

Individuals' engagement represents the second dimension to workplace participation. Despite the kinds of constraints identified above, individuals are able to exercise their capacities and discretions in ways that go beyond the constraints of what is afforded by workplace practices, as elaborated in Chapter 3. Workers are able to exercise discretion, to a greater or lesser degree, in their participation in work. Therefore, beyond the affordances of the workplace, individual engagement also shapes their participation, perhaps even in the most extreme work situations. In many ways, this exercise of agency is necessitated because, as foreshadowed, the enactment of work practice is not a behavioural and faithful rendition of an existing practice; it is the individual's construction and enactment of that practice. Within the scope of possible action, individuals have demonstrated a capacity to exercise their agency, even in apparently constraining employment circumstances. Grey (1994) demonstrates how professional workers achieve their goals through acting almost Machiavelli-like in an accountancy workplace to firstly secure employment and then work towards partnership. This is what Rose (1990) refers to as being 'enterprising selves': individuals who are entrepreneurial in presenting and positioning themselves effectively in the workplace, but potentially engaging or presenting a false sense of self to achieve those goals. Yet, whereas Grey's study suggested individuals had to subvert and deny their sense of selves in order to secure employment and promotion, this may not always be required. Within the scope of professional practice, Billett et al. (2004) noted how a grief counsellor was able to transform the practice of grief counselling in a forensic science facility to that aligned with his preferred approach (see Chapter 10). A later study identified the means by which workers were able to negotiate a space for themselves in their work activities such that there was consonance between the emerging and existing personal and professional goals of the individuals and the space they were able to negotiate (Billett and Pavlova, 2005).

Similarly, Darrah (1996) notes how the imposition of teamwork on a group of manufacturing employees was resisted and complicated by the beliefs and values of those who were supposed to work together collectively. He describes how workers in an American computer manufacturing company who were originally from Vietnam rejected the teamwork concept, as it violated their Confucian heritage values about individuals acting independently and being valued as individuals. These workers equated the request to work in teams as being analogous to communist work teams that they had fled Vietnam to avoid. "One supervisor's explanation that diverse members were to work together 'at the same level' only exacerbated their belief that communism had indeed followed them to the United States" (Darrah, 1996: 27). This example is interesting because it represents a culturally-derived value that was exercised collectively by a group of workers. Similarly, a group of coal miners rejected additional safety training that they construed as really about transferring the responsibility of mine site safety from management to workers (Billett, 2001c). However, there are also instances where the bases for workplace engagement are located within individuals' interests and sense of self.

Billett and Pavlova (2005) found that five workers engaged in different kinds of work were able to exercise a high degree of agency in their engagement in work tasks. This agency extended to individuals being able to secure goals that were important to their needs. So the negotiations that occurred between individuals and the affordances of the workplace are central to the workplace participatory practices in which individuals engage. Moreover, as is taken up in the next chapter, these processes of participation cannot be excluded from an analysis of the requirements for work performance, because these practices essentially structure "the work and learning that occurs there" (Darrah, 1997: 252).

Therefore, it is necessary and important to understand not only the objective account of what constitutes work and work participation, but also the subjective bases for individuals' participation in that work. Together, these comprise the dualities required to understand work and workplace participation. It would be quite inaccurate to view matters of engagement in workplace activities as only cognitive tasks and access to guidance as benign, without trying to understand how access to these activities is distributed, by whom and for what purposes. However, it is important not to over-accentuate the role of the individual without careful qualification, as these relations can lead to placing responsibility for the maintenance and development of skills throughout a working life on the individual.

In the sections above, it is suggested that bases for workplace participatory practices are found in workplace norms and practices, and how individuals respond to those norms and practices. That is, a consideration of participation in work needs to go beyond being considered in terms of workers responding to workplace imposed arrangements and needs to include how individuals and cohorts of individuals negotiate and engage in workplace practices. Together, these constitute a basis for considering how individuals participate in workplaces, and hence learn and play roles that permit them to exercise their selves and also perform effectively.

In elaborating the facts that shape workplace participation, the discussions above suggests that workplaces are often far from benign and supportive of participation in work and the learning arising from it. Instead, they can constitute highly contested environment. Given the contested nature of workplaces, the ability to secure many of the goals associated with work and the ability to access opportunities to participate and learn are beyond the control of the individual alone. Therefore, it is important to consider how an individual's progression throughout a working life needs to be mediated and supported by interests outside the workplace. Participation in work is more than the exercise of the workplace's affordances in terms of how individuals are permitted to work, the activities they are permitted to engage in, and the degree of support they get to assist their participation. It also needs to include the degree to which individuals elect to engage with the workplace and exercise their agency and intentionality through their work. Beyond the immediacy of the particular workplace factors, there are also societal views about work and the different status that different kinds of work are afforded.

A factor that influences both the bases for workplace affordances and how workplace relations play out, and also how individuals elect to engage in their work, is the status and standing of that work and those who conduct it.

3.   STATUS AND STANDING OF WORK AND WORKERS

The status and standing of particular kinds of work and workers influence how they are afforded opportunities to participate in work. Different categories of work are privileged in different ways in societies, for instance 'mental over manual'; across communities, for instance where that work is central to the community's existence (e.g. coalmining in coalmining communities); and within workplaces, for instance, work that is privileged in particular workplaces (e.g. academic work within universities), as discussed in Chapter 4. This privileging may shape the access to worker support, discretion, resourcing and progression. Therefore, the standing and status of the work is central to how work is valued and opportunities afforded for workers to progress. Whalley and Barley (1997: 24) claim that:

> Manual work, contaminated by its actual and symbolic association with dirt, material objects and physical labor has long been accorded low status. Even when manual labor is intensively skilled, it has still been devalued because of its reliance on oral traditions and tactile understandings rather than more formal and abstract codifications. Mental work, by contrast, is clean and relatively privileged, largely because it involves working with symbolic representations of a virtual world abstracted and distanced from nature.

They continue:

> If manual labor has historically been the work of inferiors-slaves, peasants, and more respectably, skilled craftsmen-mental labor has been the privilege of the elite: of gentlemen and sometimes ladies, of aristocrats, officers, scholars, professional and priests.

Darrah (1997) also notes how the design team in a computer manufacturing plant was taken as the 'heroes' in the workplace and, as such, afforded support and praise for their efforts. Conversely, the development needs of production workers (e.g. Board Technicians—production workers), although requiring high levels of adaptive and organisational skills for their work, were ignored, or received minimal support. Therefore, depending on workers' status and standing, they may find their capacity to participate in the workplace is either encouraged or inhibited. As Darrah (1996: 18) suggests:

> Board techs are trained through gradual exposure to increasingly complex PCBs. A lead technician ... assigns new workers to the automatic testing machine for a few weeks so they learn the characteristics of the individual tests, their sequence, and typical error messages. Then he allows them to trouble shoot simpler PCBs, such as memory or input output boards. After three or four months, technicians are able to recognise error messages and pinpoint the defective areas of the boards. Gradually, they tackle the more complex PCBs.

Yet, these production workers were classified as uninformed and unskilled staff and their contributions were seldom solicited in deliberations about improving workplace processes or performance. For instance, because of their lowly standing, their views on how computers might best be manufactured were not solicited—to do so entailed a level of co-operation that would violate departmental boundaries and occupational hierarchies. In this way, the low status of this work supported the view that production workers' skill development is 'informal' and poorly structured and this was reflected in management beliefs about their role. Moreover, Darrah (1996) comments that a lack of understanding of their work by workers of higher status, led to enhanced complications for the production workers, who had to routinely engage in complex problem-solving activities to maintain the required level of productivity. Yet, Darrah (1996) proposes that even the most cursory examination of board technicians' work reveals the demands and complexity of their activities.

From this instance, and other data about the distribution of workplace support for employees, it seems that how individuals' or cohorts of workers' work is perceived shapes the support they are afforded through their work. There is also the related issue of what work means to individuals in relation to workplace and community norms. For example, the ability to work in call centres provided opportunities for disabled workers to engage in relations with customers and clients not influenced by those clients' knowledge of their disability (Church, 2004). So, beyond the societal sanctioned views about the standing and status of work, there is also a way in which particular kinds of work will have standing and importance for workers. As shown, this might be based on localised needs or cultural practices that sit beyond the mainstream purview of what constitutes high status work. Across studies of food processing, coalmining and hairdressing, issues of personal identity were key bases upon which individuals decided to engage in work related activities (Billett, 2001c). Males in a rural community particularly valued aspects of food processing work that were seen to be highly masculine.

Thus, there is interdependency between individuals and their workplaces and there may be inherent problems with this relationship when work practices that are potentially dangerous to the individual are endorsed by community norms and values. In Somerville's (2002) studies of coalminers and aged care workers it was noted that these workers carried workplace injuries as emblems of their occupational identity. Yet as noted in these studies and elsewhere (Billett et al., 2004; Billett et al., 2005) the press of situation requirements is not uniformly felt by all workers. That is, some engage more with these norms and practices than others. In this way, the interdependency between the individual and the workplace is importantly relational, thereby suggesting that subjective accounts of work are required to sit alongside the more objective views about workplace practices, norms and affordances.

The personal standing of individuals also warrants a basis for their participation. This standing can be endorsed or inhibited by the same set of factors that affect cohorts of workers. For instance, one worker at a mine site was able to retrieve a piece of earthmoving equipment that had partially fallen into the open cut coal mine by making it operate and then using the bulldozer's own capacities to cut a pathway out of the mine (Billett, 2001c). He was hailed as a hero and was granted high levels of credibility in the workplace. Yet, workplaces can also work to inhibit or enhance the standing of workers regardless of the availability of objective measures. In particular, workplace cliques can erode or elevate the status of individuals.

The implications for this kind of societal view extend beyond the immediate workplace. It has also played an important role in shaping the social and political allegiances of the clerical labour force and in fostering the sense of cultural inferiority felt by many blue-collar workers whose education provided little access to cultural resources (Sennet and Cobb, 1972 cited in Whalley and Barley, 1997). Yet, these implications should not be taken as necessarily potent or important for individuals.

Having discussed the relations between the workplace and individuals in relational terms and focused upon participation in workplaces in terms of participatory practices, it is appropriate now to elaborate further the bases of these practices. In the next section, issues associated with changes in the ways and means of participation in work are discussed.

4.   CHANGING WAYS OF WORKING

There are no standard means by which individuals across industries, countries and cultures participate in work. Therefore, there is no easy benchmark that can be applied to make critical appraisals of how individuals participate in work and judgements about any changes to that participation.

The organisation of large numbers of individuals working within the same physically located organisation, while often seen as representing a standard way of working is an unconvincing benchmark. This is because it is far from typical and its existence and practice has occurred in different countries in different ways and at different times. For instance, much of the gathering of workers into large factories occurred in European and American enterprises in the 19th century. Prior to that most workers would have been self-employed or working in workplaces where the owner of the business employed relatively small groups of workers. Even in contemporary times, most private sector employment remains in small businesses, that is, in businesses employing fewer than ten individuals, in countries such as Australia (ABS, 2004). So, the majority of workers outside of those employed by government have always and will likely continue to work in small workforces. Yet, it is understood that in many ways these employees are denied many of the benefits which are available to those in larger enterprises.

Initially, during the move to industrialisation, in many factories a skilled tradesperson operated as a subcontractor, employing their own staff and maintaining a capacity to negotiate with the factory owner. However, skilled workers enacted changes in the organisation of work to break the control of the means to production. This eroded their power, making them mere employees (Whalley and Barely, 1997). Later, the introduction of scientific management in factory work did much to further segment and control the way workers use their skills in workplaces. However, it was this very demarcation of labour that provides a platform for employees, in the form of organised and collective labour, to play a role in how work was and is conducted in workplaces, including the degree of discretion available to both managers and workers.

These shifts from a predominant pattern of self-employment or employment in small workplaces to employment in large and highly organised workplaces have occurred differentially across the world. Currently, for instance in countries such as Korea, China, Thailand and Vietnam, and in India with its business support centres, there is a move to a form of industrialisation in which an increasing proportion of the working population now find employment within large factories. Whereas it is rare in Western countries for a large private sector workplace with 10,000–20,000 workers, such workplaces are now being established in India to provide business services to customers in America, Europe and Australasia. Similarly, the expansion of manufacturing within Western Europe is often to relatively low-cost countries such as Turkey, Uzbekistan, and Turkistan. As noted in the previous chapter, these kinds of change are reshaping the opportunities for participation in paid employment in both the countries from which the work is being exported and also those in which new manufacturing facilities are being constructed. In these countries to the east of Europe, recent changes in technology and the cost of labour have resulted in new means of working. Conversely, the prospect of lifelong employment in Japanese enterprises is now being transformed, bringing with it prospects of diverse employment over a Japanese workers' working life. Young Japanese are less interested in working the hours that their fathers are working. Consequently, there is no fixed model of what constitutes an established way of parti-cipating in working life, nor its manifestations at particular points in time.

In the two sections below, examples of changes in work participation are discussed and associated with the rise in non-standard or contingent work, and work conducted in isolation from the workplace.

4.1   Contingent work

An increasing percentage of those in contemporary Western workforces are contingent workers. Contingent workers comprise part-time, contract and consultant workers who are employed to perform specific tasks for limited time periods without the security of ongoing employment. They are often not paid for sick days or vacation, and in some instances are denied health or pension benefits. Although the type of contingent work differs widely, from low skill workers engaged in repetitive tasks to specialist consultancy workers, overwhelmingly, it seems that contingent workers are involuntary. For example, 90% of the 365 000 jobs created in America during February 1993 were part-time positions taken by workers who wanted to work full-time (Van Horn, 1996). Certainly, contingent work arrangements may suit the needs of some highly mobile workers and specific groups of individuals, for instance some women wanting to balance their work and family life (Shima, 1998). However, although women who are financially secure enough and able to negotiate part-time employment welcomed this mode of employment, overall the vast majority of contingent workers are claimed to be involuntary (Lipsig Mumme, 1996; Van Horn, 1996). These contingent work arrangements impact particularly heavily on women, migrants, non-native speakers, the lowly skilled, and, in some countries, the aged.

The rise of this contingent workforce may be a product of a labour market that currently favours employers or, alternatively, it may become part of a new workplace order. Certainly, in the past, high percentages of casualised forms of work were associated with periods of high unemployment and low economic activity in Western style economies. However, this orthodoxy has now been challenged by the sustained level of contingent workers in high performing economies such as America, Australia and the United Kingdom.

Van Horn (1996) claims the US workforce is divided into two distinct groups, comprising permanent core workers and contingent workers. Nevertheless, the existence of well-paid and high skill 'portfolio' workers disrupts this easy generalisation. These workers may be able to negotiate high levels of pay for their specific services and might be classified as self-employed.

Over time, contingent work can weaken the prospects for career development and the continuity of employment of those affected. Tam (1997) notes how women's part-time employment has led to restricted careers. Contingent workers are far less likely to participate fully and seek advancement (Grubb, 1996). In all, Harrison (1997) sees the growth of the contingent workforce as the 'dark side' of the new economy, where "... growing heterogeneity in work organisation and practices, both among and within particular employers has led to declining employment security and more uncertain wage and salary prospects over time" (p. 259).

The issue of contingent workers is not restricted to countries that have lax or liberal labour laws. For instance, Australia, despite its tradition of organised labour and workplace regulation, has the highest rate of casual and part-time employment in the OECD after Spain and very high job turnover rates (Pusey, 2003: 80). From his surveys of the Australian workforce, Pusey (2003) claims that about one in three jobs are casual or part-time. He notes that full-time employment in Australia as a proportion of total persons employed declined between 1985 and 2000 from 82% to 74%. Through the same period the level of casual employees as a proportion of all employees increased from 16% to 27%, nearly an 80% increase in this form of employment. Moreover, this work is increasingly undertaken in asocial hours. That is, it occurs at weekends, through shifts at nights and with greater job insecurity that in turn generates new pressures for the family. In Britain, over the past 20 years there has also been an expansion in 'non-standard' patterns of employment. The percentage of all employees working part-time (i.e. less than 30 hours a week) increased from 21% in 1991 to 26.5% in 2000. Similarly, temporary jobs increased from 4% to 8%, and self-employment rose from 7% to 11.6%, in the same period (UK Labour Force Surveys, 2005). At the same time, and perhaps more than coincidentally, trade union membership is reported to have declined significantly from 45.6% to 24.7% and the reported numbers of weekly hours worked increased from 40.3 to 42.9. In the United States, part-time employment has increased for women since the 1960s (Shima, 1998), yet males are now also increasingly being employed as part-time workers in increasingly contingent workforces. As noted, it is these kinds of trends that buoy claims that the norms for what constitutes standard and decent work are changing.

Instances of contingent forms of work, while impacting mainly on service work, are not restricted to forms of occupations that might be described as low skill. For instance, workplaces such as universities, banks and government departments have workforces with high percentages of contingent employees. Indeed, the outsourcing of work conducted by contractors or individuals may see the concentration of expertise and resources into particular enterprises. Another possible consequence is the fragmentation of work into small or self-employed enterprises where tasks are undertaken by casually employed workers. Small businesses with fewer than five employees are becoming typical, as are smaller units of workers and there is also a modest shift from employment in larger enterprises to smaller enterprises (Noon and Blyton, 1997). However, employment in smaller enterprises can be more volatile. Certainly, for many in the workforce, what was previously accepted about career paths and permanent employment appears to be disappearing as are ideas about mutual trust and the rewards for hard work well done (Rifkin, 1995; Kempnich, Butler and Billett, 1999). These changes and their impacts are likely to differ among categories of contingent workers. For instance, highly skilled and qualified portfolio workers may be able to negotiate far more effectively in this new work order than workers in the service and retail sectors.

Yet, the detachment from the workplace may also work against employers' interests. That is, contingent workers may have divided loyalties across a number of workplaces and between their work and other demands, such as their home life or parenting responsibilities (Hull, 1997). However, the requirement for work and provision of benefits varies across countries. For instance, in countries which have no or limited public health or welfare provisions, the benefit of a healthcare retirement provision as part of a remuneration package is of greater significance than in countries where these are provided through public provisions (for example, America where health and pension entitlements are often employer provided, as part of the condition of employment). Therefore, a contingent relationship with an employer can seriously affect an individual's provision of healthcare and pension entitlements (McGovern et al., 2004, McNair et al., 2004; Tam, 1997) in ways that are quite different from an employee in a country where these are organised through public agencies. It can also lead to a preference for particular kinds of work activities and limits in responding to available options by employers.

In sum, the traditional orthodoxy was that stronger economies would see enterprises extending tenure to workers in order to secure their labour. However, this orthodoxy seems to have been enacted in selective ways in many Western-style countries. It appears more likely that those workers whose level of skills and specialisms are central to the enterprise's activities will be offered more secure forms of work than those whose skills are easily undertaken by others. The degree to which such a principle is practiced across many enterprises and/or is permissible by labour regulations will do much to shape the labour market and the likelihood of permanent work for workers and the selection of workers for permanency. The impacts of contingent work include difficulty with career maintenance and progression, as well as uncertainty in remuneration levels over time. Also, there may well be difficulties for workers' sense of self and security arising from contingent employment conditions. The impacts of contingent work arrangements may play out differently across the community. For those families with dependable incomes, the possibilities of part-time employment, particularly when secure, provide a means for balancing work and life outside work, particularly family life (Bolle, 2001). It can also make it easier for workers to enter, leave and retire from the workforce, because it provides employment options that bridge the employees' requirements at that point in time (i.e. easing into and out of work life). Yet, Bolle (2001: 237) continues with a warning:

> Policies designed to promote part-time work and lowering its costs below that of full-time employment are likely to have the perverse effect of increasing the proportion of involuntary part-time workers, i.e. under-employment, with adverse consequences both social—especially for women and other workers already at a disadvantage on the labour market—and economic, depressing demand, growth and employment.

So although the provision of part-time work can be seen as primarily assisting the employer's capacity for a flexible workforce, it may serve the interests of some workers while working against those of others (Bolle, 2001).

For many workers, particularly those who are self-employed, fluctuating income is a common work experience. So, the idea of contingent work is not without precedent across the workforce. The problem in contemporary circumstances is that it seems to be available to many in the community who are in a disadvantaged position and this form of work may well exacerbate or entrench that disadvantage.

4.2   Remote Workers

Another form of nonstandard work participation that appears to be growing is working remotely. Changes in technology and technological applications to work, particularly those associated with electronic technology, have the potential to transform how individuals participate in work. This includes the capacity for workers to work remotely from others and their clients. This has occurred in two quite distinct ways, both associated with remoteness. Firstly, the advent of electronic communication and low-cost telecommunications and computing means individuals are increasingly able to work in locations remote from the physical location of the workplace. Most graphically, this capacity is exercised in the business support services now being offered from India to clients in Europe, the Americas and Australasia. The extent of this work appears to be growing: from the handling of electronic business administration tasks at a distance, the work has expanded to call centre services, offered in real time to clients in other continents; to the overnight transcription and filing of American doctors' voice-filed notes about patient care required for health records and insurance purposes. Even within India, this technology is now enabling women to work from home, rather than the call centre facilities that have been established in state-of-the-art workplaces in Delhi, Mombai and Bangalore. In this way, it allows women who otherwise would be denied the opportunity to continue to engage in paid work, while also performing childcare and home-related tasks.

However, there can be limits to working remotely. For instance, remote workers can have difficulties in participating fully in workplaces, being seen to be competent and accessing opportunities for advancement. Home-based workers express concerns about being 'outside the loop' of not knowing the current goals and directions of their workplace. Hence, their actions can be perceived to be not as competent or in keeping with the current norms and goals of the employer. There is a concern about being invisible or being seen as peripheral to the organisation's needs and practices. It might be seen, in some work situations, as the first step towards further outsourcing or contracting or being made redundant.

However, isolation in the conduct of work is hardly novel. Shift workers have long worked in isolation from the day shift of managers, clerical workers and professionals. For some, this isolation is quite welcomed. In a study of production workers who worked in teams and rotating shifts, a key attribute of the long night shift was the autonomy that it granted the workers (Billett, 2000a). They planned and enacted their work largely in the absence of supervisors or professional engineers who were the daytime occupants of the workplace. As an observer of their work and work practices, the collaborative and responsible way in which their work was conducted seem to have many of the characteristics of what constitutes professional work. Instead of meal breaks being used to discuss only sport and recreation, they were often the place where the team members came together to discuss their work and the allocation of tasks for the night shift. Their satisfaction and autonomy was in contrast to the day shift workers, who complained about the interference in their work by professional engineers who lacked a feel for the plant yet mandated actions that seemed counter to the experience and expertise of the production workers. It extended to them organising 'sick' rosters: convenient days when workers were sequenced to call in sick, without making excessive demands upon co-workers. However, these workers were not individually isolated—they worked together as a collective. For example, they were aware of the need to avoid situations where they might fall asleep or be placed in a dangerous situation when battling sleep. Similarly, the conduct of food process workers, many of whom would be classified as low skill workers, demonstrated high levels of responsibility and pride in their work, again trained many of the characteristics of work which elsewhere is seen to be worthy of work discretion (Billett, 2002a).

The experience of working remotely can be isolating and inhibiting or it can open up and extend prospects for employment and be supported by the social partners. So, depending upon workers' individual circumstances, their needs and the kind of remoteness that their work entails it can have quite a different impact. However, in making judgements about the quality of work performance and engagement, it is necessary to engage a subjective view of those who are participating in the work, because observations and interviews reveal that these workers are interested, engage and take their work practices as an element of their sense of self. This extends to work that others might see as being of little worth.

4.3   Separation from work processes

The other kind of remoteness comprises a separation from the means of production. Increasingly perhaps, technology mediates the actions of the worker and can provide some separation between the work and the worker. This might serve to make an easier working life as the capacity to control machinery and equipment from a distance, and away from heat, dust and noise is likely to be welcomed. However, there is also a separation between work and the worker that may degrade the worker's skills (Zuboff, 1988), that is, separating individuals from productive processes can lead to unsatisfactory outcomes. It can also threaten their work identity. Wright Mills (1973) in referring to the ideal craft worker notes:

> What is necessary for work as craftsmanship is the tie between the product and the producer be psychologically possible; if the producer does not legally own the product he must own it psychologically in the sense that he knows what goes into it by way of skill, sweat, and material and that his own skill and sweat are visible to him. (p. 11)

Such attributes are in danger of being violated by the technological separation between workers and their work (Martin and Scribner, 1991: Zuboff, 1988). Zuboff (1988) refers to the need for a 'sentient: that is, attentive-cognisant involvement' between workers and their work. Hull (1997) emphasises important social components of work such as membership of a work-based community. Yet, as the means of conducting work inevitably change there will be changes to both the kinds of work that will be undertaken and the means through which that work is conducted. In particular, technologies have changed the requirements of skilled work in different ways. One way has been to reduce the amount of physical effort required in many forms of work (e.g. powered machinery to sew, cut and finish garments; cut wood, assemble components and build houses). These innovations have transformed the immediate contact between workers and their materials and tools. They have replaced some of the sweat that Wright Mills (1973) refers to, and the injuries that he does not. Thus, the mediation of technology and a separation between workers and materials upon which they work need to be balanced with other considerations. Although physically remote and separate from the processing plant, workers in the control room claim to develop a 'feel' for the plant (Billett, 2000a), in much the same way that others kinds of workers report. These workers claimed that their knowing of the plant became so profound that they could predict the impact of wet ore and other factors on the production of magnesite crystals. They also referred to reengaging with the plant after periods of recreational leave and expressed frustration when the plant engineers ordered them to make changes to production settings that were against their intuition about how the plant best operated. The point here is that the kind of associations between the worker and materials may not necessarily be rendered totally separate by the mediation of technology. This sense of separation, likely has much to do with the previous history of the individual worker as well as the actual technology. For instance, whereas Martin and Scribner's (1991) manual labour operators might experience a sense of isolation, the new generation of machinists who were familiar with computer controlled lathes might not, given the data provided in that study. Again, it is the relationship between the workplace change and the individual's history that may determine what is seen as separation and what is seen as a basis for engagement.

This section has aimed to provide two instances of how changing work arrangements influence work practice and the means by which individuals engage with their work and with their working lives. The growing use of contingent work arrangements provides a form of separation between workers and workplaces in terms of the duration, certainty, and standing of their work that complicates how they participate in work. It may also marginalize the affordances the workplace makes for them. In a similar way, the potential growth in workers who are based away from the workplace provides a different kind of separation—physical separation and isolation. Carnoy (2001) views this kind of work as reshaping not only the conception of work but also those of workers.

> Workers are being separated both from their traditional identities built up over more than a century and the social networks that enable them to find economic security. The job and everything organised around the job—the friends of work, the after work meeting places, the trade union, even group transport—lose their social function, they are becoming as permanently temporary as the work itself. (p. 306)

As a consequence, workers may be separated from their work practices and means of engaging in vocational practice in ways that make it more complex, difficult or only partial. However, there are also consequences for work practice and workplaces arising from these arrangements. Contingent workers are less likely to be centring their attention on a workplace that only affords them limited and uncertain participation. Moreover, for permanent workers in these workplaces, there may well be a far greater range of tasks to be undertaken by far fewer full-time workers. That is, the administration and conduct of work becomes the central concern of fewer workers, making their work more intense and perhaps more broadly based. However, some of this intensity and broadening of responsibilities may be welcomed. In different ways and from different premises, the changes in participation and participatory practices will be engaged with and construed by individuals as either welcomed or potentially alienating. The picture is of more flexible work arrangements that may suit some, but not all individuals. Consistently the evidence suggests that the majority of contingent workers are involuntarily contingent. Similarly, the prospect of working away from the workplace may have advantages for some individuals or cohorts. Yet, it can also curtail the kind of participation in workplace activity that workers find the most satisfactory and easiest to manage.

Yet, beyond changes in the means of participating in the workplace, there are also changes in those who are participating. This represents another dimension of workplace participation.

5.   CHANGING PARTICIPATION IN WORK

In sum, this chapter has proposed that over time, the opportunity to engage in particular occupations will likely fluctuate, although more so for some sectors that others. It will do so in different ways in different places, for the reasons discussed above. The strength, duration and durability of economic activity do much to determine the availability of work, as can the available skills and technologies to conduct that work. Moreover, cultural mores can shape the extent and kinds of available work. For instance, in many Western countries, the last 40 years has seen a significant increase in the number of women participating in the paid workforce. In many advanced economies, such as America, Australia and Britain the percentage of women participating in the workforce is now almost equivalent to that of men (see Chapter 4). Thus, to maintain levels of employment, significant increases in the total amount of employment generally have had to occur. Yet, again this pattern of increased participation by women in the workforce also plays out differently across countries. In some countries, such as Japan, there may still be an expectation that women will relinquish their paid work upon marriage. In other countries, such as Finland and Denmark, it would be seen as quite strange for a woman, even with young children, to not be participating in the paid labour force (Tikkanen, Lahn, Ward and Lyng 2002). Moreover, changes in social welfare provision in some countries are causing both men and women to postpone retirement and work longer, and for women to return to work earlier after giving birth to children. Given the personal and professional need for full participation in the workforce, there are inevitable consequences when employment becomes scarcer during periods of low economic activity.

The means of participation in work is driven by workplace and individual factors that are in some ways quite interdependent. The goals for continuity of the workplace and individuals' work life are key imperatives. This duality ultimately constitutes enactment of paid work including how individuals experience and negotiate their working life, remake practice and sustain and develop their sense of self, thereby making participation and workplace participatory practices a core concept to understand work, learning through-out working life and the remaking of work practice. Yet, there are diverse perspectives about how ideally (i.e. what should be) work practices should be enacted and also the contemporary reality (i.e. what is), from high involvement workers to the burgeoning body of contingent workers. It has proposed that the high involvement ideal promised more broadly is only the experience of a select few. Instead, the kinds of participatory practices being employed by workplaces likely reflect the particular set of values that underpin the conduct of work and the workplace's goals. This has resulted in participatory practices that afford particular kinds of support for some cohorts of workers and some individuals. The level of affordances does much to shape how individuals are able to participate fully in the workplace.

Indeed, these relationships between the workplace and workers are the focus of the next chapter, which explores and discusses changes in who is participating in work and its consequences for them.

Chapter 7

CHANGING COMPOSITION OF PAID WORKFORCES

> Analysing changes in working life at any time in history requires an understanding of women's and men's relationship to social institutions outside the workplace, particularly family and the community. Today, this is even truer than in the past with women's massive return to wage work overtime and profound change in the workplace, in families and in communities. (Carnoy, 2001: 305)

In addition to changes in the available work and changes in forms of participation as discussed in the previous two chapters, the composition of the workforce—those who are working—is also changing. In many countries, the key change in workplaces is the increase in women engaging in paid work, including those with young children. In the last 20 years, the increased levels of women's participation in work have transformed workplaces and work practices across countries such as America, Britain and Australia. Although existing levels of women's participation vary across countries—for instance, in Scandinavia there have long been high levels of women's employment—the changes in other countries are significant in terms of occupations populated by women and working life generally and, relations within the workplace and between work and home life.

There are also other identifiable groups within different countries that struggle to participate effectively and fully in work and working life. These groups include migrants, non-native speakers and indigenous populations. Often lower levels of education and language proficiency hinder their full participation in work and working life. This has consequences for their capacity to position themselves well within work and to secure the kinds of work and working life that meets their needs and, supports and exercises

149

their full potential. Then there are the ambiguous circumstances of disabled workers who are afforded opportunities to work by new technologies and service centres, yet may remain marginalised within their workplaces. There is also an increasing participation by older workers. However, often their participation is set within contradictory discourses, while encouraging and claiming to value their participation (particularly in certain kinds of service work), the same workplaces will tend to favour and support younger workers in preference to those who are older. This is particularly evident in the distribution of training support. Against predictions of previous decades, it seems that individuals' working lives are likely to become longer in many countries. Longevity, changing demographics and the reduction of public provisions all combine to suggest a societal need for longer working lives in many countries. Also, the changes to social welfare benefits in many countries are prompting a circumstance where the onus for a long working life is being converted from the societal to the individual level, as increasingly older people will be required to rely on their own resources. Yet while it is easy to characterise cohorts of workers under common titles (e.g. women, disadvantage, older), those categorised in this way are not homogeneous. Instead, their experiences, purposes, capacities and means of engaging in the world of work are likely to be as diverse as any other group. These issues are discussed in turn here.

1.   WOMEN'S PARTICIPATION IN WORK

The gradual increase in women's participation in the labour force represents a significant changes in many Western countries over the last half 50 years. The increase of women's participation in the American labour force during the 30-year period between 1970 and 2000 was quite dramatic. Participation by women aged 16 years or older increased from 43% to 61%. Over the same period, participation by males in the American labour force declined slightly from 78% to 74% (Department of Labor, 2005). This increasing participation is closing the gender gap in the US workforce, with women comprising 47% of the labour force in 2000, and predicted to shortly become the majority of the American workforce. In Australia, the proportion of young women aged between 25 and 34 engaged in the labour force has increased by three quarters in only one generation (1970 to 1996) from 41 to 71% (Pusey, 2003: 84-85). Pusey (2003) claims that with the relative decline in male earnings and increased family indebtedness; female earnings are now required to help Australian families cope and get ahead. Similar patterns also exist in Britain and Canada. Female participation in the labour force has increased from 42% in 1980 to 47.3% in 2000 in the United

Kingdom. However, this increase is largely in paid part-time work, with women comprising. 81.6% of part-time workers in Britain. It seems that, like in Australia, in both the United States and United Kingdom, women are participating in the labour market because of low or declining real wages (Bosch et al., 1994). These authors conclude that 'emancipation through the market' does not lead to good work for women, when compared with countries that have a strong welfare provision. However, this pattern of contingent work is also reflected in male employment with an increase from 2.3% to 8.4% of men being employed in part-time work (McGovern, et al., 2004). Being married now has less effect on women's participation in work. For instance, in the US labour market, there is now a convergence between participation in the workforce by women, regardless of marital status and age of youngest child. In 1960, fewer than 20% of women with children under the age of six participated in paid work. Currently, 60% of these women and over 75% of women with school-age children are participating in paid work thereby making their level of participation consistent with that of women generally (Jacobsen, 2004). This increased level of participation indicates a dramatic transformation in the lives of women as they divide their time between paid work and unpaid family activities.

In the United States, the decline of male participation is claimed to be associated with additional Social Security benefits that encourage retirement at the age of 65 (Department of Labor, 2005). However, the increase in female participation is held to be more complex and likely a product of expanded job opportunities for women and/or compulsion to enter the workforce. In Australia, early retirement and redundancy combined with increased longevity (about 10 years more since the 1950s) has reduced the relative span of working life for Australian males (Pusey, 2003), thereby increasing the proportion of nonworking males. Shah and Burke (2003) also claim that a much greater percentage of Australian male workers are exposed to global labour markets than female workers. As elaborated in Chapter 5, Shah and Burke (2003) have categorised forms of work into those that are advantaged by global competition and technological innovation, those that are relatively insulated from these factors and those occupations that are vulnerable to global competition and technology. Many of the occupations that are insulated from global competition and technology are those that provide 'in-person' services while the most vulnerable occupations are those that could be performed by workers from overseas or by technology. These vulnerable occupations comprise many of the forms of work mainly conducted by males. These include skilled trades persons, clerical workers, machine operatives and production and process workers. Although it is possible to find exceptions to the identified occupations, Shah and Burke's (2003) principles appear to provide a useful predictor. The point is that the concentration of traditional male work in the vulnerable category indicates fragility in the male labour market, and potentially their erosion as a proportion of the labour market. However, the concentration of women in 'in person' services work may well be doing much to buoy the proportion of females in the workforce.

The usual distinction between male and female working life cycles is that the former are typified by the continuous working life between school and retirement, whereas the latter are characterised by interruptions of employment brought about through marriage, childcare and caring for elderly relatives (Bosch et al., 1994). Jacobson (2004) proposes that the cause of changes in gender difference in the labour force participation in the USA is most likely found within critical moments in and relations with family life, that is, changes to the timing and nature of interruptions to women's working life. Jacobson (2004) proposes that 20 years ago, women were more likely to marry younger, interrupting their college education to do so, and have children and engage in child raising earlier. This resulted in movement in and out of work, largely constraining women to part-time employment. Moreover, their work was a job to provide additional resources for the family, rather than a career focused on their needs. In contemporary times, however, these circumstances are held to have changed. Women marry later, have children later, are more likely to go to college, less likely to interrupt their education for marriage, and are more likely to have a career before marriage (Jacobson, 2004). Moreover, women now have fewer children and childcare is much more widely available, in some places. In short, "family structure variables have less exposure power in female wage and participation equations than in the past" (p. 7). Women have also benefited from their increased participation in education to secure more generously remunerated forms of work (Loutfi, 2001).

Yet, contemporary accounts also suggest that women are still far more likely to be employed in part-time work than their male counterparts, and that this work still leads to truncated and unsatisfactory career options. Tam (1997) concludes that part-time work constitutes "a trap which lowers women's lifetime employment prospects and earnings" (p. 243). She argues that "it is unwarranted to characterise, in a sweeping manner, part-time work as being secondary employment" (p. 241). However, Shima (1998) concludes it is not all part-time work that disadvantages, with quality part-time work not necessarily constituting a disadvantage. Instead, it can provide a desirable alternative to non-employment or full-time employment. As noted in Chapter 6, part-time work is viewed differently in different countries and for good reason. For instance, in the US it engages concerns about loss of benefits that are provided through employment. However, in Europe (e.g. The Netherlands, Denmark and Sweden), part-time work is viewed positively as a satisfactory alternative. In these countries there is also significant movement between full- and part-time work (Blossfeld and Hakim, 1997). If individuals can choose whether they work part- or full-time and are able to exercise that choice in a balanced way, it becomes a very distinct work-life choice. This is quite different to the scrambling and non-voluntary options of women as contingent workers (Bolle, 2001).

Given the enduring growth in patterns of women engaging in part-time work, which for some may be welcomed but for others are less than satisfactory forms of employment, it is important to know in what ways this increase in participation in paid work has furthered the scope, opportunities and benefits to women. That is, understanding how the issues about non-standard work, play out for women as an increasing and potentially the majority of participants in future workforces.

1.1   Outcomes of increased participation by women in the workforce

The biggest change in occupational structure of the American workforce is a result of the increased participation of women in managerial, administrative and professional occupations (Department of Labor, 2005). However, despite these categories of employment being seen as prestigious and well rewarded, the increased representation of women in these sectors is not without problems, particularly for women themselves. Firstly, women workers are still concentrated in particular occupational fields. Nearly 25% of American women report being employed in administrative support positions, compared with 5% of males. Also, whereas 20% of working men report being employed in work categorised as precision production work, only 2% of women worked are so categorised (Department of Labor, 2005). Further, although a higher proportion of working women are now classified in work categorised as professional, much of this participation actually comprises primary and secondary school teaching and nursing, areas traditionally dominated by women. Loutfi (2001) claims that there have been significant gains in women's share in professional and managerial employment in the last two decades in many countries (e.g. Australia, Canada) as well as the United States and suggests some general progress by women into occupations traditionally dominated by men. The data on benefits, however, remain equally mixed. American data on median wages suggest that there has been some reduction in the gap between women's and men's wages.

Certainly, there have been some relative increases in the parity of women's remuneration over time. In 1966, the ratio between men and women's salaries was 0.60 and currently it is 0.86 (Jacobson, 2004). She claims that this rise in women's earnings is due to increases in: (1) women's educational attainment, particularly in postgraduate education; (2) work experience and lifetime hours worked; (3) remuneration in some female dominated occupation and sectoral shifts in relative demand and supply; and (4) measures to combat blatant forms of gender pay and promotion discrimination. However, other research indicates that for a group of women who were able to secure more specific job training, it did not make a lot of difference. It did not get them more jobs, better paid jobs, better benefits or even, for the most part, jobs for which they were being prepared (Merrifield, 1997). So, as with men, the advantages and benefits of education are not played out equally among women. Yet, against these gains, it is suggested that the gap between men and women's wages is largely accounted for in the stagnation or fall of men's earnings during recent periods of economic recession. Jacobson (2004) concludes by claiming that recent cohorts of women workers (e.g. younger women) have benefited most from changes in the labour market. However, women's wages remain lower than men even within the same occupational categories. As in America, McGovern et al. (2004) claim that British employers were able to exploit women because of existing patriarchal attitudes within the community. Moreover, women in Britain are more likely to experience poverty in old age because of a marginalised and intermittent working life (McNair et al., 2004). Equally, despite much being made of the relative emancipation of the Nordic workforce and women's role within it, Melkas and Anker (2001) claim that occupational segregation is relatively high in these countries. It is these kinds of assessments that led Loutfi (2001) to propose, that actual equality has not been achieved anywhere. So, despite the convergence in the levels of men and women's participation in the labour market, the differences in the rewards are still distinct. This is distinct in levels of remuneration. Given the almost equal levels of participation, women's medium pay is estimated to still range from between 75% and 85% of pay that men receive. There is also evidence that work that becomes characterised as women's work may lose some of its status, thereby also potentially leading to a reduction in benefits.

So new work practices and relationships are arising that are not always sensitive to the emergence of increasing percentages of women workers who are employed on a contingent bases, work in relative isolation and have family responsibilities. There is also little evidence in America to suggest that the increased participation of women in workplaces has led to significant changes in work policies that are inherently family-sensitive and supportive. Similarly, in countries such as Australia, government support for childcare provisions seems to be evaporating. For many workers, the 'traditional' relationship between the individual and the workplace has been made more tenuous, anxiety ridden and/or peripheral by a lack of societal support for their transition to work. In short, it is made unsatisfactory by the current kinds of participation practices encouraged by enterprises and government.

Jacobson (2004) identifies how changed circumstances affect female participation in the labour market. She notes that family life has innumerable complications and distractions—despite entering into it freely a person becomes engaged in a situation where their capacity to act independently is constrained. She suggests that the changing patterns proposing a move away from women's role within the family, serve to complicate the task of understanding the implications, because of the variation and differences that arise from women's negotiations between family and working life. Carnoy (2001) claims that family life has been a traditional social integrator. However, although the role of the family in society has changed there remains an expectation that families and the community will continue to preserve social cohesion. This era of change coincides with change within the family, including a redefining of men's and women's roles. Carnoy (2001) suggests that coinciding with the increase in women's participation in the workforce has come the rejection of the identity of them as homemakers which was generated by industrial society. Extrapolating this view, Jacobson (2004) suggests that shifting from a more uniform pattern of participation in the labour market constrained by early marriage and child rearing, has led to a greater range of employment choices and, hence, decision-making. Yet, rather than easing the conflicts between family and working life, this is likely to open up more options and potential negotiations between work and family life. For instance, changing work patterns and changing jobs may have repercussions for other family members. In some instances, flexibility of work practices assist with securing this balance. In other circumstances, dependable work patterns and practices might be more important. For example, an ex-nurse reported having to resign from nursing, despite liking the work, because she could not be guaranteed a reliable finishing time which made problematic the organisation of child care and meeting children after school. Here, certainty and reliability in working hours rather than flexibility were required to balance work and childcare responsibilities. Such differences are evident across the provision of support available to working parents that shape how women are able to participate in work and how family life progresses. For instance, some countries have publicly funded and subsidised childcare facilities that ease the participation of women in paid work and the more distributed roles and responsibilities within contemporary families (Carnoy, 2001). In other situations, the family still plays a significant role, with the long hours worked by Japanese males being supported by a disengagement from their workplace by their wives.

In proposing a view of understanding participation in the labour market beyond one premised on objective measures, Jacobsen (2004) notes:

Human capital theory leads to a framework in which discrimination is modelled as continuously lower payoffs to one's human capital (measured in years of education, experience, and tenure) the critical junctures of the framework is one in which discrimination currently operates by generating lower probabilities of success at different career junctures for the discriminated-against group. Thus discrimination need not be an all or nothing phenomenon in which, for example, women are never hired or never promoted or always paid less than men, but instead a phenomenon in which women are hired and promoted at lower rates and are likely to receive lower pay than do men. (Jacobsen, 2004: 13)

So while women are increasingly populating workforces, this trend may play out in different ways. For instance, some countries may still expect women to leave the workforce upon marriage (e.g. Japan) (Carney, 2001), while others have different societal expectations including high levels of participation in the workforce by women (e.g. Scandinavian countries). The greater participation of women in the workforce per se, does not necessarily lead to changes throughout all forms of work. The consequences are likely to be particularly strong in some forms of work and less so in others. Moreover, as is noted below, these consequences can lead to the marginalisation and erosion of the standing of work that is inhabited by women. Thus, the increasing participation by women has not necessarily been converted into better jobs for all women.

In summary, the experience of work for women is likely to be highly varied. The emerging forms of participation by women workers have consequences for them, their work and workplaces, as well as their families and communities. They may render improbable individuals' desire for a positive and sustained work identity. Work and work practices may become differentiated for those who are full-time and permanent and those who are contingent. Individuals may invest their time and energies in different ways, or circumstances might press them to work towards transforming that identity. The degree to which they will receive support and from whom, becomes contested in the changing relationships between the workplace and the work. Consistent with the case made throughout this book, there are significant issues for individuals and for work and workplaces arising from these changing patterns of participation. There is also the prospect that, like their male counterparts, women's work will be increasingly divided into that which is highly remunerated and that which is lowly remunerated, thereby reflecting the hollowing out of the middle of the labour market. The remaking of work practices and work competence is firmly embedded in individuals' engagement in and learning through work. So the continuity of workplaces, the evolution of work practices and individual learning is likely to be shaped by these changes in patterns of workplace participation.

Participatory practices are also a key element of work requirements, as individuals need to negotiate and practice—participate—in these environments. That is, the need to work with others, understand changes in workplace goals and the requirements for performance are salient for both the workplace and the individual. Therefore, in order to advance an understanding of the requirements for work, learning through work and workplace pedagogical practices, it is necessary to illuminate and elaborate further these reciprocal participatory practices.

2. CHANGING WORK AND DISADVANTAGED GROUPS

Changes to work and working life likely play out in different ways for the disadvantaged, yet with perhaps greater potential to entrench or further exacerbate their disadvantage. In the USA, African-American and Hispanic populations disproportionately participate in low wage work—with the emergence of an 'underclass' and precipitous declines in their labour force participation (Bernhardt, 1999). The Employment Policy Foundation (2003) claims that education levels have risen in all American occupations. In 1940, the vast majority of the labour force (75%) had less than a high-school education, yet by 2002, American workers who have not completed high school constitute only 10% of the adult labour workforce. Moreover, individuals with college or graduate degrees in 1940 comprised only 6% of the labour force, whereas by 2002 American workers with at least one college degree made up the largest group of the labour force aged 25 and over (31%). The consequence of this is that, as workers develop more highly specialised skills and knowledge, they gain greater flexibility and leverage in relation to their employers. The concern here, of course, is that those without high educational achievement may struggle to find a worthwhile role in their paid work. In particular, this suggests that African-Americans who are using education as a means to enhance their economic mobility are confronted with factors that go beyond human capital in the distribution of opportunities and the cushioning of recession.

A concern is however, that the impacts of changes in workplace requirements do not fall equally or solely on the basis of human capital (e.g. level of education). McBrier and Wilson (2004) claim that downward occupational mobility is more likely to affect African-Americans more than their white counterparts. They noted that white middle-class males were more insulated from the fluctuations in demand for the white-collar professional category of work than their African-American counterparts. This insulation took two forms. Firstly, white professional workers were likely to enjoy lower levels of downward mobility within white-collar work than their African-American counterparts; and secondly, they were less likely to descend into blue-collar work than their African-American counterparts. In a sample of 1000 American managerial, administrative, professional or technical workers, who had not quit their job voluntarily, overall 68% of these workers had stayed in work at the same level. However, African-American workers were reported at 56 % and their white counterparts at 73%.

Overall, those reporting having experienced downward mobility, but remaining within white-collar occupations were at 17% with 21% of African-Americans experiencing downward mobility compared with 15% of white Americans. Downward mobility into blue-collar work was experienced by 15% overall, with African-Americans reporting 23% and white Americans reporting 12% levels of downward mobility. These data indicate how the consequences of shifts in economic activity have different impacts that go beyond human capital. This is what McBrier and Wilson (2004) referred to as 'minority vulnerability'. The reasons they propose for this vulnerability resides within practices in workplaces that reflect cultural mores. They suggest that, firstly, employers likely rank workers on the basis of what they believe to be characteristics of productivity and collegiality, with white workers being seen as higher on these measures. Secondly, the African-Americans' recent participation in these kinds of occupations likely sees them to be at lower level, low paid roles that might restrict their capacities to gain promotion and weather economic changes (McBrier and Wilson, 2004). That is, they are more vulnerable to downsizing. Thirdly, they refer to informal networks that might operate to marginalise African-Americans, because, for instance, most supervisors are white.

In these ways there is a danger that the changing character of work can be extending the disadvantage of groups of workers that have long endured social disadvantage. So, the risk of changing and emerging forms of work for those who are structurally disadvantaged is to entrench and exacerbate that disadvantage, unless they are afforded opportunities to participate equally and fully in contemporary workplaces. Certainly, the workers' levels of education and the low standing of some forms of work make these groups particularly vulnerable.

3. OLDER WORKERS PARTICIPATION IN WORK

There are clear trends in a number of Western countries towards workers having extended working lives and older workers being essential components of the national workforce. Sometimes the need for an extended working life arises out of financial necessity and sometimes because of the prospects of continuing work. Against some predictions, the lengthening lifespan of individuals means that a longer working life is a reality and in some cases a necessity. As countries with social welfare provisions struggle to fund the healthcare provisions for its older citizens and the costs are being increasingly borne by individuals themselves, there is a growing likelihood that individuals will now need a longer working life to sustain the standard of living to which they aspire. Also, with the difficulties of recruiting younger workers, particularly in the service industries, older workers are now being seen as a likely source of labour (McNair et al., 2004).

However, older workers appear to face a contradictory discourse in their extended working life, particularly where their accumulated human capital is not easily deployed because of different kinds of work or changed working circumstances. These workers are seen as a 'last choice'—needed, but not of first preference (McNair et al., 2004). Certainly, there is an issue associated with the privileging of youth that is cultural (Giddens, 1991), but likely to become exacerbated, as younger workers become a relatively small component of the labour force. The concern is that while workers are required to work longer, they may experience limits in support for their continued working life. That is, they will not be on top of the list of employers' preference for training and development opportunities. Just as with workers of colour, older workers may well be denied the kinds of support and affordances that will assist the continuity of an effective working life. Also, it is likely that older workers are far less mobile than their younger counterparts. If enterprises change locations or centralise their operations or the available work shifts to distant locations, older workers may be most disadvantaged by changes in geographical location.

Importantly, and as rehearsed earlier, regardless of whether work is becoming more or less demanding, many accounts of contemporary work refer to the constant change in the requirements for performance. Maintaining and developing further work competence now likely includes engaging and negotiating with different and new ways of working and means for working. Consequently, ongoing learning is now required throughout working life. This requirement probably plays out in different ways for different cohorts of individuals given their work, the degree and frequency of its change, their background, gender, age, skill levels and the support provided by their workplaces. For older workers there are particular challenges. These include the redundancy of their skills as familiar ways of working and goals for work performance change. For these workers, new learning may sit alongside the displacement of existing capability, with the attendant risks to their sense of self. Not that this new learning is necessarily disempowering, alienating or marginalising (Billett and Pavlova, 2005). Yet, it may be distinct for older workers, because of the impact of the displacement of existing competence, and the relative lack of support they may encounter in maintaining their competence.

Moreover, although the evidence on the capacities of older workers is quite optimistic, that there is not necessarily a decline of cognitive and per-formance related functions per se, there will be some declines in processes and ways of functioning. Much remains unknown about the prospect for older workers to remain fully competent throughout their working lives. The literature on human development across the lifespan suggests that whereas maturation processes are helpful in expanding the capacities of children and younger adults, they work against older workers. There is an inevitable decline in a range of human functions such as speed in reaction time, processing of novel ideas and the active engagement of memory, and also physical strength. However, the evidence also suggests that older adults have developed significant memories and capacities that are highly effective in resolving problems and performing effectively in work-related roles. This capacity can compensate for slower nervous systems (Baltes and Staudinger, 1996), because the level of performance is not dependent on processing capacity alone. For instance, while typing speeds might decline with age, older typists are as efficient as younger typists, possibly because their wealth of previous experiences allows them to predict and execute the typing task more efficiently than the younger counterparts: "…while older adults may well experience some basic processing shortfall, they may well have developed specialised knowledge and strategies that may compensate for these losses." (Sigelman, 1999: 229)

This view is supported by functional and relativist preferences on thinking and acting (Baltes and Staudinger, 1996). That is, functional applications that are central to work are also consistent with the preferences for adults' organi-sation of knowledge and bases for performance (Tikkanen, et al., 2002). Rather than abstracted or dis-embodied forms of knowledge, functional applications seem to be central to what motivates the engagement with an organisation of adults' knowledge. Moreover, increasingly rather than viewing knowledge as formalisms—being a set body of knowledge that is objective, as in an objectively definable domain—increasingly, knowledge is seen to be associated with individuals' construal and construction, that is an individual domain of knowledge. This constitutes the relativist claim.

Cognitive performance does not necessarily decline with age (Sigelman, 1999). So even when older humans have been found to be slower with problem-solving activities, very brief training may be able to improve cognitive abilities (p. 186). This suggests cognitive capacities may endure, yet are required to be engaged and/or reactivated. So, as the potential of these capacities remains, this means both the opportunity for and desire for their exercise come to the fore. In the absence of development coming from internal maturation processes (Baltes and Staudinger, 1996) it is necessary to seek support from social and cultural sources outside the individual. Yet, perhaps, at the heart of older workers' capacity to remain competent throughout their working lives is the potential power of their agency and intentionality in exercising their capacities and engaging with the kinds of support, albeit quite indirect, that are available. The exercise of this agency will, in part, be subject to and conditional on support provided in the workplace.

Nevertheless, despite their increasing presence within the workforce, there is some cause for pessimism about the level of support which older workers may be afforded. Certainly, the increase of women in workforces in many Western countries has not necessarily seen an increase in support to make women's working lives easier. Family-friendly policies, as argued above, seem to be the exception rather than the rule. Therefore, it is questionable whether the need of employers to hire and retain older workers alone will necessarily enhance their workplace affordances. One outcome of highly contested workplaces is that workers needing support may be reluctant to seek it, to avoid drawing attention to them. Church (2004) refers to disabled workers who have particular needs and yet are strategic and cautious in their demands for support from their workplace and co-workers. They fear being seen as liabilities in a cost conscious working environment. Least this example seems extreme, Church (2004) reminds us that for most workers old age and disability come together at some point. Moreover, European employers are more likely to spend funds on training the young and well-educated, than older workers (Brunello, 2001; Brunello and Medio, 2001; Giraud, 2002). True, some European countries in northern Europe have mature attitudes towards and claim a strong sense of obligation to older workers (Bishop, 1997; Smith and Billett, 2003). However, elsewhere, there is little evidence that legislation (Giraud, 2002), national sentiment or government edict (Bishop, 1997) are able to influence how enterprises expend resources on their employees. So, despite older workers' preference to learn through practice and with workplaces representing potentially effective learning environments, this may not be forthcoming from employers.

So, while there is a growing interest in retaining older workers in the workforce, this is set in an environment that ultimately is likely to remain not particularly supportive. This sets older workers the task of 'cheerful striving'—as it does disabled workers—as they work around values that are not supportive of that striving. As these affordances shapes the support they are likely to be able to access, this suggests that it is likely to be individuals' agency and capacity to be agentic that will become the key determinant of older workers' capacity to maintain competence throughout working life.

Given the need to maintain their competence throughout working life, possibly in circumstances of inhibited access to support within the workplace and against the societal privileging of youth, the essential component of older workers' capacity is their personal agency. This agency is central to both their engagement in work tasks and also the learning they are required to do. There is agreement across constructivist theories of learning that the intensity with which individuals engage in activities is consonant with the level of learning outcomes. That is, individuals' full-bodied engagement is likely to lead to far richer learning than if their engagement is superficial and dependent upon others. There are, however, conflicting views about the degree by which this development is dependent upon on direct interpersonal guidance, rather than individual agency alone. However, it seems that even strongly socially sub-jecting situations, such as heavily monitored workplaces, are unable to con-strain the exercise by individuals of their agency and intentionality (Fenwick, 2002; Billett, 2003a; Hodkinson and Hodkinson, 2004). When faced with difficult employment situations such as unemployment or under-employment, it is likely to be the older workers' personal agency (Bauer, Festner, Gruber, Harteis and Heid, 2004; Smith, 2004) that has the potential to provide effective responses. Yet their sense of self identity which ultimately directs this agency is threatened and, at times traumatised, by such employment situations (Billett and Pavlova, 2005; Hodkinson and Hodkinson, 2003).

There are four premises for the important role of individual agency and intentionality will play in maintaining older workers' competence. Firstly, individuals' engagement with tasks and interactions is a necessary basis for the process of learning and development (Billett, 2004). The process of learning and everyday thinking and acting are in many ways the same. In both, the degree to which individuals engage and deploy their cognitive capacities and experiences shapes whether rich or weak learning transpires. Such outcomes are a product of the degree to which individuals elect to exercise their energy and intentionality when engaging with tasks and in interactions. So individuals' epistemological activities need to engage with critical reflection to consider what is strategic and important for them. Workers in a textile-printing factory and in a forensic psychiatric clinic (Van Woerkom, 2003) demonstrate differences in their scope of critical reflection. While some workers like to think about organisational policy and 'the broad lines', others concentrated more on their work tasks at the minutiae level. Yet, both in different ways underpin the importance of this form of personal agency.

Secondly, the contributions to individuals' learning and development from social practices and social partners are distributed in different ways and by different degree. As noted, the very kinds of gifts that older workers sought from the workplace may not be available or may be inaccessible. This suggests the need to be agentic and critical in engaging with and reflecting upon social sources and also strategic in determining what knowledge they need to gain through interactions with social partners and social practices. The social genesis of knowledge and development is founded in a relational interdependence between individual and social contributions to individuals' learning (Billett, 2003a, 2005). From the individuals' perspective, engagement in this interdependence needs to be informed in ways that are functional, purposeful and critically agentic. So they need to interact with the social world in ways that position them as informed, selective and canny participants.

Thirdly, individuals through their interactions with social partners and social practices play an important role in construing and constructing from the social experience (Billett, 2005). Some claim that there is a significant mismatch between older workers' views of their employability and effectiveness and the perceptions of those who employ them (Patrickson and Ranzijn, 2004). That is, individuals' sense of self is important in how they conduct their engagement. This is doubly problematic because it is these workers' ability to be agentic in making contacts and developing further their skills that are held to be the likely basis of them achieving employment at the level that they believe reflects their capacities and contributions (Patrickson and Ranzijn, 2004). So society's gift is not made uniformly, it is made through the interaction between the social experience and individuals' construction of that experience, and their subsequent engagement with the social world (i.e. how they engage in and learn through their work). Because individuals' subjectivity and intentionality are an embodiment of their agency, it remains central to the process of learning and development, including the constant remaking of workplace practices. This remaking of cultural practices needs informing by critical reflection. This can serve to refine and improve work practices as societal conditions change. So, work can be remade in ways that serve the needs of older workers.

Fourthly, and because of this, the degree to which individuals will exercise their interest (i.e. agency and energy) shapes not only the learning process but also the kinds of knowledge that are learnt (Billett and Pavlova, 2005; Hodkinson and Hodkinson, 2004). External press does not wholly determine individuals' exercise of effortful and demanding thinking and acting. Individual interest and intentionality also plays an important role. Moreover, the kinds of critical reflective activities older workers engage in will be shaped by their sense of self (van Woerkom, 2003).

Picking up the theme addressed throughout this book, it would seem that it may well be older workers' agency and intentionality that is their energy, productivity and cleverness that will be the bases for their continued engagement in workplaces and their effective practice as paid workers. Fundamentally, what these sets of propositions reinforce is that work needs to be understood from the perspective of the worker, not only from some process that seeks to quantify and measure work and workplace performance. That is, the subjective experience of workers is the individuals' and collectives' need to be considered in accounts of work. This is not to exercise a half-hearted attempt at acknowledging workers' contributions. Instead, it suggests that the experience of work and working life cannot be uniform across workforces and the conduct of work. Starkly, as women become the majority in the workforce and as older workers become a greater component of the paid workforce these cohorts simply cannot be put to one side as aberrant

4.   CHANGES IN THOSE PARTICIPATING IN WORK

It has been argued in this chapter that the profile of those who are participating in working life has changed. Workplaces are increasingly populated more evenly across gender, although work segregation continues regardless. Yet, as with the suggestion elsewhere about the 'hollowing out' of the labour market generally, it seems women workers are experiencing this phenomenon in different ways. That is, while participation in some forms of work is providing high levels of pay, and secure high skilled jobs, for many women, the increased opportunities for work are being found in insecure low paid service work. This issue of disadvantage in the labour market is also reflected in other groups whose options are sometimes limited by low levels of education, but by factors that go beyond human capital. This includes race, ethnicity and language skills. Given this and the prospects for a longer working life it seems that workers' experiences in workplaces will increasingly be characterised by difference depending upon the bases for participation. For some, an extended working life will be focused on continuing a professional practice which is important to the individual's sense of self. In some countries, the demographic change will see an increasing valuing of some kinds of work and some kind of workers thereby buttressing the prospects for a rich and well-supported extended working life. For others, an extended working life will be largely focused upon meeting basic needs of food and shelter as state based provisions for retirement become wholly insufficient. For both kinds of workers, there will be an ongoing need to maintain competence throughout working life. Yet, as argued in the next chapter the requirements for workplace competence are changing. There are likely to be quite different bases for how individuals are able to maintain workplace competence. While those in high demand high status work will receive support to maintain competence through an extended working life, they can be no confidence that older workers and those otherwise disadvantaged will be recipients of such levels of support.

Chapter 8

CHANGING REQUIREMENTS FOR WORK PERFORMANCE

> situated accomplishment, and an activity oriented toward and coming from a course of action, rather than an intellectualised pursuit. (Trogon and Grusenmeyer, 1997: 87)

> ...negotiating behaviour, knowledge claims and interpersonal interactions will play a greater role in determining workplace outcomes and the economic opportunities of workers. (Leicht, 1998: 45)

Not only are the kinds of work available and participation in work changing, but what constitutes work and work performance are also marked by change and difference. What constitutes the performance requirements for paid work is a product of changing cultural need, as elaborated in Chapter 2. Work and work requirements are shaped by those requirements, emerging technologies and the acts of a generation of workers remaking those practices, at particular points in time. However, beyond acknowledging that work and work requirements are changing, it is important to identify these changes and how they reshape work and the experience of working life. Without this understanding, it is difficult to advise how individuals, enterprises, governments and the like should, respectively, plan their development for working life, the continuity of the workplace, how education systems need to act to prepare and develop further the capacities of workers, and how enterprises and individuals might best exercise their resources in maintaining their capacity for effective work practice.

As proposed in Chapter 2, to understand the changing requirements of work, there is need to account for factors and changes to cultural practices and norms that together manifest what constitutes performance in particular workplaces. Cultural and situational factors are themselves subject to constant change and these are manifested in the circumstances where they are deployed in meeting cultural needs: particular workplace settings. Moreover, because of situational factors, these requirements are likely to be diverse in some ways, even when the same occupational practice is being enacted (Billett, 2001b). So, accounts of workplace requirements that can inform government, education systems, enterprises and individuals need to identify factors that can articulate the scope and intensity of change in the requirements for work, while also acknowledging the situated, diverse qualities of workplace performance.

However, observable and so-called objective bases for understanding the requirements for work represent only one dimension of work requirements. There are also the more subjective and person-dependent bases by which individuals make sense of, interpret, and use their capacities in order to fulfil these work requirements. As discussed in previous chapters, it is this subjective experience that shapes how individuals participate in work and in doing so constitutes the enactment of work that has historical, cultural and situational sources. Individuals' engagement in their work and how they exercise their capacities in work activities and interactions is often not included in so called objectives accounts of work that focus on tasks and activities. Yet, ultimately work is something which is undertaken by individuals as they make sense of the tasks they are engaged with and complete them deploying their procedures, understanding and valuing of those activities. In this way, the human engagement in and conduct of work is an essential facet of all work and what constitutes working life.

Using the example of technological change, the changing requirements of work here are shown to be both diverse and highly situational, and shaped by factors that suggest they will continue to be diverse and dynamic: subject to continual change (see Chapter 2). As Darrah (1997) suggests, these requirements are so diverse and peculiar to particular workplace that they defy easy generalisations. Certainly, how occupational practices are enacted in specific workplaces suggests that even what might be taken as common forms of work, are manifested in particular ways in each workplace, because of the array of situational factors. Nevertheless, following this discussion and drawing upon diverse perspectives, some common bases to understand changes across diverse kinds of work are identified in this chapter.

1. CHANGE, TECHNOLOGY AND WORK

In order to illuminate the scope of changes to work in terms of subjective experience, the impact of technology on work provides an instance with which to consider the kinds and scope of change to work and workplace performance requirements. Advances in technology are transforming work in ways that are not readily categorisable as leading to either up-skilling or down-skilling. For example, the introduction of computers into hospital wards has provided a range of changes in how nurses work (Cook-Gumperez and Hanna, 1997). It may remove some tasks associated with the routine monitoring of patients and extend nurses' practice requirements to monitor and respond to a broader range of health care activities. Computers can also make health records available to patients, thus transforming aspects of the nurse-patient relationship.

Another change that technology may well serve to support is the increasing professional status of nurses (Etzioni, 1969). Nurses more than providing for the immediate care of the sick are now "expected to be a link between the depersonalized activities of professional medicine and the nurses' ability to treat the whole person" (Cook-Gumperez and Hanna, 1997: 320). Thus, nurses' engagement with electronic technology serves to transform how their work is being viewed. This technology, and its application to nursing, challenges in a positive sense the ways in which nursing has been viewed as "women's work". Since computer technology has never been viewed as women's work, this appropriation allows the discourse on nursing to take a major shift—to establish a revision of its standing as professional practice (Cook-Gumperez and Hanna, 1997). So, the impact of technology includes transformations to nurses' work, the scope of their activities and also serves to undermine gendered conceptions of work, through boosting the status of nursing work. Yet, the transformation of nurses' work is not solely through technology. For instance, the demand to reduce hospital costs is leading to patients staying in hospitals for a shorter time, with convalescence occurring at home or in other places away from the hospital ward. Consequently, nurses' work in hospital wards has become more intense as all patients in the ward now require more intense treatment. Doubtless, as discussed below, nurses' work has become more intense through this period of change making it more demanding, and potentially more stressful. This suggests that the consequences of change to work cannot easily be categorised as either up-skilling or down-skilling, but rather change in the work undertaken, its organisation and its standing.

Similarly, but more pervasively and with wider implications, banking work is also being changed by the extended use of electronic technology. These changes are transforming bank work leading to a reduction in front counter jobs and an increase in backroom jobs, often conducted in centralized locations well away from the physical bank branch. Workers in these centralised roles have different kinds of skills from those of the traditional front counter bank tellers. Here, the suggestion is that there has been a downskilling in the work of bank counter staff. Certainly, the requirements for work performance have been transformed by these changes. Yet, within such changes it is possible to identify dimensions of work that need to be accounted for in discussions of work practices and their requirements. Although the range of tasks to be conducted by bank counter staff may be more restricted in some ways, there are components that are made more demanding. With transformations in the banking sector has often come the removal of specialist staff from a bank branch. The experienced managers, accountants and advisers are absent now and their counterparts are to be found in locations that are physically remote from the bank. Yes, information is accessible to the bank counter worker through a small visual display unit. Yet, both of these changes (i.e. the absence of specialist staff and information being made available through representational and symbolical means) constitute a more demanding work environment, because the support for and means of working are now more remote, absent or just more difficult to access. So, beyond the changes to bank workers' tasks and activities, some consideration needs to be given to the changes in the prospects for interactions that also assist them in fulfilling their requirements for work performance. This is because work is changing in many ways, and not only for those forms of work that are often described as 'knowledge work'.

2.   KNOWLEDGE WORK

Descriptions of the current era being an 'information age' in which 'knowledge workers' come to the fore are not particularly helpful. There is little discussion about what delineates the characteristics that set this era apart from others. Certainly, each age has required the extensive use of knowledge and the current one is no exception. Analyses of work have suggested that this era relies more on technology and occupations where information and services rely on means that are increasingly remote from humans (Barley and Orr, 1997; Heath and Nicholls, 1997; Zuboff, 1988). That is, a reliance on the possession and utilization of knowledge that is remote from human experience and needs to be learnt with the assistance of an individual who understands and practices that knowledge. However, previous eras also have required knowledge that is not easily accessible. For example, earlier understandings about the principles associated with building houses, churches and even the great cathedrals of Europe were dependent on individuals' memories and concepts, not written plans or diagrams (Gimpel, 1961). Consequently, this knowledge was remote and difficult to access and often only learnt about through participation in socially-shaped occupations, and over long periods of time. However, even in current times, it is worth considering the very remote and hidden knowledge used by, for instance, Vietnamese rice farmers or aboriginals hunting and gathering in environments that are seasonal, hostile and demand specific skills for survival. Both of these kinds of practice require rich bases of knowledge that are historically and culturally developed and learnt over time through engagement in culturally defined activities, though when the term 'knowledge workers' is used these are probably not the kind of workers that immediately come to mind.

Claims about the requirements of the 'information age', like the rhetoric about 'knowledge workers' have become commonplace. Yet, helpful definitions that inform these concepts are hard to locate. An early reference to 'knowledge workers' is that by Drucker (1973). However, his classifications appear to lack conceptual or categorical clarity. His examples of 'knowledge workers' include systems engineers, information specialists and health care professionals (e.g. nurses, dieticians, X-ray technologists, social and psychiatric case workers, physical therapists). This broad grouping appears quite inclusive, yet fails to offer a coherent way of differentiating between those who are and are not knowledge workers. Best (1973) suggested another view of knowledge workers as those whose "job is to discover, integrate, process and find applications for our constantly exploding reserves of knowledge" (Best, 1973: 101). However, here again, this could apply as much to the indigenous hunter and gatherer as to the rice farmer as to the researcher, bank worker, and so on.

The difficulties with categorising particular kinds of work as 'knowledge work' still persist, probably made more difficult by associations between knowledge work and computer operations and applications. For instance, Barely and Orr's (1997) efforts to define technical work retreat into a similarly broad definition that could have far wider applications than perhaps they had desired. They proposed four traits that define technical work. These are: (i) the centrality of complex technology to the work; (ii) the importance of contextual knowledge and skill; (iii) the importance of theories of abstract representations of the phenomena; and (iv) the existence of a community of practice that serves as a distributed repository for knowledge of relevance to practitioners (Barley and Orr, 1997: 12). Yet, as with all the above, work has always required knowledge, its application and development through practice. The issue now is whether in contemporary times, this knowledge is in some ways now of a different kind. For instance, is it more symbolic in character and thus difficult to access and therefore to understand, learn and subsequently deploy effectively?

3.   CHANGE AND WORKPLACE REQUIREMENTS

The changing requirements for performance in workplaces brought about by technology are characterised by both change and difference. Some of the driving forces behind these changes are attempts to reorganise work—increasing the outputs of paid labour and reducing its cost, with an emphasis on competitiveness through improved performance (e.g. enhancing workers' skills and fully utilising those skills). Elsewhere, the source is held to be a low cost, low skill, productivity and cost workforce with low levels of valued added contributions (Noon and Blyton, 1997). A related interpretation is the two tier one, with some jobs upgraded while others are not, instead being routinised and de-skilled. This suggests a hollowing out of the middle levels of workers, as a number of commentators propose. Yet, Darrah (1996), referring to Spenner (1988) and Cyert and Mowery (1989), concludes that there is no compelling evidence for either a massive upgrading or downgrading of skill requirements. Instead, they propose that the changes in work are best viewed as just that—changes—that require a re-skilling, rather than higher or lower levels of workforce skill.

In this way, regardless of whether contemporary work is becoming 'up-skilled' or 'down-skilled', the requirements for work are changing on both the objective (i.e. observable) level and the more subjective experience. Characteristics of these constantly transforming workplaces usually are held to include: new products and technologies; short production cycles, changing production concepts, a high discretion workforce and strategies of rationalisation (e.g. Darrah, 1996; Ellström, 1998). However, as noted in Chapter 6 there seem to be few enterprises reported in the literature that can be described by these characteristics. Some studies report work practices with some of these attributes, but not others; they cannot be taken as a common or comprehensive listing. Yet, although patterns of changes in the kinds of work being undertaken, the requirements for work and how individuals engage in work are referred to in the literature, there is little consensus that can lead to a basis for understanding the requirements of particular workplaces. Hence, claims about terms such as the *'information age'*, *'new workplace'* and *'knowledge workers'*, need to be treated skeptically. Also, distinctions among workers such as trades, technicians, professions or 'un-skilled' based on these kinds of categories are questionable. Instead, categories of work might be more effectively classified in terms of the kinds of activities and interactions that comprise the work practice, not as some objective differentiation of the nature of work.

Yet, it is briefly worth returning to consider whether the requirements of contemporary work are, in fact, more or less demanding than in earlier times. In some ways, there can be no easy basis for comparison because the requirements and the capacities of those who undertook that work cannot be easily understood. The requirements for work and subjectivities of those conducting work do not stand as phenomena that can be objectively appraised. For instance, assumptions about the limited requirements of certain kinds of work (i.e. those categorised as low skill) are also sometimes contested by examinations of their actual requirements (e.g. Darrah, 1997; Billett, 2000a). Bernhardt (1999) found that in more upscale retail work or products requiring degrees of expert advice—the 'soft skills' to build relationships with customers and the ability to and knowledge to make decisions on their own—led to work that is remunerated well and enjoys above average benefits for the industry. She uses the example of Home Depot (a hardware chain store) workers who earn more than the industry average, enjoy extra benefits, and experience a low turnover. Hourly paid sales associates can make decisions such as ordering stock of significant value. Further, with technology, which is reported as being increasingly pervasive in contemporary and emerging work, the replacement of observational learning with the need for learning acquired through symbols has become more commonplace, making work tasks more demanding (e.g. Martin and Scribner, 1991; Zuboff, 1988). Those classified as technicians are now required to represent the structures and processes of their machines symbolically in their heads (Berryman, 1993). Also, it is important to understand how participation in work has changed and the demands this makes for individuals to maintain the currency of their skills throughout their working lives. Also, a clear trend associated with the growth and continuity of contingent work is that the traditional associations between employers and workers are breaking down, with a series of consequences for learning throughout working life. Consequently, workers have to engage in independently organised and directed learning to maintain work competence.

Similarly, the conceptual demands of computer driven work tools are not easily comparable with those of a manual era. The former may be more symbolic in their representation, but the requirements to work without the array of contemporary technological aids also have their own demands— these requirements are different, at least. However, regardless of whether it is considered up-skilling or downscaling, commonly work is held to be changing in its requirements more frequently than in previous eras. Importantly, and neglected in much of the accounts about changing work, the very fact that work is changing in its requirements means that workers need to acquire new ways of knowing and working more and more frequently. Given that workers have existing knowledge, practices and ways of conducting their work, changes to the work bring demands for continual learning. Bailey (1993) refers to accelerated production cycles, a proliferation of products, heightened levels of uncertainty and changing work practices. Consequently, the requirements for work practice are probably greater than they have been credited.

Taking stock of the actual requirements of work, rather than assumptions premised on common assertions, reveal them to be highly demanding in terms of their scope and requirements for performance. These requirements can be found in the need to accommodate constant change, as well as the intellectual demands for work in terms of their conceptual (symbolic) requirements and procedural bases. Put simply, the requirement for constant change alone can render work practice to be inherently non-routine. Therefore, claims that some forms of work are 'unskilled or semi-skilled' are open to challenge. All this leads to a more demanding work environment, because work is less routine. Such changes are structuring employment and the requirements for effective work performance. The shift to service industries, changes to the character of employment, down-sized workplaces and non-standard forms of employment all serve to transform and make dynamic (and, therefore, more demanding) the requirements for performing work (Noon and Blyton, 1997). Because of this constant transformation, changes in work include relinquishing past practices, with the displacement of existing competence and confidence. It is in these ways that the demands of work are both different and increasing in frequency in the scope and depth of change.

This person-dependent premise of change foreshadows the other dimension of understanding workplace change, that is, the need to go beyond objective analyses of work as a set of observable tasks and interactions whose requirements can be recorded and ordered in some ways, to embrace a view about a person's engagement with those work tasks. To the Vietnamese rice farmer who has grown up observing the changing seasons and growth and hues of rice plants, predicting the moment of harvesting is achieved through a rich repertoire of knowledge secured through rice farming, and understanding the timing of seasonal, and potentially harvest-wrecking weather. However, for individuals without that way of knowing, the task of predicting the time for harvesting is quite a different proposition. Essentially, the bases of knowledge or ways of knowing that individuals bring to a particular task also play a key role in what constitutes the requirements for work. The gap between what is required and what the individual knows is played out in different ways across work practices (as discussed below) as is the degree of dissonance or change that has been brought about by the new circumstance, such as a different way of working.

4. DIVERSITY IN CHANGING WORK REQUIREMENTS

A complex of cultural and local factors shape the degree and scope of change across workplaces, thereby leading to diversity in requirements across workplaces even those enacting the same occupational practice: "...jobs seem so diverse as to obviate the need for generalisations about how people perform work" (Darrah, 1997: 249). Rather than being homogeneous, there is inherent diversity within the same occupation when it is enacted in practice (Billett, 2001b). While there are concepts, values and practices that are common across the application of an occupation—the canonical knowledge of the occupation—within a particular culture or country they may vary in their application, as discussed in Chapter 2. Moreover, there are also quite diverse requirements for performance in specific work situations. This suggests occupational classifications need to account for the breadth of the applications required within the occupation, in order for this practice to be comprehensively understood. It is, therefore, helpful to understand something of the range of performance requirements of individual work-places, and the likely requirement for the individual to apply their occupational knowledge in different workplace settings throughout their working life.

Therefore, in attempting to understand and identify the changing requirements for work practice, it is necessary to acknowledge and accommodate the prospect of diversity in performance requirements across enterprises, industries and countries in how these changes are manifested. There are factors at the national, cultural, local and enterprise level in what is required for work performance. It is these factors that shape the observable and material form of changing requirements of work and workplace practices: the objective account of workplace requirements.

4.1 National differences

Across different countries and cultures there are quite different means of working and changes in work. For instance, Japan has a highly automated and computerized car manufacturing industry, in which robots are used extensively. Yet, clothing manufacture in Japan is often undertaken in the old-fashioned bundle system (Bailey, 1993)—where the component parts are bundled together by machinists and then passed to another who first unbundles them and performs an operation and re-bundles and so on, thereby requiring high levels of handling and highly specific machining skills. So in the country that developed and applied the 'Just -In-Time' approach to work processes and maintaining low work-in-progress inventories, there are garment factories where large amounts of stock are in production at any one time. The logic of the production processes in the Japanese garment industry is associated with the limited working life of female Japanese garment workers, who are expected to leave the workforce upon marriage. Yet, as Bailey (1993) points out there are quite different bases for how an industry such as garment manufacturing proceeds across countries. In contrast to the Japanese approach, the German garment manufacturing industry is highly mechanised and uses automated equipment to not only construct the garments but also move garment components through the manufacturing process thereby minimising the relatively high labour cost of German garment workers. In this way, technological developments and cultural mores, such as the ones referred to above, shape how the same work is organised in two distinct cultural milieus.

The requirements for work at a national level may also extend to the particular moment in their resources or climate, for instance, the demand for some facets of occupational work are played out differently in countries that have hot summers and frigid winters. Some of the mechanical tasks required of automotive engineers in northern Europe, Canada and northern American states are unlikely to be undertaken by their counterparts in most places in Australia, southern American states or other warmer climates, and vice versa. So there are sets of cultural factors that are constructed and influence the conceptions of work and its organisation in different ways weighs across countries.

4.2   Differences within an industry sector

Differences for work requirements within an industry sector in the same country are illustrated by retail work in America. For instance, some retail work is highly segmented and routinised as in American pharmacy chain stores. Yet in others, such as in hardware stores, the expertise of the retail worker is prized because they are expected to provide advice to customers about products (Bernhardt, 1999). Also, different bases for remuneration exist. In America, retail workers in exclusive fashion stores are often paid on a commission-only basis. Their skills are focused on making sales and selling the kinds of goods that have the best margins between wholesale and retail price, and also through establishing relations with key client groups. Their work is about building relationships with clients, and making sales. Yet, despite the prestigious nature of their business, their remuneration can be perilous because it is on a commission only basis. Perhaps surprisingly, of all categories of American retail workers, it is those working in hardware stores that are the highest paid and enjoy greater tenure and other workplace benefits. Because their hardware knowledge is highly valued in terms of the advice they provide to customers, they attract a higher level of pay and greater bases for tenure (Bernhardt, 1999). Interestingly, other workers who provide advice and regulate sales in the retail settings also attract higher levels of remuneration. For instance, pharmacists provide similar services yet, would not be labeled as retail workers—their knowledge is codified as professional in contrast to hardware retail workers. So, in work that might be categorised as comprising the same occupation, there are also variations that reflect diversity in the cultural practices in requirements of those workplaces.

4.3   Difference in workplace requirements

The particular requirements for work performance will also likely vary from workplace to workplace, because of localised factors. In investigating what comprised hairdressers' work it was found that in each salon, the goals for hairdressing had distinctive features across four salons, three in Australia and one in the United Kingdom (Billett, 2001b). As previewed in Chapter 2, observations and interviews revealed the characteristics of the vocational practice included the requirements for performance in each salon and how localised factors shaped the cultural practice of hairdressing in particular ways. In a fashionable inner city salon, the key goals for performance were to transform the clients' appearance, and to offer new cuts and colours. The interaction with clients in this salon was a product of the clientele and the hairdressers' interests and values (lifestyle). In a salon in a low socio-economic suburb, an important requirement was to manage a precarious business with an absent owner, two part-time senior hairdressers and a clientele that included those who demanded complex treatments, yet did not subsequently care for their hair, and where cost was a predominant factor. A key requirement here was to manage these 'awkward' customers when they returned complaining vociferously and forcefully about their treatments. In another salon, the clientele comprised elderly women who came to the salon fortnightly, perhaps as much for companionship as for hair treatments. Here, the hairdressers' knowledge of clients' personal histories, knowing the names and circumstances of family and friends, was an important component of practice. The fourth salon was in a provincial town in a rural region that was enduring a three-year drought. The goals here included providing good value to maintain the clientele and managing the difficult balance between eliciting additional service (e.g. colours and perms) yet not causing clients to choose between the cost of a hair treatment and groceries for home (Billett, 2001b). So it was localised factors that shaped performance requirements in each of these salons in quite distinct ways and generate quite different practices across these vocational practices. These factors also shaped the likely changes occurring in each workplace. For instance, shortly after the research was completed, there was a change in ownership and management of at least two of the salons with the focus of business activities being re-shaped in one of these. Beyond changes in technologies (e.g. new hairdressing products) and changing societal preferences (e.g. away from chemical hair treatments), there are also salient local factors that shape what constitute work requirements.

Similarly, across six open cut coalmines owned by the same large company, different performance requirements were evident in mines where the same tasks of coal mining where being enacted (Billett, 1994). The work practices in each mine site, and therefore requirements for work performance, were premised on different kinds of industrial affiliations and demarcations (i.e. distribution, organisation and division of labour). These had developed over time in each particular mine site, shaped by the age and production stage of the mine (e.g. the depth of the coal seam below the ground). Also, the previous history of mine ownership had led to particular workplace arrangements and union affiliations that shaped the work practices that were not likely to be changed or made uniform, because of rival interests in demarcated workplaces. Moreover, beyond these institutional facts, was the brute fact of the direction and angle of the coal seam that shaped the production costs and viability of the mining operation, and the timing of the shift from open cut to underground mining operations. So the requirements for work performance differed across these six work sites as did the kinds and extent of change likely to be brought about by brute or institutional facts that locally shaped these requirements. So while there are clear changes in the requirements for work, how these changes are going to manifest themselves in particular workplaces, can be responses to the localised factors.

Although there are many differences in work requirements, even in the same industry sector or occupational practice, there are also requirements that are more or less common. There are trends in the changing character of work requirements that need to be understood. As a number of studies describe contemporary work practice as having both complex workplace work tasks and organisational dimensions, it may be helpful to identify changes in terms of work tasks or activities and their organisation. To identify the former, the requirements for work tasks are considered in terms of activities, and workplace organisational activities in terms of workplace interactions. All this suggests that change in the requirements of work is likely to be quite different across and within countries, industry sectors, communities and enterprises. Moreover, the factors constituting these work requirements will likely change in different ways, at different paces, for different purposes and with different scopes of change.

However, before proceeding with the identification of emerging qualities of contemporary workplaces it is important to understand that work is also a subjective process which shapes participation and engagement: that is individuals' work practice. The analysis so far in this chapter has emphasised the objective view, that is, the observable and quantifiable changes to work requirements and their diversity are proposed as a set of objective requirements for participation in paid work. These are the institutional facts (Searle, 1995) that comprise paid work. So, the requirements for performance—expertise if you like—are likely to be highly situated. Yet, these are also fleeting. This is because the circumstances that constitute the requirements for performance in particular workplace settings are subject to constant transformation. Notwithstanding all this, there remains a significant gap in understanding the requirements for work and its diversity, that is, the subjective and person-dependent basis upon how individuals engage in work.

5. WORK REQUIREMENTS AS SUBJECTIVE AND PERSON-DEPENDENT PHENOMENA

While the objective view of work provides a benchmark for performance, albeit highly situated and fleeting, the requirements for performance are also shaped by the capacities, interests, perspectives and agency of the individuals who populate workplaces and perform workplace activities and interactions. Ultimately, it is individual workers who engage in work, make sense of what is required and deploy their capacities in workplace participation and the remaking of work practice. Take, for instance, the examples of how computer and numerically controlled (CNC) lathes have transformed metal machining or nurses' work has been transformed by technology. Martin and Scribner (1991) make clear, the requirements for operating a CNC lathe are closer to the skill requirements of a computer operator than a manual lathe operator. The rich subjective experience of an experienced manual lathe operator is rendered largely ineffective by the changing technology. Therefore, the understandings, nuanced bases of performance and agency of the manual lathe operator and their sense of self competence may be challenged by the change in how they are supposed to work. Moreover, the challenge is likely to be person-dependent. Individuals do not bring to or engage in tasks with a uniformity of experience and ways of knowing. Instead, they bring diverse bases for conceptualising and construing what they experience in the workplace. Here, it is worth noting the differences in attributes and experiences that experts within a domain of knowledge might bring, compared with relative novices. For example, in a project that sought to identify difficult-to-learn tasks in the workplace, tasks identified by those who had recently learnt them were different from those identified by experts (Billett and Boud, 2001). That is, those who had recently engaged in the learning of these tasks were able to identify the particular difficulties related to their learning compared with those who had learnt them long since and used them repeatedly. There are explanations associated with cognitive processes that explain these differences (Anderson, 1982; 1993), but nevertheless, it would be mistaken to believe that individuals bring the same cognitive resources to work situations thereby providing a platform for objective decision-making about the relative complexity of such tasks.

As elaborated in Chapters 6 and 7, there are also likely to be quite diverse conceptions of what constitutes work practice across different kinds and categories of workers. This includes contingent workers, whose access to comprehensive workplace knowledge might be quite restricted—home-based workers who are struggling to understand the overall goals; disabled workers, who deal with knowledge in their own and sometimes difficult ways (Church, 2004) and older workers who have to confront turbulent work situations while struggling to apply their existing knowledge to changed circumstances (Tikkanen et al., 2002). This prompts caution in being able to identify the objective qualities of work, because individuals each bring their experiences to engage with the work tasks. Ultimately subjective processes shaped participation in work. Perhaps only through understanding the subjective experience of individuals that the performance of work can be fully and comprehensively understood. For instance, in the clothing industry, a common task was 'rate setting' of clothing machinists performing specific operations. In many ways, this is emblematic of attempting to provide the objective account of what constitutes work. A methods officer would time a machinist performing a sewing task ands this would be used to determine their performance and possibly bonus. The machinists would attempt to secure a generous time allowance for the operation, as this would deliver a bonus. A standard approach was to work slowly when being timed. The methods officer, of course, knew this and would attempt to calculate at what level of potential performance the machinist was working when being timed. Of course, the machinist also knew that the methods officer was conducting such an additional judgement and would act to appear to be working very quickly while foxing on actual speed. Often the methods officer also knew that the machinist knew this to be case and so on and so on. The simple point here is that the conduct of work is premised on work being enacted by an individual that includes their experience, capabilities and intentionalities, and also the judgement of the observer. So even in a situation where there is a quest to identify the objective character and qualities of work, it needs to be mediated between the observer and the actor. The actual performance of work is ultimately a subjective process. This helps explain diverse practices in the conduct of work, even when the same workplace processes are being undertaken and the goals for work performance is the same.

So it is not just work performance task requirements, such as technological change per se that reshapes the requirement for work, it is the relationship between workers' existing capacities and conceptions through which they make sense of and respond to workplace activities that is central to workplace performance requirements. Having some objective basis through which to understand work requirements is helpful, but incomplete without considering the relationship between those requirements and the individuals who are supposed to perform those changed requirements. That is, enactment of work requirements is a lived process; it is more than their representation on a piece of paper as a statement of work requirements. It represents the actualities of enactment of work, 'what is', not just statements of intents or ideals, 'what should be'. This includes the diverse challenges faced by workers in responding to changes to their work practice and ways of knowing and doing. Moreover, the objective view represents a snapshot, whereas the relationship between the individual and the workplace reflects the ongoing transformations and negotiated nature of those transformations in terms of what is encountered within the work and across working life. Therefore, in identifying ways in which the diverse and dynamic qualities of workplace change can be understood it is necessary to account not only for the objective and observable facets of change, but also the impact upon those who are enacting workplace performance. To consider one without the other is to deny the actualities of the live work experience, and to render it as something devoid of human experience.

The following sections takes up the first part of this challenge by attempting to identify some bases of workplace performance that capture both its objective and subjective dimensions. They do so by drawing upon a diverse body of research into work, work requirements and individuals' engagement with work from disciplines associated with the sociology of work, anthropology, cognitive studies of work and human resource development. The key elements of this analysis comprise a consideration of activities and interactions.

6.   ACTIVITIES AND INTERACTIONS REQUIRED FOR WORKPLACE PERFORMANCE

This section uses categories of activities and interactions to propose some ways of understanding contemporary workplace performance requirements. In doing so it goes beyond requirements of the particular occupational practice and situational factors to identify means to understand the changing requirements of work. In the following sections, some of the emerging changes to requirements in contemporary workplaces are drawn together as a set of conditions that may more or less account for the reality of all forms of paid work. Taking Darrah's (1997) advice about the diversity of work practice, the concern is not to articulate a set of generalisations, but to identify factors which in different ways (i.e. to greater or lesser extent) may impact upon instances of all work practice and workplace requirements. These characteristics of work activities and interactions can be apprehended through understanding the quality and degree of their: (i) routineness; (ii) specialisation; (iii) intensity; (iv) conceptual requirements; (v) discretionary qualities; and (vi) complexity. Interactions in workplaces are premised on enhanced engagement with tools and artefacts, and with others. These qualities of contemporary work are seen to apply more or less across work of different kinds, and in particular situations.

6.1   Workplace activities

6.1.1   Routineness of work activities

There is much evidence that work across industry sectors will become increasingly subject to change as the needs for goods and services transform, and the means of producing or providing them change through new technologies and ways of working. A key factor is the degree by which the work that individuals undertake is routine or novel, because the frequency of non-routine action indicates the level of change. This is because work will become less routine and the requirements for performance are subject to constant change. One such characteristic of contemporary work is the shortening of production or service cycles. Shorter production cycles means that work becomes less routine, thereby requiring all workers to have higher orders of knowledge and the capacities to analyse, understand and respond to emerging and possibly novel work requirements. That means workers will be faced more frequently with the need to engage in and learn new tasks and processes. This includes the requirement not only for learning new techniques and ways of working, but also the formation of new identities and the displacement of existing capacities and the comforts of a stable occupational identity.

For instance, skill requirements for technologies change as the technology moves through the life cycle stages of introduction, growth, stability and decline (Bartel and Lichtenberg, 1987; 1991; Flynn, 1988; Mincer, 1989). Yet these life cycles associated with technology may become increasingly shorter and overlap each other so that the desirable 'stability' stage is barely reached before it transforms into more uncertainty and change. Hence, in this way, a particular skill level or workplace competency might be associated with a particular technology, at a particular period of its life cycle. Bartel and Lichtenberg (1987) claim that the educational levels of Americans have risen in response to the demands of new technologies. This conception of technical life cycles also suggests that skill requirements are not a given or objective fact. Individuals' interaction with technology is premised on a negotiation between the life cycle of the technology and their knowledge and experience with that technology. For instance, a mechanic spoke of getting to know the nuances of particular models of automobile as they went through a succession of versions (Billett and Somerville, 2004). This nuanced knowledge was developed over time from working on the specific models of automobiles. However, when that model was no longer being produced, and hence serviced by the mechanic, that knowledge was rendered redundant. The more frequently the models of a car change, the more frequently nuanced knowledge has to be developed and then discarded.

In a study of information technology helpdesk workers (Billett et al., 2005) this concept of transitory knowledge was made particularly apparent. These workers have long since abandoned text based manuals, and even help facilities within software applications. Instead, they work from constantly transforming web sites to gain information about the latest applications and updates, and then share this information with co-workers. For these workers, the idea of valuable knowledge is configured, in the ever-changing and ephemeral knowledge that is drawn down from web sites supporting software and hardware products. So the issue of permanency of knowledge is associated with helpful web sites and histories of particular interventions in operating system in which they work. Here, the only permanency is the constant updating of information.

Aligned with the concept of novelty in work activities is the capacity to be flexible, that is, being able to adapt to non-routine situations and not necessarily be constrained by past practices. Worker flexibility has been identified as the most prominent source of workplace re-organisation measures (Waddington and Whitson, 1996), with teamwork, for instance, being seen as having lower utility in workplace effectiveness than flexibility. That is, the capacity and interest to engage in novel ways with workplace tasks, particularly tasks which are new to them is more important for workers' performance than the need for collective effort. However, again the relational argument arises. What comprises novelty, is likely to be person-dependent in some ways. So, the advent of a new technology, way of working or workplace procedure or being flexible has particular impacts and implications for those whom it affects, not whether it is entirely 'new' to a country, community or workplace.

In a study of how small business operators responded to the implement-ation of the goods and services tax in Australia there was evidence of the diverse impact of having to conduct administrative arrangements to organise business administration through computer-based processes (Billett et al., 2003). For those familiar and confident with the use of computers and business administration software, the novelty of the tasks required to administer the goods and services tax were considerably less demanding than for those who were not. One small business operator had administered his business from the 'green' book he carried in his pocket. The requirement to move to an electronically based business administration system was hugely novel and disconcerting for him. Eventually, in an effort to make the process work, he placed the computer on his shop's counter. He later recalled his frustration and that of his customers when on the morning he commenced using the system it failed to operate as he had planned. He spoke of the anguish he felt as his queue of valued customers became longer and longer, and watched as they eventually left the shop without purchasing. Even worse was his belief that some of his longstanding and valued customers had taken their products without paying. The point here is that beyond the change in work requirements and technologies as an objective fact (the need to implement electronic systems of business administration), there is also the subjective experience of these changes in the degree of novelty for the particular individual.

In sum, the degree by which work is routine or is attempted to be rendered routine is central to understanding the requirement for work performance. Non-routine activities require higher levels of work-related capacities to respond effectively to new tasks and performance requirements. More routine activities, suggest a reduced requirement for workplace performance, and perhaps lower levels of remuneration and control over work activities are likely to follow from work being made more routine.

6.1.2   Degrees of work specialisation

In keeping with what has been argued earlier about changes to the organization and conduct of work (e.g. downsizing, up-skilling), it is likely that both specific and more general skills are required in different measures in different work situations. Being a good technician or skilled practitioner alone may no longer suffice in some work situations. Instead, a thorough understanding and being able to communicate this to others; and an ability to consider how innovative practices might proceed, as well as account for practices which ensure safety and are sensitive to the environment might also be required. For instance, the extended warranty now being offered by automotive manufacturers appears to be changing the relationship between car dealerships that sell and service automobiles, and those who purchase them. A four or five-year warranty on a new automobile weds the dealership to the client, and if the relationship can be maintained they may well subsequently purchase another car from the same dealership. A manifestation of this is that motor mechanics may become more skilled in communicating with the customers of the dealership. In a study of changes to work and worker's identity (Billett and Pavlova, 2005), a mechanic who had previously worked as a roadside emergency repair mechanic and possessed interpersonal skills and an interest in addressing client's needs became highly valued in one such dealership. He was able to work across the boundaries between the mechanical and sales departments. His broad based skills permitted him to establish a crucial role as the relationship between the dealership and its customers changed. Also, as workforces become smaller or leaner there is a likelihood of them having to perform a more diverse range of tasks. Cabin crews on budget airlines are required to clean toilets, handle luggage and undertake tasks that their counterparts in major airlines would not be expected to perform, for instance.

Yet in many work situations highly specialised skills still remain valued. Airframe and engine mechanics might only be licensed to work on particular models of airplanes, pilots only certified to fly particular routes because of the specific requirements for that work. Conversely, in another study, an information technology worker was able to enjoy enhanced work status and job security because of his specialist knowledge (Billett et al., 2004). His knowledge of the state education department's standard operating system made him indispensable across five primary schools in which he worked. Earlier, his computer skills and knowledge had been used widely by administration and teachers, but had failed to secure him permanent employment. However, when a computerized administration system was implemented, his work became more specialized and his role was transformed from assisting teachers and administrative staff to being indispensable to the running of the schools. It was his specialist knowledge that led to pay increases, permanency and a titled position.

Lewis (2005) refers to mechanical queries on trucks as having to be referred to experts in Scandinavia where the trucks are manufactured. Such is the complexity of the trucks' design and functions that the manufacturer prefer to support expertise located within their facilities in Scandinavia, and these are communicated electronically to service staff in other countries. In some ways, this approach is an exercise in the evolution of occupational practice and its changing needs, and particular specialization of skills and capacity to provide access to that expertise via electronic means. Similarly, electricians' work is being transformed by the requirements to understand electronics and electronically operated equipment. This creates, at one level, niche areas of expertise and the evolution of new occupations. However, for other electricians, perhaps working well away from where such expertise might exist, this work becomes the expansion of electricians' day-to-day work practices. So, particular circumstances and situations will make these requirements different across different work settings.

Then, there will be requirements for workers to be both highly specialized and broadly skilled. The mechanic in a small country town will be required to be competent in a range of mechanical repair tasks that would not be expected of city-based counterparts. Yet, there might also have highly specific and specialized skills as well, because of the circumstances of being the only mechanic. For instance, the mechanic Mike who worked in the mechanical and customer service role referred to above had highly developed diagnosis skills (Billett and Pavlova, 2005). In fact, as well as being broadly skilled as a mechanic and being a go-between between mechanics and customers, he prided himself on fixing persistent faults and hard to identify noises, sources of inconsistent performance and frequent breakdowns. It may well be that, again, a binary of either being highly specialized or broadly skilled will explain contemporary and emerging requirements although they may play out differently across workplace requirements. They may even play out differently in the same workplace with expectations of both highly specialized and also broadly applicable capacities.

6.1.3   Intensity of work activities

The intensity of work brings with it additional demands. As well as being able to undertake and manage a number of tasks simultaneously, it also may require a temperament that is able to adapt to intense working situations. The intensification of work practice likely arises from the requirement for exacting quality standards and greater competition in many forms of working life, yet often with fewer workers performing a greater number of tasks (Noon and Blyton, 1997). Consider, for instance, the intensification of nurses' work referred to earlier. Within hospitals, patients are now having shorter stays than in previous times, as they are recuperating at home or elsewhere. Consequently, most patients in a hospital ward are likely to now require higher levels of care. Hence, nurses' work has been made far more intense.

In the banking sector, computerisation is said to have brought about a reduction in routinised activity, thereby also making this work more intensive (Bertrand and Noyelle, 1988). Hence, for nurses, bank workers and others, work has come to include the management of more intense activities. As a consequence, the capacity to work at higher levels through completion of non-routine activities and with increased accountability may be required. However, this change is unlikely to be uniform, with the intensity of work varying across and within workplaces. Consider the intense periods of activity in hospitality work during times of service, compared with more measured preparation time.

In other workplaces, emerging performance demands might be associated with higher quality standards, a smaller workforce and a wider range of tasks required of 'multi-skilled' workers. In a study of the paid part-time work undertaken by school students (Billett and Ovens, 2005), they were quick to point out the intense moments of service work (e.g. on particular days, or at particular times of the day), the impact of that work upon them (e.g. feeling hassled, dealing with demanding customers) and their diverse reactions to those intense work moments (e.g. "feel like running away"). The male students, in particular, greatly resented anybody being rude towards them. So there were individual responses to stressful and intense working situations. So these are not wholly objective phenomena, they are subjective to some degree.

In summary, a dimension of emerging work practice is its intensification requiring an ability to monitor and prioritise which activities demand non-routine and creative thinking, rather than merely deploying standardised procedures. Also, the need to possess a wider range of capabilities and apply that knowledge across a broader range of tasks is often required. Further, a capacity to manage intense work activities is likely to be a common work requirement. Moreover, how individuals will respond effectively to the demands of the intensification of work will be dependent upon their personal capacities and dispositions, including their prior experiences. So, again what constitutes intense work and its impact of those participating in it is, in part, person-dependent.

6.1.4 Work requirements are becoming more conceptual

Because of the advent of increased use of electronic technology whose operations are hidden, remote and not easy to access and understand, work requirements may also become more opaque, difficult to comprehend and perhaps increasingly reliant upon conceptual and symbolic knowledge.

Technology such as computers can have a profound impact upon work because it: (i) reconfigures work tasks; (ii) transforms the division of labour; and (iii) introduces unanticipated asymmetries to communications (Heath and Nicholls, 1997). As noted earlier, Cook-Gumperez and Hanna's (1997) study of the impact of technology on nursing provides an instance of the reconfiguration of working tasks. They note the potential changes to nursing work brought about by the introduction of technology that monitors patients' health and progress. The introduction of bedside computers to monitor, document and chart patients' conditions reshapes nurses' work through, among others, changes to the representation of the requirements for nursing knowledge. Firstly, there were concerns by nurses about competence with 'difficult to learn' technology that represents patient data in ways that are unfamiliar to nurses. Secondly, as nursing work requires interpretation of several sources of data to present a unified provision of care, some nurses felt their ability to deploy this competency was being challenged by technology that might be privileged as being correct. Thirdly, nurses identified the loss of personal and professional identity associated with nursing work through the introduction of technology. Yet, they also identified positive dimensions to the introduction of the bedside technology. They stated that the computer undertook the generation and recording of routine and accurate patient information that otherwise represented a labour intensive activity. This, it is claimed, provided an opportunity to advocate for the whole-patient approach to nursing with nurses co-ordinating information provided by the technology and their nursing knowledge. In this way, it enhanced the standing and status of nursing work. Moreover, bedside computers facilitated more democratic patient-nurse interactions. The screen served as a visible and accessible domain in which the patient could have access to records that were previously inaccessible, and provided a platform for elaboration of the patient's condition. Furthermore, the nurse's place at the bedside was confirmed by this technology, they did not have to go elsewhere to record information. The bed became even more the focus for the nursing activity because of the bedside computer (Cook-Gumperez and Hanna, 1997).

In this way, the introduction of technology both challenges and supports the essential role of nursing work: patient care, as discussed in Chapter 5. Bedside-located technology frees nurses from a range of mundane monitoring tasks and also can be used to avoid moving patients for particular kinds of testing. It also provides an opportunity for patients to monitor their own progress. Yet, it brings particular demands, some of which make the task of nursing more complex. Moreover, technology has the potential to transform work, making nurses closer to what Barley and Orr (1997) claim is the increasing technologising of work. The increased use of technology in work applications makes invisible the knowledge required to understand its operation (Zuboff, 1988). Consequently, this knowledge is more difficult to learn and deploy because it is difficult to access. These procedures are likely to be more demanding when workers are required to be more broadly skilled, because developing conceptual knowledge takes time and effort. Similarly, Bresnahan, Brynjolfson and Hitt (2002) conclude that there are positive aspects as well as limitations associated with information technology's impact on workplace organisation that serve to create jobs with great diversity and autonomy. So, while technology has the potential to reconfigure work, these changes need to be understood in terms of their overall impact on the work to be done and the acknowledgement that work is likely to change, as well as the impacts upon individuals' identities as workers.

Nevertheless, some technology can also make performance at work more rather than less demanding. Even though the technological tools may ease some tasks and undertake them with greater efficiency, there may well be cognitive demands associated with the technology, as the studies of nurses (Cook-Gumperez and Hanna, 1997) and truck drivers (Lewis, 2005) have proposed. There is also often a requirement of the technology and the separation between the individual and the object that is being worked upon by the technology (Zuboff, 1988) that can make the task of understanding the requirements for performance more difficult. Certainly, there is evidence that even when electronic equipment is monitoring processes, those who are relying upon the information provided by the equipment need to understand how it operates. Perhaps most spectacularly, this was demonstrated by the incidents at the American nuclear power station at Three Mile Island. A malfunction in the nuclear power plant resulted in incomplete or inaccurate information being provided to the operators of the power plant. Then, even though the operators sensed something was wrong with the power plant operation, they were largely reliant on the (incorrect) information provided by the electronic systems. This allowed the power plant's malfunction to go on longer than if the correct information had been supplied to and acted upon the operators.

The President's Inquiry into the Three Mile Island Incident (US Department of Commerce, 1994) concluded that the plant operators lacked a conceptual understanding of the operation of the power plant. They were reliant for their understandings on the symbolic displays provided in the control room, rather than understanding the power plant's operation. Moreover, even when they realised there was a problem, the operators lacked the skills to be able to quickly respond to the malfunction, because of their lack of understanding. The important point here is that the operators' understanding of the operation of the plant was premised on the displays of information that they monitored, rather than the actual operation of the plant. Hence, they did not know how to respond to the non-routine situation of a failure within the plant. Developing the required level of understanding, of course, is made more difficult because the workings of nuclear power plants, like many other forms of industrial processes, occur in spaces where humans cannot go to observe their processes. As noted below, such conceptual requirements are difficult to access and learn.

Interaction between technology and work organisation is also dependent on other factors including the enterprise's institutional history, its size and internal labour management relations and products (Bailey, 1993). Also, there is a relationship between the technology and individuals who are working with the technology. For instance, in a study of a secondary processing plant (Billett, 2000a), the original plant operators were initially hired to assist in the construction of the new plant, with their employment continuing through the commissioning phase to the final stage where they became the operators of the plant. This process of engagement with the plant provided these workers with a rich understanding of the operations within the kilns and the furnaces that, once in operation, became inaccessible to humans. Consequently through their experiences in the construction phase, the workers developed a comprehensive understanding of the plant and its operation. In contrast, workers who came later did not have these sets of experience and their understanding of the plant's operation was premised on very different bases (e.g. drawings and videos of what was occurring within the kilns).

Martin and Scribner's (1991) study of CNC lathe operators found these workers required high levels of conceptual and symbolic knowledge to operate these lathes. Also, the knowledge was harder to access and learn because the workers were separated from the information provided by manually-operated lathes. This includes the vibration, the colour of the swath, the smell of the coolant as it contacted the metal, and other visual clues such as the colour of the metal and tool as the cutting commences. All these clues informed the operator of a manual lathe about the machine's operation and progress. With CNC lathes, this kind of information is not useful in organising the operation of the lathe. Rather, because the machine has to be preprogrammed, understandings of its operation need to be deployed before the commencement of the job. However, operators who had previous experiences with manual lathes worked from very different bases to understand the computerized lathes' operation than lathe operators whose experiences were solely with computerized lathes. The different kinds of experiences had led to different ways of understanding and dealing with the new technology. Arguably, the experienced manual lathe operator's were disadvantaged because they lacked the symbolic and conceptual capacities of those more familiar with computer operations. Such demands suggest that workers need to develop, deploy and apply conceptual knowledge of a kind than was not required by more manual applications of work where the worker was more closely positioned to the objects and artifacts with which they work. Whether these new requirements are inherently more complex and demanding is yet to be resolved. However, they are different. So, the previous experiences of each group of workers generated particular sets of understandings and capacities to comprehend the technology that was being deployed.

Moreover, the kinds of knowledge required to operate computer-controlled machinery may be more difficult to learn because they are more opaque. They may need to be deliberately made visible and concrete to be understood as representing symbolic forms of the required knowledge. In addition, taking the work task from the engineering plan through to digitally organising the lathe's work requires a high level of conceptual and symbolic knowledge in realising the product. Similarly, Lewis (2005) notes how the increasingly computerised functions of truck driving are requiring them to understand a greater range of operational functions within a truck (hundreds in fact), which can be represented on a visual display which replaces the format that truck drivers are used to working with. So the task of truck driving has become more complex, but the means by which this complex task can be understood is symbolic and in some ways apparently detached from the truck's functions. This requires the truck drivers to have enhanced conceptual capacities. In Lewis' study there was little to suggest that the experience of truck driving in terms of years was a predictor of successful understanding of computerised trucks' operation.

Again, the issue of particular requirements, the degree and extent of the use of technology, and its criticality will differ across workplaces and have greater meaning in some workplaces than others. Moreover, the ability to learn to use technology effectively was also shaped by the workers' previous experience, ways of knowing, if you like. Individuals' ability, interest and means of construing an engaging with this work will be person-dependent in some ways. Therefore, beyond objective accounts of what constitutes highly conceptual work, will be the subjective bases for understanding symbolic and abstract knowledge. So here, despite the fact of technology, the capacity to engage with it was at least, in part subjective.

6.1.5   Discretionary qualities of work

The capacity to exercise discretion within paid work is a defining characteristic of its standing for many commentators (Carnevale, 1995; Davis, 1995; Howard, 1995) and perhaps most workers. That is, the scope of workers' capacity to be able to make decisions and organise their work is important to their sense of self. This is the high discretionary work referred to in Chapter 6. Certainly, what distinguishes work that is termed 'professional' from other kinds of work is the degree of discretion afforded to the practitioner. McGovern (1996), for instance, claims that professional engineers were distinguished from crafts workers and lower level technical staff by the trust and discretion afforded them. In this way, a key facet of understanding work requirements, and changes to them, is the degree to which individuals enacting that work are able to exercise discretion in its conduct. Noon and Blyton (1997) suggest that a key attribute of so-called new work is that the worker is able to exercise significant discretion in their work and workplace activities. This is sometimes referred to as work expansion. There are at least two dimensions to the degree of discretion a worker has. The first is the degree of responsibility that the individual is required to demonstrate in their work role. Junior workers are often constrained in the execution of their work. For instance, in a hairdressing salon, there will always be tasks that are the preserve of senior staff. These include controlling the hairdressing supplies in some salons and performing specific treatments in others. Moreover, it is likely to be the owners or senior hairdressers that go beyond the norms of the salon's particular scope of hairdressing styles (Billett, 2003a). The other dimension of discretion is the space that individuals make for themselves in their work. For instance, in a study of five workers engaged in different kinds of work, some of which were closely supervised, each was able to make roles for themselves and more able to exercise discretion in 'being themselves' (Billett and Pavlova, 2005). Yet, even in workplaces that have the capacity to monitor workers' activities, there are still discretionary spaces. For instance, in the hairdressing salons referred to earlier, one salon had a regime of management that even forbade the hairdressers initiating conversations with their clients (Billett, 1995). It also had a strict work regime about how the work of the hairdressers should be conducted and divided. Yet, despite efforts to secure consistency and adherence to the salon's norms and practices, hairdressers still were able to exercise their discretion in their negotiations with their hairdressing clients about the kinds of cuts and treatments they gave. This included the hairdressers exercising their preferences for particular treatments and cuts.

However, employers are sometimes quite ambiguous in their approach to workplace discretion of both these kinds. On the one hand, they want workers to exercise their capacities fully, engage effectively in their work and work activities and exercise their energy, creativity and intellect. In this way, the worker's discretion is most welcome. This is the work expansion thesis advocated by human resource development specialists in Chapter 4.

Similarly, Smith (2004) noted the necessity of new workers to exercise their agency and discretion in learning how to be effective in new workplaces. He illustrated the important role of these new workers' epistemological agency in securing the capacities to be effective in their new jobs. However, this discretion may be less welcome if it is seen as challenging the manager's or owner's, or even other workers' control of or standing in the workplace. Indeed, the new lean workplaces now present in many Western economies were expected to deliver dividends in the form of increased professionalism brought about by the flattening of hierarchical relationships, the management of integrated work areas, budget responsibilities and the advent of continuous improvement (Bonazzi, 1998). However, Lowe (cited in Bonazzi 1998) found that although workers might have greater responsibilities, the content of their work remained largely unchanged. Similarly, their distance from management remained unchanged and there was claimed to be widespread uncertainty due to their scant preparation for the new tasks. These workers are now required to have technical, work participatory and decision-making skills of a high order. So, these work requirements demand a higher level and broader scope of decision-making than in more restricted forms of employment, yet the preparation for these roles and their benefits may not be apparent to workers.

Yet, much work is intended to be low discretion by its employers. Hughes and Bernhardt (1999) suggest that some retail work is deliberately down-skilled in order to secure low levels of pay and maximise the opportunities of using part-time and contingent workers. For instance, massive technological investment by the retailer Wal-mart has been use in product management and to keep its inventories responsive to turnover patterns. For example, some tasks are being transferred to suppliers who can re-supply stores based on access to records about product sales (Bernhardt, 1999). Yet, these changes have been driven by technological and process innovation—not on the basis of a human resource model. Although these are not high performance workplaces, the company's performance is highly profitable: "It is hard to see the advantages of taking the 'high road' in the retail industry" (Bernhardt, 1999: 16). She continues:

> What would convince McDonald's to shift its production-line system to one based on skilled workers, given the enormous start-up costs and the amount of capital it has already sunk into designing its kitchen around low-skill labour? How would Macy's go about creating work teams that are productive enough to support higher wages, given its sales staff makes money by interacting with customers and the cash register, not with other workers? (p. 16)

So, whereas teamwork and smaller work teams, and even the opportunity to work from home, may require and emphasise the importance of workers' discretion in particular ways, it is far from likely to be deployed universally. However, it is also important to acknowledge that discretion is not something that is purely a workplace affordance. Just as critiques of Braverman's (1974) de-skilling thesis suggested that he had failed to take into account worker resistance against management attempts to de-skill and marginalise them, it seems this principle is applicable far wider. For instance, in detailed studies of workers' lives (Billett et al., 2004, Billett and Pavlova, 2005, Billett et al., 2005) there is clear evidence of workers being able to exercise their agency and creating discretionary practices for themselves. There will of course, be instances when discretion afforded by the workplace and that required by the individual come together. For instance, the goals of the primary schools and that of the information technology worker in those schools were quite compatible (Billett et al., 2004). Similarly, in the same study, the work requirements and personal goals of the union worker were also consonant in many ways.

All this suggests that the discretion required for work and for work performance is in many ways a negotiated quality between the individual and the workplace. Again, there is an interplay between the objective requirements for work and the subjective needs of individual worker that shapes how they experience and engage in work.

6.1.6   Complexity of work activities

Along with the requirements of constant change, greater intensity and the requirement to access, understand and deploy conceptual and symbolic knowledge, work can become increasingly complex. Complexity refers to the number of compounding factors that need or potentially need to be taken into consideration when considering the work task. Barley and Orr (1997) claim the growth and commercialisation of science has shifted the balance of employment towards technical work in three ways, all associated with enhanced complexity. These are: (i) an escalating demand for scientific knowledge which has led to employment opportunities for scientists, engineers etc, and hence, scientific concepts and knowledge; (ii) requirements for specialisation; and (iii) a tendency for scientists and professionals to allocate more routine duties to somewhat less trained individuals. Technology often brings about complexities for work practice. For instance, as foreshadowed earlier, Lewis (2005) notes how truck driving has been transformed into the management of a transportation device that has to comply with environmental issues (e.g. levels of emissions and noise), be operated in a way which maximises fuel efficiency and requires the monitoring of potentially hundreds of functions to ensure the truck's best and safest operation. This includes the requirement to move easily from an automatic gearbox to manual controls based on the driver's assessment of load factors and the capacity to maintain speed around corners and up inclines. So, more than managing traffic and locating destinations, the truck driver's job has become one of managing an expensive transportation asset, with that management being mediated through symbolic representations on the truck's dashboard. Complexity here refers to the compounding number of factors or processes or goals that need to be accounted for and conceded for those forms of work that have increased complexity there is the requirement to possess a wider range of capabilities. This may occur when the work activity, including decision-making itself is subject to multiple factors, processes and goals. So, for instance, high levels of complexity are involved not only in planning and enacting an integrated form of work (catering arrangements, medical care, building project), but also, the apparently simpler daily tasks such as driving a truck.

In addition, modes of work organisation can lead to greater complexity in the conduct of work. For example, when enterprises reduce the size of their workforce, they tend to expect workers to perform a wider range of tasks than previously required. In Australia, this is referred to as multi-skilling. It means that workers are required to perform a wider range of tasks in the workplace. However, more than simply having more skills, it can also require the judicious use of skills and their pertinence for particular work tasks. That is, it requires a greater understanding not only of different areas of work, but also the relationships among those different areas of work requirements.

> ...the production workers simultaneously performed multiple tasks, which management described as flexibility, also a desired skill. The workers indicated that this minimized the value of planning and reduced the opportunities to demonstrate initiative, since their workload was largely imposed upon them. Thus planning, initiative and flexibility existed in an uneasy tension, and workers were hard pressed to demonstrate each. (Darrah, 1997: 264)

This issue of enhanced complexity is particularly relevant to changing requirements for work because a change to the organisation of work and down-sizing is associated with removing workplace demarcations that are either industrial or professional. Such a view supports the idea that much of the change brought about by liberalising workplace practices leads to up-skilling rather than down-skilling. For instance, there is a trend for hairdressers now to become sole operated businesses in hairdressing salons, rather than being an employee of the salon. This expands the job and makes it more complex, as they need to manage their own books and clientele and so on. Moreover, as Darrah (1996) suggests, the pessimistic assessments of down-skilling were premised on the use of work organisation and technology to reduce worker discretion in an era of mass production. Now a shift to flexible modes of production is accompanied by fundamental changes in the organisation of work and in the skills required of workers at all levels in the organisation.

The important point here is that work which might otherwise be categorised as a relatively low skilled on examination is revealed to be highly complex. This may be because of the demands brought about by work expansion, or even activities aimed to more closely supervise and monitor workers' practices. Even so, the assessment of the complexity of the work situation will still be, in part, a product of individuals' perceptions and capacities. For those workers who have regularly engaged in expansive work and broad discretionary roles, (as often occurs in small businesses for instance), changes to work practices that expand job roles may not constitute such a challenge.

The complexity of a work role might be embraced as being personally significant and important by one individual, yet rejected by another. One hairdresser discovered he was partially colour blind and so the organisation of work and management of clients involved working closely with a junior hairdresser who particularly enjoyed working with colours. Later, this same junior hairdresser became a sole operator and despite having to learn new skills about managing a small business, reported enjoying the added complexity of her work because it suited her needs as a worker and her identity as a hairdresser. She stated that she now had her own clientele, which was as important to her as deriving benefit from her efforts and capacities. Conversely, some workers might actively reject the expansion of their work roles, even when others propose enriching it for these workers' betterment. For instance, a group of production workers in a German factory rejected an offer to expand their work roles. Although a member of the management team had assumed that these workers would welcome greater variety and richer forms of work activities, the workers, who were largely engaged in highly routine activities, said that they preferred such activities as they could listen to the radio and talk to their friends while they worked. So, there will be subjective bases for how changes to the complexity of work are likely to be engaged with by those who are subject to them.

6.2   Work and work activities

The listing of the characteristics of work activities provided above, sets out something of the scope of considering paid work activities. They include the degree to which work activities are routine or novel, the requirement for specialisation and diversification, the likely intensification of work activities, the increasingly conceptual or symbolic knowledge underpinning contemporary work, and prospects for enhanced discretion and complexity. Many of these qualities are generated by the social world, what Searle (1995) refers to as institutional facts. That is, the changing requirements for vocational activities make work increasingly subject to change, thereby more frequently presenting workers with novel tasks. Moreover, in different ways, the intricacies of occasional knowledge in practice, on the one hand, demand greater specialisation, yet, on the other hand, often require a broader range of activities to be conducted by workers within the workforce.

The dynamic nature of work is a product of changing cultural need that, by most accounts, is accelerating, leading to work activities becoming increasingly intense. Coupled with the increase in technology that arises from social sources is the requirement for workers to comprehend and deploy forms of conceptual knowledge that will allow them to represent work activities of this kind. With shifts in views about the organisation of work have come, for some workers, greater discretion in the conduct of work. And, whether through adversity or specialisation, intensity or the requirement to understand symbolically represented knowledge, there is seen to be an enhanced complexity about contemporary work tasks. In many ways, these represent facts that all workers will experience to a greater or lesser degree.

However, there will also be personally subjective constructions of these characteristics. Depending upon the individuals' previous experience, tasks will be more or less novel, and specialisation or diversity will represent a greater or lesser challenge to individuals as will changing patterns of discretion and complexity. So, although these characteristics are presented as institutional facts that individuals cannot wish away, the degree by which these characteristics shape individuals' construal of them still remains a subjective event. In the next section, the kinds of interactions that shape and organise work are discussed. Because these emphasise interactions, which necessarily mean some form of exchange (with others or with artefacts), they are two-way processes which of necessity include individuals' subjective construals. So, as with the characteristics of work activities laid out above, the subjective experience of the workers comes to the fore, in particular ways.

6.3 Workplace interactions

Beyond the categories of activities referred to above, there are also categories of interactions that stand as important aspects of work. Some commentators claim these are becoming increasingly a part of contemporary and emerging work practices. Some, are also concerned that interactions as a component of work are underestimated, misunderstood and not always considered within conceptions of work: "… efforts to understand the nature of the skills required in the technological workplace … often fail to honour the extent to which people function as part of a system in which knowledge and competent action are distributed" (Resnick et al., 1997: 6).

Workplace interactions are a central requirement of much workplace performance, albeit to a different degree across different kinds of work and workplaces. These interactions are an important facet of paid work and something often sought by workers, even when management work against them. For example, in a study of office workers where all interactions were supposed to take place through telephonic communication, workers subverted this requirement because of their need to engage face-to-face with colleagues. Increased levels of interpersonal skills and decision-making are required to be effective in these kinds of work environments (Berryman, 1993). Less-hierarchical approaches to work organisation (e.g. self-managed teams, 'green field' work sites) are premised upon high degrees of work and interaction. Less direct forms of work organisation and the need to respond to constant change in the workplace require greater frequency of workplace interactions. There are also greater demands arising from team-based or collective forms of work favoured in some workplaces. Similarly, for some workers, innovations in technology and the demands of responsiveness and flexibility in the production of goods and services (Wall and Jackson, 1995) are heightened not only through face-to-face interaction, but also those interactions that are technologically mediated.

However, it is probably premature to view these changes as being universal shifts in patterns of work and the means by which work has to be undertaken. For instance, small enterprises (particularly those managed by owners) are unlikely to fit into simple patterns of workplace transformations with flatter organisational structures or with the technology mediating interactions that might be found in larger enterprises (Kempnich, Butler and Billett, 1999). In other circumstances, these transformations will be patterned differently accor-ding to the requirements of the particular workplace or work situation. For instance, in a study that identified the requirements for work across four hairdressing salons (Billett, 2001a) quite different patterns of workplace interactions were identified for each salon. In one salon, the hairdressers were to conduct the hairdressing process as a production line with a number of hairdressers working with a client throughout their haircut. There were a complex set of rules that allocated work to the most skilled worker who became available at any point in time. However, all of this was to be con-ducted without any oral communication among the hairdressers. Interactions in this salon had to be organised through gestures because of the owners preference for there to be 'no yapping' (i.e. talk by the hairdressers). The hairdressers here found ways of operating around these work requirements. This included using a physical space within the hairdressing salon where beverages were prepared (as were chemicals and hair colourings) and to talk discreetly about clients and the owner. In this way, in the public space they found methods of interacting that did not breach the performance requirements in the salon itself, while in more private spaces they operated under different norms.

Taking another similar instance, the armed forces and emergency services will likely want to maintain a 'command culture' which is 'top down' and hierarchical, rather than one that aims to be open and democratic. Interactions in these forms of employment, therefore, are based on set rules premised on rank and command. Yet, there may also be differences across these forms of work. For instance, although fire fighters are under the command of an officer at an emergency incident, the bases for their interactions may be quite distinct. A specialist fire fighter, such as a ladder operator, has greater discretion and interacts in a different way with the senior officer than those working with hoses on the ground (Billett et al., 2005). In this instance, enhanced discretion arising from particular expertise leads to a different kind of workplace interaction albeit within a highly regulated work environment. This suggests that interactions in the workplace are central, subject to change and not easily categorisable on the basis of existing conceptions of workplace hierarchies. Undoubtedly more experienced and expert workers exercise interactions more strongly than novices, but there are always likely to be spaces for negotiation. That is, the bases for interactions are relational, perhaps made more so by the constant change that renders redundant much that was earlier prized. So these conditions may lead to more relational interactions in workplaces.

In the following two sections, the requirements for workplace interactions are elaborated in terms of interactions with others, and also with tools and artefacts.

6.3.1 Working with others

The literature on work practice requirements often refers to some forms of work now having less direct hierarchical management or supervisory control. Certainly, there seems to be a growing expectation that employees will be good at 'working with others'. Discussion of workplace skills necessarily tends to focus on individuals and how they accommodate each other at work. Yet, workers need to do more than just accommodate each other, they typically participate in interpersonal networks that generate, retain and transmit crucial work related knowledge. Working within such networks may require more than simply getting along with co-workers—as they form a social practice which may be central to the enactment of work in that work practice or workplace (Darrah, 1997). Employers identify the capacity for workers to engage in collective and shared workplace processes and interactions to complete their work tasks, (even if it is not always exercised) as a key quality for performance in contemporary workplaces. It is suggested that innovative approaches to workplace organisation are characterised by a breakdown of traditional functional roles, flatter organisational hierarchies, decentralization of responsibility and greater involvement at all levels within workplaces (Dertouzos, Lester and Solow, 1989; Hayes, Wheelwright and Clark, 1988; Zuboff, 1988). Sometimes, the requirement to work with others is shaped by a pressing need to operate as a team, for instances in fire fighting, underground coal mining and flight attendant work. In other instances, this need arises out of a belief that collective efforts are inevitably superior to individual efforts. In modular or team-based work, supervisors and engineers, Bailey (1993) suggests:

> can no longer focus on workers in isolation, but must consider the effect of the action of each worker and the design of each task on the functioning of the group. Workers must become involved with the quality and pace of production of their co-workers. (Bailey, 1993: 41)

One effect of teamwork is for some workers to perform a variety of tasks, the multi-skilling that often accompanies the reduction of the number of workers in a workplace and the concentration of work tasks on the remaining workers. Moreover, there are requirements to not only interact with the immediate team, but also across other teams when the work process is shared.

> ...the conversation process creates an implied social relationship through shift work on the various operational levels. The two laborers working on a machine in 3 eight hour shifts must exchange information and share their respective actions. They are required to construct a common history regarding their relationship with the machine, which is not too far removed from reality. The intricacy of the textual and logical processes of this operative conversation is thus also the overall accomplishment of their work, this time, however, on a social and economic level. It is a social and global process. (Trogon and Grusenmeye, 1997: 107)

Such processes are also required where jobs are shared. However, requirements for working together and a greater emphasis on communication and interactions in workplace settings, while generally seen as being desirable for individuals and offering benefits to employers, can also serve to disempower and reinforce disadvantage. Hull (1997) reports how the lack of English skills disempowers workers in contemporary American workplaces:

> Not being able to speak English means not being able to defend yourself in the workplace when you are accused of a mistake, …reduced chances of promotion, even when you do your current job very well. There are no Korean supervisors in this high technology workplace where international certification standards require that manufacturing processes be written, read and communicated in English. (Hull, 1997: xiv)

The social nature of work also challenges the concept of required skills. Workplace cliques, for instance, may deploy strategies of judging individuals by how the strategies suit their purposes. For instance, the conscientious and hard working might be dismissed as being workaholics or over-ambitious or not working for the collective good. Such behaviour is used to isolate and diminish the achievements of those outside the clique. Such cliques may be more powerful and necessary for their own purposes in workplaces where views of workers are held to be central to their achievements. Here, as above, the issue of the relational nature of interactions becomes apparent. The basis upon which workplace interactions occur, whether initiated and intended by employers for productivity purposes, or by supervisors for engaging or maintaining control, or by workers or cliques of workers to include or exclude other workers, there is a relational basis to these interactions. In this way, the interactions required for working with others stand to make some aspects of work more complex, and accentuate the importance of workplace interactions. Yet, these interactions are inevitably based on subjective construals and bases for their enactment.

Moreover, interactions within workplaces are not only among humans, they are also between workers and artefacts and technologies.

6.3.2   Interactions with tools and artefacts

There is seemingly an increased reliance upon access to work and work processes as mediated through technology and tools. Workers have always used tools and artefacts to shape products of the natural, physical and social worlds. However, over time, interactions with cultural tools and artefacts have potentially become more important as these tools now perform a greater array of functions and with a requirement for greater consistency and effectiveness. The evolution of nurses' work provides an instance of this. Early in the development of nurses practice

> (Nightingale, 1859) observed that informed observation comprising patient's physical appearance, activities of daily living (i.e. eating, sleeping, elimination, physical mobility) and other basic needs both

physiological and psychological. (Cook-Gumperez and Hanna, 1997: 322)

In the century after Nightingale, a shift towards written forms of documentation occurred (Cook-Gumperez and Hanna, 1997). This shift essentially alters the representation of nurses' knowledge base and the practices that are premised upon the knowledge base. Earlier, observational skills were primarily made through the senses (i.e. sight, sound, touch, and smell) and from a technological perspective, monitoring of the vital signs (i.e. temperature, pulse, respiration, and blood pressure), were the extent that to which mechanical devices were used. Now, observations are documented with notes and on charts for the vital signs. However, increasingly it seems electronic devices that collapse the interactions between the sense and the technology from which decisions about the patients' health are made mediate nurses' work. The depth of diagnostic and observational information is now required in a systematised form as the professional accountability of the nursing work grows.

There is also the issue of separation between the individual and the function of their work by mediating technologies. This suggests the need for workers' capacities to interact with technology to overcome the isolation that technological, specifically electronic artefacts might create. For instance, Zuboff's (1988) study of changes in technological systems associated with the paper milling process suggests that rather than working directly with the equipment, workers are located in glass booths and their work mediated by algorithms and digital symbols, a computer interface, and reams of data.

However, in human-machine interactions Suchman (1997b) suggests "The point is not to have the price of recognizing the agency of artefacts be the denial of our own. Agency—and associated accountabilities—reside neither in us or in our artefacts, but in our inter-actions." Thus individuals not only exercise their agency in their interactions with technology, but such interaction is necessary.

So the requirement to engage with artefacts and tools and to overcome the limitations that these might generate, may well be becoming an increasing component of work. If, as other commentators suggest, with the wholesale use of electronic technology into work generally, the issue of the mediated interaction between humans and technologies will increasingly come to the forefront of work requirements. If this is the case, changes to technology, which seem to be inevitable, will bring about the ongoing demands for responding to new practices in ways in which the individual is, in some senses, abstracted from practice. So interaction with tools and artefacts is a subjective process.

7. ELABORATING REQUIREMENTS FOR WORK

This chapter has identified ways in which contemporary and emerging forms of work are changing and experienced in different ways by workers. Hence, the requirements for work and work practice are being transformed by these changes, albeit in different ways, degrees of intensity and scope of change across workplaces. In addition, the timing and case of these changes will likely differ and fluctuate across and within workplaces. The key proposition is that regardless of whether work is being made more or less demanding by these changes, the impact of the frequency and intensity of changes is rendering contemporary work as being more demanding. This conclusion is supported not only by objective analysis of the requirements of work, and the scope and degree of change of work activities, but also the impact upon workers, their need to continually learn, reshape their practices and their work identities and sense of self as workers. That is, the changes have person-dependent impacts and implications. These changes are brought about by and rendered diverse by combinations of transformations in cultural need and situational factors. In combination then, requirements for work within a particular country, how that work is manifested in a particular workplace and individuals' capacities as workers or need accounting for in elaborating the requirements for work. The bases for describing, elaborating and appraising that work advanced here—work activities and interactions provide a means to engage both the objective observable character of work as well as workers a subjective experience. It is perhaps only in accounting for both of these kinds of experiences that work and working life can be comprehensively and effectively apprehended.

In the next chapter, the first of the next section, these ideas are developed into a framework that can be used to understand the requirements for work.

SECTION 4: DESCRIBING AND ELABORATING WORK

The fourth section of the book, *Describing and elaborating work* consists of three chapters.

Chapter 9—A framework for describing work—synthesises the discussion in the previous four chapters and proposes a framework for describing and illuminating the requirements for work practice, and informing the development of curriculum responses and the design or pedagogical practices able to address these requirements. The framework comprises categories of *activities* and *interdependencies*. These, it is argued, provide a mechanism to understand the requirements for work practice and participation in that work practice. This framework has been used and evolved through describing the work of individuals in diverse kinds of workplaces (Billett, 2000a; Billett et al., 2004). The categories of *activities* include dimensions associated with the routineness, homogeneity, complexity, multiplicity, intensity and discretion that constitute the particular work activities. These dimensions are used to describe the kind of tasks that constitutes work activities. The chapter also includes a consideration of the accessibility of the knowledge required to perform these activities. The categories of *interdependencies* comprise dimensions associated with: working with others, engagement in work, status and standing of work, reciprocity of values and access to participation. This framework goes beyond describing work activities to include the requirements for and bases by which individuals participate in work. Participation is seen both in terms of needs associated with work performance and the way in which the work activities have meaning for those who participate. In all, the framework elaborates what constitutes work life more comprehensively, than just through an account of work activities. Overall, it provides a useful basis for the development of vocational and professional educational provisions that can respond to these needs.

Chapter 10—Changing work practice and work requirements: Case studies—draws upon accounts of individual agency and affordances being exercised in the workplace to propose that individuals are not merely subject to the social suggestion and press of workplaces. Instead, individuals are active in seeking goals of different kinds from their participation in workplaces. Participation, therefore, is intentional and guided by individual subjectivities and their agencies. These accounts are drawn from a study of workplace participation over extended time periods (Billett et al., 2004).

It was found that there exists a complex relationship between the affordances and direction of the workplace and individuals' capacities to negotiate and progress in workplaces. Against some recent predictions about the alienating nature of contemporary workplaces (Bauman, 1998; Grey, 1994), their capacity to disempower (Rifkin, 1995), of socially saturated individuals (Gergen, 2000) and rendering individuals as anxiety ridden (Giddens, 1991), these studies indicate that workers lives and trajectories are not subjugated. Instead, it was found that they were able to negotiate and advance their circumstances even when confronted with strong social press within the workplace. In some instances, individuals were able to realise important personal and professional goals (i.e. being themselves) through their own agency at work, even during turbulent times of workplace change. For others, the exercise of personal agency remains significant, even if these individuals were not able to secure all their personal goals and aspirations. Moreover, in these studies, it was as frequently the exercise of individual agency as much as the agency of the workplace that threatened the continuity of the individual's employment or their developmental goals. Here, the concept of the 'enterprising self' is seen as an empowering metaphor, albeit one enmeshed and intertwined in relationships between the social practice of work and individuals' goals and trajectories. However, more than identifying and exercising a 'sense of self' from work, the humanist goal of 'being oneself' arises when there is concurrence between individual and workplaces' goals and trajectories.

The final chapter, Chapter 11—Work, learning and identity—revisits the key debates, premises and conclusions drawn throughout the book and synthesises their collective contributions. It summarises the purpose and outcomes of the theoretical discussions and also the empirical work throughout. It posits some deductions for education and learning as key concluding contributions. Here also, considerations for practice in terms of organising participation in learning through work are advanced.

Chapter 9

A FRAMEWORK FOR DESCRIBING WORK

Despite a vast and heterogeneous literature, relatively few studies of skills are based on direct observations of people at work or on interviews with workers. Instead, conclusions about changes in skills are generally inferred from formal job descriptions that ignore the exigencies of life in specific workplaces and the practical expertise developed by ordinary workers (Halle, 1984; Kusterer, 1978). ... While studies of skilling may reveal gross skill levels, they do not provide sufficient resolution in order to assess how actual workers perform in their jobs. (Darrah, 1997: 252)

This chapter draws together the contributions of the previous chapters to propose a framework for describing and illuminating the requirements for work performance, and individuals' experience of work. The scheme is premised on a framework comprising dimensions of work activities and interdependencies, generated from the bases for describing the experience of work identified, elaborated and discussed in the previous chapters. It goes beyond just describing work activities or tasks to include the requirements for and bases by which individuals interact in work with others and tools and artefacts. It also sets out to capture both the objective character of work as activities and interactions, and the subjective experience that constitutes work for individuals. This includes the premises for their participation and interaction, and their contribution to workplace performance, which are labelled here as interdependencies. In this way, participation is seen both in terms of the conduct of work and the ways in which the work activities have meaning for individuals, thereby mediating engagement in workplace activities and interactions. A framework to describe work has to be comprehensive enough to capture the key requirements in terms of the tasks that constitute the work to be done and the interdependencies that constitute the doing of that work. The dimensions of activities and interdependencies offer discreet, yet interrelated ways of understanding the requirements for work practice.

In preview, the categories of Activities comprise their: *(i) routineness; (ii) homogeneity; (iii) complexity; (iv) multiplicity; (v) intensity; and (vi) discretion.* These are used to describe the kind of tasks that constitute work activities in a particular work setting or work practice. They also include a consideration of the accessibility of the knowledge required to perform these activities. The categories of Interdependencies comprise: *(i) working with others; (ii) engagement in work; (iii) status and standing of work; (iv) access to participation; (v) reciprocity of values; and (vi) artefacts and tools.*

In elaborating this framework, the chapter is structured as follows. Firstly, a rationale is presented to justify the need for this framework. Next, contributions from earlier chapters are used to justify the foundations of activities and interdependencies upon which this framework is premised. Following this, the framework comprising dimensions of activities and interactions is advanced and elaborated. The framework is then described and detailed, and its application discussed.

1.   NEED FOR A FRAMEWORK TO DESCRIBE WORK

The need for a comprehensive way of describing the experiences of work that can be used across workplaces and work practices has been advanced in earlier chapters. These chapters have mapped an array of factors required to understand work and work practices, and inform decisions and judgements about the paid work in which individuals engage. This need arises because previously judgements about work have often been premised on assumptions and conventions, and in the absence of comprehensive analyses of work requirements. For instance, the variations in the requirements for work practice which have been articulated in the previous chapters, suggest that to describe and delineate them fully needs to go beyond identifying common characteristics of work such as that of an occupation, or a set of work competencies (e.g. working with others, being multi-skilled) that are held to be able to account for workplace requirements (Waterhouse, 1998). Instead, it is necessary to understand how these requirements are manifested and the differences in their manifestations within and across workplaces, even when the same occupational practice is being employed. Without this, descriptions of work will fail to capture the diversity of what constitutes occupational practices, different kinds of occupations and the diverse requirements across workplaces and work practices. In this way, it stands to enrich the accounts of the practices that comprise occupations, rendering them as diverse and possibly unique enactments of a set of culturally derived and sustained practices, rather than some uniform category of work as presented in tables of workforce participation.

Collectively, more comprehensive understandings about the experience of work can be used to make judgements about the requirements for work, how these might be rewarded or recognised and also how best educational and instructional responses might be organised to meet these requirements. Consequently, the aim here is to propose a framework that can be used to delineate the requirements of work practice universally. This is an ambitious undertaking and claims to be universally applicable are likely to be easily tested. However, such a framework offers greater promise than relying upon the analysis of workplace tasks, or seeking to identify sets of common or generic qualities or disembedded occupational categories, as objective facts that deny the subject experience of people performing at work. As identified through earlier chapters, there is a fourfold need for developing such a framework.

Firstly, there is a need to go beyond categories of occupations. While useful as historically derived bases for understanding the genesis and ordering of work, existing categories of occupations as discussed in Chapter 5 are premised on precedents that may have not kept pace with the changing nature of work and work requirements, including how they have been transformed by technology. There is a need to generate occupational categories that are more reflective of the current and emerging manifestations of work. Further, as noted, the level of analysis offered by occupational categories is inadequate for understanding how these occupations are enacted in particular workplaces, the particular demands for performance and the bases by which they change. It is within these workplaces that the requirements for performance are generated, need to be enacted and are the means by which they are to be judged. So there is a need to go beyond occupational categories and the occupational level of analysis of work and work practices, to understand individuals' experience of work.

Secondly, work performance requirements are both situated and diverse. Even with the diversity of workplace requirements as identified and elaborated in the previous chapters, there is a need for comprehensively accounting for what constitutes the work activities and interdependencies in particular work practices and how these translate into workplace performance requirements. As proposed in Chapter Eight, it is through understanding such specific and diverse instances of practice that decisions such as those associated with the relative value of work can be made, thereby relying less upon subjective and socially contrived accounts. Such a mechanism may also assist to critique the ways in which work is currently categorised (i.e. unskilled; low skilled, semi-skilled) as discussed in Chapter 5. Through a combination of objective and subjective accounts of work activities and interactions, all kinds of work practice can be considered in terms of their characteristics and qualities, rather than assumptions about those practices. This is more likely when the qualities and complexities of the work being enacted can be identified and elaborated. This may well assist in the future in overcoming the haphazard way that labels such as non-skilled or semi-skilled are applied and exercised.

Thirdly, the complexity of all work requirements might be more fully described through this process. Given the kinds of discussions in the early chapters about the complexity of work requirements and the experience of work, particularly those associated with workplace interactions, there is a need to go beyond viewing work in terms of narrow task analyses. Instead, a more comprehensive account is required to understand the interactions and engagements, including collective work, which underpin much work and, consequently, the requirements for workplace performance. Traditional task analysis approaches to identify the requirements for work, such as those often used in vocational education curriculum development activities (e.g. DACUM, Skills Analyses, Training Needs Analysis), often fail to accommodate the nature of interactions in workplaces as a central and essential part of work activities. Because these interactions are less easy to specify than workplace tasks, it becomes even more important to find a way of accommodating these components of work through identifying and elaborating their requirements for work. This is made more so because many of the interactions in workplaces and work practices are with others and artefacts, that stand as necessary and central components of workplace requirements, not merely niceties about having convivial work environments. Interdependencies comprising interactions with others and socially derived tools and practices are essential for performing and learning the required practices, and need to be included in accounts of work and work requirements.

Fourthly, there is a need to explicitly link activities and interdependencies. Given the importance of engagement with work activities and interactions in the conduct of work, there is a need to develop a way of understanding work that includes and is sensitive to: (i) the relations through interactions that comprise work; (ii) understanding how the values that are central to this work are enacted; and (iii) the means by which individuals engage in work. For instance, contingent workers who do not enjoy tenure or full-time employment stand in a different relationship to the workplace in terms of the quality and duration of their engagement than those who are tenured. The latter are more centrally located within the workplace, and more likely to be subject to its affordances and support. Therefore, issues of status and standing in the workplace are also required to be considered as these are the bases through which the requirements for work and its affordances to conduct that work are mediated, as articulated in Chapter 5.

2. BASES OF THE FRAMEWORK

The two key organizing bases for describing the experience of work—activities and interdependencies—are used here as analytical tools. While avoiding generalisations about the requirements for work, it is useful to have some common way of describing and analyzing work practice and delineating the requirements for work performance. Some components of these dimensions (e.g. working with others) may well reflect what has been proposed in some accounts of generic work competencies. But the concern here is to use these dimensions to identify how work practice is manifested in particular workplaces. In this way, the framework is intended to have utility for identifying the requirements for performance at work in each work practice, (since the framework can be used to describe and illuminate those requirements), rather than the framework being a prescription for the requirements for work performance as proposed for the generic or core competencies. Their selection is based upon the premises that follow.

2.1 Activities

The activities individuals engage in are manifested as a product of historical, cultural and situational sources that reflect evolving cultural need and situational factors, as articulated in Chapter 2. The activities of workplaces are prescribed by the cultural practices that it constitutes and enacts. Moreover, it is performance with work activities that are situated in and are a product of that work practice which is central to its continuity and development. These activities are directed towards the provision of goods and services within workplaces and work practices. The conduct of the work activities will shape the viability of the workplace, and also the continuity of workers' employment and careers. Activities in workplaces are responsive to situational factors, forms and priorities that shaped those requirements.

The use of activities as a key dimension is also consistent with both cognitive and social cultural analyses of work. Both acknowledge the centrality of goal directed activities as a key element for and product of the deployment of individual's capacities. In proposing activities as a principal dimension to understand the requirements of work, there is consistency with the focus on tasks that has traditionally been the platform for occupational analyses. However, here, it is anticipated that the categories of activities proposed provide a richer account of task requirements than those offered through inventories of work skills, because they tease out the different qualities and characteristics of activities.

Thus, the activities required for workplace performance are the manifestation of tasks (goal-directed activities) in the work practice. They are manifested in particular ways by situational factors that shape how sociocultural practice (e.g. occupational knowledge) is required to achieve the particular workplace's goals and continuities, as illustrated in Chapter 2. The dimensions of *activities* permit analyses of the goal-directed activities that individuals might engage with in the workplace, their requirements for performance and the bases by which they might change to be identified. This capacity for learning is important in responding to workplace change. Participation in non-routine workplace tasks (i.e. those that are new to an individual) requires workers to have highly developed knowledge of the vocation. Moreover, it is through engagement in these kinds of tasks that individuals extend what they already know, that is, they learn new knowledge and develop the knowledge required for non-routine work activities. Accordingly, those individuals afforded access to non-routine activities are likely to have richer developmental opportunities, particularly when afforded support and guidance, than those individuals whose work is restricted to only routine tasks. However, if individuals are confronted by too much non-routine activity, and lack support to respond positively to these new tasks, then work can become overwhelming. Similar issues exist with knowledge that is difficult to learn (i.e. conceptual knowledge that is hidden).

These kinds of conceptual and procedural knowledge are important for performing non-routine tasks. However, such knowledge is unlikely to be learnt by discovery alone. It requires the guidance of more experienced social partners (e.g. experts, more experienced workers), to assist individuals' access to that knowledge and to learn to practice it. Without access to that guidance, the knowledge may remain remote from the learner or be constructed in ways that are so idiosyncratic as to render it incommunicable or unsustainable in any shared context (Newman et al., 1989). For instance, in earlier chapters reference has been made to the symbolic knowledge required to operate CNC lathes (Martin and Scribner, 1991), in manufacturing processes (Zuboff, 1988) and to drive automated and computerised trucks (Lewis, 2005). Consequently, the activities and support individuals access will influence what they learn through work activities. The reliance on this access emphasises the significance of the second principal dimension: interdependencies afforded by the work practice, not only in the form of more experienced workers but also the array of socially-sourced contributions to thinking and acting located in paid work.

2.2   Interdependencies

The interdependencies between workplaces and works constitute a set of salient requirements for work. Drawing on Marx, Scribner (1984) noted that work always engages those who work, with the social world. She described the apparently solitary task of a lighthouse keeper as the epitome of social work. That is, the need for the lighthouse keeping task, its practice and performance are inherently beyond the individual and require the individual to engage with the social world to operate the lighthouse equipment, to understand its purposes and monitor its performance. The knowledge required for work has its genesis within the social world, as discussed in Chapter 2. However, as discussed in Chapter 3, social suggestion is not always projected uniformly or in comprehensive or comprehensible ways. Therefore, individuals need to actively engage with the social world to discern meaning, understand practices and make judgments about performance requirements. Yet equally, to be enacted, socially derived knowledge needs to be engaged with by individuals. Moreover, it is this engagement that maintains the currency and works to transform that knowledge when confronting new circumstances and goals. Socially-derived knowledge requires a process of appropriation by individuals. In doing so, they enact the contributions of the social world and through their enactment remake and, potentially, transform that knowledge. In this way, there is interdependence between the socially derived knowledge and the socially shaped worker. Without the individual there would be no change to socially derived knowledge; it would become moribund and redundant.

So, as elaborated in Chapter 3, this interdependence is essential because there is a need for individuals to engage with others and socially derived tasks and artefacts (e.g. tools) to conduct and re-make their work. Interdependence has been used to refer to "the extent to which unit personnel are dependent upon one another to perform their individual jobs" (Van de Ven, Delbecq and Keonig, 1976: 323). However, here the term is used perhaps more broadly and emphasises the interdependency of agent, activity, world, meaning, knowing and learning (Lave, 1990), between the individual and socially derive knowledge. This view of interdependence holds that interactions and tools do not simply facilitate an existing mental function while leaving it qualitatively unchanged (Wertsch, 1991), nor is the social practice changed by individuals' appropriation and enactment. Thus interdependence is a key defining basis for understanding performance and change. Likely, the nature of interdependence can only be accounted for through a situated basis for the social organisation of work, which can detail the bases for access to, participation in and mediation of knowledge by situational factors. Even then, there is a need to understand relations between the individuals' values and goals, because the consonance between these dispositions and the requirements for work will shape how individuals will enact workplace requirements.

Yet, in addition to forming a key frame to understand the enactment of work, interdependence also, like activities, informs about how individuals are able to or are inhibited from learning about the work practice. The role of social practice in the mediation of knowledge is essential to understanding how individuals will engage with or remake that practice or learn through participation. The relationship between the mind and the social world may be understood by a focus on mediational means, between individuals and others, as well as on socially shaped artefacts, tools and practices. Recent theorising such as distributed cognition (i.e. cognition that is shared with others and objects) (Solomon, 1997), neo-Vygotskian perspectives and sociocultural constructivist perspectives (Scribner, 1985a; Cole, 1998) and recent shifts in cognitive psychology (e.g. Resnick et al., 1997) all include a convergence between the mind and social practice. These also privilege, in different ways, mediation between social sources and the individual. That theoretical and conceptual convergence is commonly held to be associated with both close interpersonal interactions as well as the influence of the broader social and cultural world. Yet, individuals' engagement in goal-directed activity, of necessity includes engagement with others and socially and culturally situated tools and signs. So how work is engaged with and workers learn and remake work practice is socially mediated. Hence, interdependencies are central to how we come to perform and transform work.

Workplace interactions are also processes where power and control reside, are exercised, deployed, and shape how the social organisation of work is explicitly or implicitly determined. Whalley and Barley (1997: 27) propose that the distinctions between mental and manual work are cultural frames of great power; "They affect the way we see, think about and value the work we do and have important social and practical consequences." Similarly, Hull (1997) has shown how language and literacy skills influence workers' participation in workplace activities, thereby influencing their work roles and ability to perform and learn. Equally, workers who are contingent, short term or peripheral are likely to be inhibited in their participation and interactions. As discussed in Chapter 3, workplaces are highly contested as forms of power and control are exercised and negotiated. In this way, engagement with activities may be made more precarious in the contemporary world because of the contested and truncated nature of engagement and experiences. How support and access is afforded (e.g. Darrah, 1996) shapes the prospects for individuals and cohorts of individuals' engagement, learning and remaking the work practice. Danford (1998; 412) proposes, "management may exploit the new labour flexibility imperatives of team working to disempower workers; that is, by imposing a mode of team organisation which dismantles traditional shopfloor controls over the regulation of labour". He suggests that assumptions about teamwork becoming enriched in a 'de-Taylorised' factory floor need to be carefully appraised. Rather, "… in the context of a low skill and repetitive labour process in lean mass production, shop floor labour may in different ways find itself subject to increased work intensification and heightened subordination to a regime of direct management control" (Danford, 1998: 413).

In seeking to develop a framework to describe and illuminate work, activities and interdependencies are central to the social genesis of work and, in part, reflect accounts from psychological theory about work performance requirements. These dimensions are consistent with activity theory as pro posed by Leonteyev (1981). They also reflect the work of others. For ins tance, Resnick et al., (1997) use of conceptual bases comprising Activity, Discourse and Tools are not inconsistent with the dimensions proposed here. Ellström's (1998) bases for work performance (i) individual attributes; (ii) job requirements; and (iii) interaction view, provides a view of competence for work practice premised on individual acts, yet also has elements that are consistent with what is proposed here. However, the dimensions of activities and interdependence proposed here, build upon yet are elaborated beyond those Ellström proposes.

In the following section the scheme comprising categories of activities and interdependencies is described and elaborated.

3. FRAMEWORK OF ACTIVITIES AND INTERDEPENDENCIES

The scheme for describing the experience of work comprising dimensions of categories of *Activities* and *Interdependencies* is as follows.

Activities within work practice can be described in terms of their:
- *Routineness*—the degree to which work practice activities are routine or non-routine thereby requiring robust knowledge
- *Homogeneity of tasks*—the degree to which tasks in the work practice are homogenous. Similarities may provide for greater support (modelling etc.) in development of the ability to perform
- *Discretion*—the degree to which the scope of activities demands a broader or narrower range of decision-making and more or less autonomous practice

- *Intensity*—the degree to which work is complicated by having to perform multiple tasks simultaneously, thereby requiring high levels of managing, monitoring and prioritizing work activities
- *Multiplicity*—the range of activities expected to be undertaken as part of work practice
- *Complexity*—the degree to which decision-making is complicated by compounding variables and resolution of tasks requiring negotiation among those variables; and
- *Accessibility* (opaqueness of knowledge)—the degree to which knowledge required for the work practice is either accessible or hidden.

Interdependence within work practice can be described in terms of:

- *Working with others* (teams, clients)—the ways work activity is premised on interactions with others
- *Engagement*—the basis of employment
- *Status of employment*—the standing of the work, its perceived value and whether it attracts support
- *Access to participation*—the attributes that influence participation
- *Reciprocity of values*— the prospects for shared values
- *Artefacts/external tools*—physical artefacts used in work practice upon which performance is predicated.

The justification for these descriptors is now provided through an elaboration of the characteristics of each of the dimensions.

3.1   Characteristics of work activities

In the sections that follow, the characteristics of dimensions of work activities are defined, elaborated and discussed.

3.1.1   Routineness of work activities

The degree and frequency that work practice requires workers to engage in non-routine activities is indicative of work that is highly demanding and requiring capacities to respond to new activities (Chi, Glaser and Farr, 1982). The key principle is that it is probably easier to fulfill the requirements of tasks that comprise routine activities because they are familiar to the worker. Once the task is understood and can be practised effectively it can be conducted with relative ease and, in many cases, may make little demand upon thinking and novel responses. However, conversely, when tasks comprise non-routine or new activities, then these tasks are likely to be much more difficult to conduct because they require a wider and changing set of capacities. For example, in the cognitive literature it is held that the possession of higher order procedures and deep conceptual knowledge in the domain of work activity is required for non-routine activities in order to transfer existing knowledge to new tasks and situations (e.g. Groen and Patel, 1988). Take for example, motor mechanics. In some workshops their work will involve routine maintenance or service checks on the kinds of vehicle with which they are very familiar. In another workshop, the mechanic will be faced with a range of different kinds of vehicles and types of mechanical tasks. These might range from maintenance work, through to repairs that require fabricating components and other engineering tasks. In this way, the work in the second workshop is more diverse and likely to provide quite novel engineering tasks more frequently. Hence, the greater the demand of non-routine activity, the higher the demand for domain-specific procedures and concepts as well as the deployment of higher order procedures to conduct this work.

In addition, there are dispositions required to engage in the kinds of transfer required for non-routine activities. That is, the requirement for effective work will be underpinned by a disposition associated with understanding how best to respond to novel situations and to what degree particular responses are appropriate or worthwhile, for example, concern with precision in engineering tasks and making decisions among possibly expensive options on a failing vehicle. Other evidence from anthropological (Lave, 1990) and cultural studies of work (Billett, 2003b) indicates that the more the demands of non-routine performance, the greater the likelihood that specific, but potential highly accountable work activity has to be undertaken.

However, there is also a personal dimension to routineness. What is novel to one individual is routine to another. For the novice, or individual moving into a new work area, every task will be new in some way. So, while an account of work needs to understand the degree by which tasks are changing and present workers with novel tasks, this also needs to go beyond a survey of the frequency of change and novelty of activities in the workplace, to understand what this means for individuals in the workplace.

In sum, there are likely to be differences in the routineness of activities in workplaces that make different demands in the orders of knowledge that workers require. In this way, rather than assuming that some kinds of work are inherently low skilled and require lower levels of capability, it is important to identify the degree and frequency by which the tasks that workers engage in are new to them. Moreover, as work tasks are likely to be constantly changing, the demand for performance and the capacities required for effective performance in most kinds of work will be of a higher order than in the few in which the tasks are unchanging. Therefore, it might be a mistake to believe that only particular categories of workers engage in activities that require higher orders of knowledge. Rather, the activities in the particular workplace will determine the degree to which tasks are routine or non-routine, and, in particular, the degree and frequency of each. It is also important to acknowledge that what constitutes novel tasks can be viewed in terms of their novelty to the workplace (i.e. "such a problem has never occurred here before") or else on an individual basis (i.e. "I have never had to face this problem before").

So the frequency and degree to which work tasks are either the same as experienced before in the workplace or are novel to the workplace and individual indicate the demands to conduct that kind of work.

3.1.2   Homogeneity of work task

The degree to which the workplace activities are homogeneous across the workplace will shape individuals' ability to source guidance and support from other workers. The more diverse the kinds of work being conducted, the greater variety in the requirements for work. There are consequences for workplace requirements and also managing change arising from differences in the homogeneity of work activities. For example, in Lave's (1990) study of tailoring apprenticeships in Angola, the apprentices learnt through participation in workshops that were inhabited by tailors and tailors' apprentices performing the tasks that the novices were learning. There was abundant direct and indirect guidance resulting from the easy access to these activities. Moreover, the apprentices lived in the master tailors' houses and these houses and the workshops were set in a street that was full of tailors' houses and workshops.

Consequently, the apprentices were immersed in tailoring practice, providing a rich environment to learn not only the techniques but also the norms of what it meant to be a tailor. There would also be very clear guidelines about how to proceed with tasks. Where all workers are engaged in similar tasks they may well be a range of options to observe, imitate, secure guidance in the performance of work and be guided through activities which are non-routine for the particular individual. Conversely, individuals could find themselves as the only individual practicing their occupation within the workplace, and therefore the scope of their tasks may well be far wider and the limits of guidance and support will be quite distinct from were all workers are engaged in the same activity. For instance, within local government in Australia, workers are often the sole or one of a few practitioners in fields of practice such as health regulation, bridge repair, road grading or word processing (Billett, 2000b). Therefore, the prospects for access, guidance and support for these workers are likely to be quite different from the support provided to the tailors' apprentices referred to above. Within these affordances there will also be the personally subjective experience of what is similar or different. For instance, experienced workers (i.e. experts) may well be able to see greater similarities across workplace tasks than novices. Experts' previous experience might well permit them to understand the requirements for work and respond to those tasks more easily than those without that experience (Ericsson and Lehmann, 1996). In this way, the experience of work and organising workplace performance will have person-dependence.

The degree to which the activities in the workplace practice are of a similar kind will determine not only the range of activities individuals can engage in, but also the nature of the practice itself and the kinds of support and guidance available to participate in fully and transform the practice. In this way, the commonality of work activities stands as an important basis to appraise the requirements for work, and the demands it makes upon individuals. These will shape how they experience and engage in work.

3.1.3 Discretion in work

The amount and scope of freedom an individual has within their work to make decisions and to enact those decisions shapes the range of decision-making workers are able to engage in. Workers with a broader discretionary role are more likely to be participating in work that requires a wider set of capacities to conduct it effectively. This discretion is likely to be determined by the culture of the particular workplace and its division of labour. If permitted only limited discretion, workers may be unable to deploy the full range of their capacities, perhaps only needing to make routine decisions. However, if the requirements and expectations are for broad discretionary action then a far wider range of decision-making capacities may well be required. Moreover, the way workers engage in work practice influences their discretionary activities. For instance, workers who are isolated or sole specialists may be required to exercise high levels of discretion, because there are no other workers to assist their decision-making.

High discretion workers are more likely to be engaged in making decisions, requiring deeper and higher forms of knowledge than when they are subject to close supervision. For example, a high discretion worker may set their own goals, periods of work and means of achieving those goals. Hence, they are enmeshed in a greater diversity and scope of decision-making and problem-solving than those not permitted wider discretion. For instance, in a study of a secondary processing plant (Billett, 2000a), the workers in the fusion areas had very wide discretion in their work. This included the timing of furnace operations to access less expensive 'off-peak' night-time electricity as well as changing costly imported carbon electrodes. In particular, the workers on the night shift had wide discretion and operated in the absence of the engineers who were mainly employed during the day. Yet, elsewhere in the same plant, workers in the control room reported feeling frustrated and disempowered by the removal of some of their discretion, when the professional engineers overrode their decisions about the plant operation. In the hairdressing salons also referred to earlier, discretion was quite different across and within the four salons (Billett, 2001b). For instance, in two salons the owner/managers refused even highly experienced and long-serving staff discretion in accessing and order hairdressing stores (e.g. shampoos, conditioner, turning solution, tints). In these salons, the owners claim that if they did they would go broke, presumably referring to the potential for wasteful use of these by the hairdresser. In one instance, a very experienced hairdresser who had 20 years experience in the salon was not permitted to order and distribute stock. Yet, in another hairdressing salon, the job of ordering and maintaining the stock was an apprentice's routine task. So the division of labour in each salon determined the array of discretionary tasks and decision-making.

Yet, the evidence was that these hairdressers still exercised discretion through their practice (Billett, 2003b). Even in the most tightly controlled hairdressing salon, junior hairdressers were able to exercise their preference for particular kinds of hair treatments through the process of negotiating with clients about hair styling. That is, within the scope of discretion afforded to them they were able to exercise their personal and professional preferences. In similar ways, it was found that workers across a range of occupations (Billett et al., 2003, Billett and Pavlova, 2005, Billett et al., 2005) were able to exercise discretion in their work that was associated with their exercise of self and was aligned to personal goals and trajectories.

In this way, the discretion required and afforded by the workplace stands as a key component of contemporary and emerging work life. In sum, the breadth of discretion that work tasks require or that workers are able to exercise can influence the scope of the tasks and decision-making that workplaces require for their continuity and the breadth of workers' potential engagement in work. In addition, the engagement by the individual in work is shaped by their need to exercise discretionary capacities.

3.1.4   Intensity of work activities

The intensity of work activities represents another dimension of emerging and contemporary work practice, with particular requirements for workplace performance. To work intensely may require an ability to plan ahead and prepare in order to manage the workload. It may also require the ability to prioritise and to deploy strategies which best manage the workload at a particular time. This includes monitoring and conducting multiple tasks simultaneously. Although there have always been intense periods in work activities (e.g. the hotel kitchen and restaurant during service periods), work in many situations is becoming more intense as workforce size is reduced and workloads increase. As noted earlier, a good example of the increased intensity of work is that conducted by nurses. Increasingly, contemporary hospital practice is for patients to have only short stays in hospital and to recuperate at home or elsewhere. This has changed the workload for many nurses. Previously, in any hospital ward there might have been a number of patients who were recuperating from operations or convalescing. As these patients required only minimal levels of care, nurses were able to spend more time with critical patients who required higher levels of attention. However, in contemporary practice, with patients recuperating elsewhere, the ward is more likely to be occupied by patients who all require high levels of care. In this way, unless additional staffing has been provided, the work of nurses has been made more intense by the requirement to look after a greater number of patients needing high levels of care.

Managing an intense workload might include delegating, prioritizing or staging activities in order to balance the intensity of the workload. Hence, in the restaurant and kitchen, preparatory work is done ahead of the service period. Judgments have to be made about what kinds of preparation are required. Similarly, hairdressers may attempt to avoid booking treatments that will take time and space during a busy period. During such periods they will monitor their time and even deploy waiting strategies (e.g. sit clients at the wash basin) to best manage the workload. Darrah (1996) noted that when components were not delivered on time to a computer manufacturing company the workers scavenged parts from machines that were either complete or semi-complete, to maintain required production outputs. Here, production workers who were seen as low status engaged in intense and multiple problem-solving tasks to meet production quotas and schedules.

Again, the demands of intensity are likely to vary from situations where planning and existing procedures can be deployed, to those in which creative and rapid responses are required. Particularly in the latter instances, managing intense workloads requires higher and specific applications of procedures and dispositions to meet workplace requirements. Consequently, the level of demand for intense engagement in work will determine the requirements to manage multiple tasks simultaneously, monitor their performance and that of others. Moreover, as studies of part-time workers in the service sector shows, the capacity to deal with intense work will vary across individuals (Billett and Ovens, 2005). Individuals work experience that has included intense periods of work may well lead to the development of specific capacities that will assist and ease the demands of intense work.

Some jobs will have regular episodes of intensive activity, as in restaurants at service time. Elsewhere, work might be highly intense throughout its duration, as potentially with nurses. So intensity as a descriptor of work requirements stands as a helpful and important base to understand the requirements for work. It needs to account for the different kinds of intensity comprising work, how individuals experience and respond to that that intense work.

3.1.5 Complexity of work activities

Complexity in work activities can best be seen as the degree and scope of the requirement to understand and respond to multiple variables in making decisions and conducting practice, that is, the complex of factors that need to be accounted for in any decision-making. Some tasks will require a resolution of a greater number of compounding variables, and in some situations more than in others. In this way, the number of variables that have to be balanced in task completion forms another dimension of work practice. For instance, planning for an evening's service in a restaurant may have more or less variables depending on the range of dishes offered in the menu. The task of dressing the hair of a wedding party, where the same style is required regardless of the suitability of the style for all members of the party and to meet a particular deadline, presses the hairdresser to consider a wider range of variables. This may make the task more complex than a single, even demanding style. The design and construction of a piece of equipment, item of clothing or building requires the individual to consider a range of variables in producing either the plan or the manufactured article. Equally, the application of technology to a service previously conducted manually may require consideration of a range of variables to ensure the full range of functions has been included in the technological version. A feature of the kinds of knowledge that doctors and lawyers need is an understanding of the complex of factors that shapes a legal position or a medical condition. Their capacity to understand, weighing up the merits of different factors and advise courses of action is a hallmark of the professional standing of their knowledge. Accurate diagnoses and solid opinions based on the consideration of a complex of factors are what are expected of such workers.

Complexity of work might also be related to the conditions under which the work is conducted. For instance, if the individual is one member of a large team of people conducting the same work there may be resources available to assist and ease the compounding variables within the complex work task, including specialist skills and capacities. However, when the individual is a solitary worker or without access to appropriate expertise, the situation may become more complex because of that isolation. For instance, the solitary electrical, hairdressing, hospitality or business studies teacher sent to a small provincial vocational college would be required to undertake the range of tasks that a far bigger teaching team in a large metropolitan college would undertake collectively. A similar situation exists for nurses who work in medical facilities in provincial centres or remote locations. The absence of doctors in such locations means that the role of nurses has been expanded, in some instances even to permitting them to prescribe some pharmaceuticals. In this way, the work of these nurses may well be far more complex than their counterparts' work in other general nursing situations. The nurses maybe called upon to conduct medical tasks that have ranges of compounding variables that need to be considered.

Again, there is a person-dependence aspect to work complexity. The expertise and experience of some workers will allow them to identify and respond to the complexities of the workplace task in ways that will be quite different than for novices. Indeed, novices may not even recognise the complexity of the work task (Chi, Glaser and Rees, 1982). That is, they may not be aware of the range of variables that comprise the work task. It is held within the cognitive literature that depth of understanding is associated with links and associations within domains of knowledge (Glaser, 1990; Gott, 1989). Yet, this only arises through rich and frequent experiences within the domain of activities overtime. So the complexity of work activities is not an objective fact. It is also a subjective and personally based phenomenon.

So, the range of variables that individuals might confront in their work tasks establishes their work as being either more or less complex, thereby making quite different demands upon workers and has different requirements for procedures and practices.

3.1.6   Opaqueness of work knowledge

The degree to which the knowledge required for work performance is accessible, contributes to understanding the demands of performing that work role. Knowledge that cannot easily be accessed is referred to as being opaque: hard to access, understand and utilise. There have always been aspects of work requirements that are difficult to access and learn about. The physician's knowledge of anatomy and physiology arises from understanding knowledge that is often highly conceptual, as is the lawyer's case. However, it is not restricted to the work of those occupations dubbed as professions. For instance, the hairdresser's understanding of the structure of hair that they want to shape through chemical or heat treatment requires conceptual or symbolic understanding rather than an observable basis for decision-making. The knowledge of forces that engineers use are also hidden, as is the stitch formation of a sewing machine for a machinist, the thickening of the chef's sauce and the accumulation of bacteria in a food preparation environment. At the secondary processing plant, many of the processes used within the plant were unobservable because they were hidden within kilns, pipes and furnaces (Billett, 2000a). Quite deliberately and necessarily, these processes have to be hidden because of the heat and forces involved in the production process. Consequently, like electricians, these workers have to develop symbolic representations of these processes to conduct their work tasks. Therefore, the degree to which the work task has elements that are hidden or opaque will also determine the requirement for developing rich understandings, through symbolic processes that are more demanding and abstract than those which are observable.

As noted earlier, there is a growing concern about the opaqueness of knowledge to be learnt arising from the increased use of technology (e.g. Martin and Scribner, 1991; Zuboff, 1988). It seems, that with the increased use of electronic technology, the knowledge required for work is less readily accessible through observation because it is hidden within the technology. To be made accessible, understood and best utilised this knowledge requires being transformed to a symbolic medium. Hence, this knowledge is not always easy to learn about, develop or deploy. Moreover, because the symbolic representations are abstracted from something not visible or tangible, they are likely to be constructed by individuals in quite idiosyncratic ways. This is because the lack of visible models and capacity to speak about them in a uniform way make it more likely for them to be uniquely constructed. There will also be the influence of prior experience that may influence how the individual construes and constructs this more opaque form of knowledge. For instance, in Martin and Scribner's (1991) study of lathe operators, it was found that those operators who have had experience with computer operations were more readily able to adapt to the introduction of computer aided lathes, than those whose experience had been solely with manually operated lathes. That is, the kinds of experiences that these workers had previously encountered, construed and constructed had a cognitive legacy that shaped their subsequent capacity to deal with symbolic forms of knowledge.

It is through interaction over time that common or shared meaning—intersubjectivity—is held to be secured (Newman et al., 1989). Yet, the conceptual knowledge likely to be associated with expert performance is often not readily experienced in ways that are likely to lead to easy or comprehensive intersubjectivity. This is because of the different and person-dependent premises for subjectivity to occur and experiences in contemporary workplaces when dealing with technology and remote forms of working which makes the task of shared understanding more difficult.

It follows then that the degree to which the knowledge required for work practice is opaque will be more or less dependent upon workers' capacity to conceptualise and transform processes that are not readily observable into symbolic forms. As suggested, the more opaque components of work there are, the more demanding the requirements for effective work practice might well be. Certainly, learning and communicating about opaque knowledge and achieving shared understandings with co-workers is likely to be far more difficult than when the knowledge required for work performance is easily observable and can be used as clues to assist performance.

3.1.7   Multiplicity of work tasks

The scope or multiplicity of tasks that comprises individuals' work roles will in many ways determine the breadth and depth of their requirements. If work is very singular in purpose and process, it may have a lower level of requirements than if it involves multiple tasks. Of course, some singular tasks carry high levels of accountability (e.g. piloting ships in the same waterway) and discretion (e.g. piloting a plane on the same route, day in and day out). However, conversely, the broader the range of tasks the more likely it is that a greater range of work requirements, and range of skills are required to perform that work. In many workplaces, the numbers of workers has been reduced leading to what is referred to as 'multi skilling' or 'broad-banding'. This means that the work of any one individual is conducted over a greater range of tasks. For instance, in some Australian workplaces workers have been allowed to be trained and certified in two trades (e.g. Electrician- Fitter) that permit them to engage in a wider range of tasks in demarcated workplaces. So with downsizing or reduction of workforces, the array of tasks is often shared across a small pool of workers. For instance, textile workers are now expected to diagnose and report loom problems (Bailey, 1993). Then there is the range and specialisation of nursing work (Cook-Gumperez and Hanna, 1997) and work within organisations with flat structures requiring the engagement in a range of communication and negotiating tasks which previously were the province of supervisors, not all employees (Berryman, 1993). So, more than being required to engage in a wider range of tasks comes the added requirement to be able to make judgements about priorities, and monitoring and completing tasks, in ways that are akin to its complexity.

As in the other categories of activities that will also be person-dependence in what constitutes the multiplicity of tasks for the individual premised on previous experience and understandings. For the mechanics who have learnt their mechanical skills in the small country garages dealing with different types of motor vehicles, automotive repairs and the need to fabricate or repair automotive components will be the norm. However, this may be less true for their counterparts in metropolitan dealerships. So, beyond the interpretive processes individuals will engage in about the range and scope of their capacities to effectively engage in work, there will also be the personal histories of the individuals involved in workplace tasks.

3.2   Work activities as objective tasks and subjective experiences

In these ways, these categories of routineness, homogeneity, discretion, intensity, opaqueness, complexity and multiplicity all stand as means by which work activities can be described and illuminated. In each instance, the degree to which these qualities are evident in individual's work determines the level of workplace requirements. For instance, broadly it is held that the less routine the activity, the less heterogeneous, the more discretion that is required, the greater the intensity, the more opaque the knowledge required, the more complex and the more components that are integral to the work, the greater the demands for work requirements. Such an analysis is based upon an understanding of the requirements for the work at any given time, and through some reasonably objective process of understanding and illuminating these qualities. However, it is important to recognise the scope and depth of the requirements of work that individuals carry out on the basis of these categories rather than to assume that certain kinds of work are more demanding than others.

However, there will always be personal factors operating within a scheme such as this. Beyond the objective analyses of the activities that constitute work, are the bases by which individuals come to the experience of and engagement in work—the essential qualities of work performance, as opposed to work activities. That is, the degree to which the individual is used to handling non-routine activities, wide discretion, intense work with many variables and roles and requiring hidden knowledge will make different demands upon novices and more expert practitioners. In addition, common across all of these categories of activities is the degree to which they change. Although captured in the category of routineness, it is important to highlight the consequences of work that is in constant transition. Regardless of whether it is objectively describable in terms of high or low levels of demand, the frequency of change will render all work more or less demanding. That is, the constant requirement to learn even routine tasks, engage in work supervised by others, of low levels of intensity and complexity will still require the development of capacities to undertake that work.

Because of these needs and the interdependence between workers and workplaces in the experience and conduct of work, it is necessary to go beyond the set of workplace tasks or activities, and acknowledge that a key dimension of work activities are the relations between the workers and workplaces. These characteristics are discussed in the next sections.

3.3   Characteristics of work interdependencies

The dimensions of interdependencies discussed here are those associated with (i) working with others, (ii) the bases of engagement in the workplace, (iii) the sharing of values between the individual and the workplace and (iv) interactions with socially derived artefacts and tools. These are defined and elaborated in turn.

3.3.1   Working with others (teams, clients)

Engagement in work practice involves interacting and negotiating with others. These interactions go beyond the close interpersonal interactions that constitute workplace communication and include more distal interaction (i.e. those through observation and at a distance). It is through both close and more distal interactions that much of the knowledge required for workplace performance is articulated and shared, and through which, for instance, common understanding about enacting outcomes and interactions is developed (Newman et al., 1989). These interactions can be premised on formalised hierarchies associated with the vocational practice (e.g. airline crews, dental teams), forms of demarcation based on affiliations (e.g. a work site delineated around trade or professional practice) or collaborative work with peers, such as in self-managed teams. In addition to any 'formalised' structures associated with interactions, such as those mentioned above, how interactions proceed may be determined by workplace cliques, gender, affiliations of a historical kind and so on that determine access to activities and guidance in workplaces. Interestingly, the high levels of discretion often claimed to be associated with 'new work' practices (e.g. see Rowden, 1995; 1997; Carnevale, 1995; Wall and Jackson, 1995) offer the promise of broader opportunities for engagement in activities and interactions in the conduct of work. Typically, this kind of participation is contrasted with work practice where work is closely supervised and comprises mainly routine activities. Arguably, some work requires sensible limits on discretion. Taking an example from dental work, there are tasks that are clearly delineated between dentists and their assistants; in a similar way to that between cabin and flight crews in commercial aviation. Hence, in these circumstances individuals' participation in activities and guidance and support to succeed may, in part, be premised on the basis of their standing in a hierarchical arrangement.

In one study of a secondary processing plant (Billett, 1994), in some work areas self-managed teams selected leaders based on their expertise. These workers enjoyed broad discretion in the planning and conduct of their work. However, in other work areas, supervisors intervened, thereby eroding worker discretion and engagement in tasks (e.g. range of tasks, decision-making responsibilities, and possibilities for practice). Elsewhere, there have been reports of supervisors' concerns about being made expendable by enhanced worker discretion that have led to the dismantling of these arrangements (e.g. Danford, 1998), or management concerns about loss of control. So there are patterns of engagement with others that are deliberately structured by the work practice that shape the kinds of participation that are permissible and how they are distributed.

Views about co-workers' standing may shape the basis of workplace interactions. For instance, members of a work team may find their participation is premised on the acceptability of their gender (Solomon, 1999), ethnicity or language (Hull, 1997). Workplace cliques and interpersonal relations also determine how individuals are treated and afforded tasks, and also how their performance is perceived. Such contested relations seem common to most workplaces. These factors influence access to activities and support afforded to individuals. Individuals who are denied opportunities to participate or access to information required for their work may be less likely to perform as well as those more centrally involved and 'in the know' as the goals for performance may not be made known to all workers. Also, values about how work should proceed within the workplace influence the conduct of activities. For instance, an enterprise may well adopt a team-based approach to work organization, yet, there can be no confidence that the team members will either wish to or be able to interact in the way intended (Darrah, 1997). There is also the fear of more experienced workers about displacement by the less experienced workers they are guiding (Lave and Wenger, 1991). Other kinds of interactions with co-workers, such as peer pressure can also influence engagement. For instance, Bailey (1993) reports novice or slow workers continuing to work through meal breaks in order to keep up with team-based performance demands. Similarly, disabled workers feel the need to hide their shortcomings and do additional work, or take work home in order not to be seen as being a liability to the team (Church, 2004).

There are practices and structures associated with 'working with others' that are premised on work hierarchies, workplace values, mores and beliefs, concerns about displacement and interpersonal relations which influence individuals' participation at work. Given that much of the engagement in and performing effectively in work is premised on direct interactions with others and less direct social sources (e.g. tools, artefacts, the workplace, observation of co-workers), the degree of inclusiveness afforded learners is crucial to their learning. However, this inclusion is often determined by others, and premised on factors that are outside of the control of individuals themselves. These include how individuals are able to engage in the workplace.

3.3.2   Engagement (Employment basis, Status of employment, Access to participation)

The bases for individuals' engagement with workplaces does much to shape how they are able to participate, contribute and access opportunities for development and also transform the practice. These bases include the nature and status of their employment and shape how they are able to engage with and interact in the workplace, including how they can access workplace activities and guidance. This is perhaps no more evident than for workers whose employment is part-time, contingent or contractual, or whose language and literacy skills or gender presents barriers to their engagement in work activities (Hughes and Bernhardt, 1999). These workers may find participation more difficult than those who are full-time and whose standing and acceptance in the workplace is core. In addition, home-based or isolated workers experience difficulties engaging in workplace discourses in ways required for full participation or advancement (Hull, 1997). Put simply, beyond stating a set of workplace requirements, achieving these requirements may be far easier for some workers than for others. Therefore, given the more expansive conception of workplace performance being advanced here which includes the conditions shaping the interdependency between workers and workplaces, the bases for and quality of workers' engagement in the workplace are a central component of work performance. Ultimately, how individuals engage in and conduct work is premised on subjective and person-dependent bases.

As discussed in Chapters 6 and 7, there are consequences for individuals whose engagement is marginal or marginalised. Part-time work diminishes women's lifetime career prospects (Tam, 1997). Also, most part-time and contingent work is involuntary (Lipsig-Mumme, 1996; Grubb, 1996) making the kind of engagement undesirable for the individuals themselves. The few exceptions include women from comparatively privileged groups who voluntarily work part-time in order to also participate in non-paid work activities such as parenting or community activities (Shima, 1998). However, other women (e.g. migrants, non-English speakers, low paid) view part-time work as undesirable alternative to full-time employment. They are often forced to work a number of jobs and relinquish preferred non-paid work roles such as child care in order to fulfill economic needs (Hull, 1997), thereby distributing their energies and interests across a number of work-places. Yet, their capacity for participation in work is therefore contingent upon these distributed sets of interests. They may not be directing their energies and interests to a particular workplace. Consequently, the basis of individuals' employment and engagement in work has implications for their participation and performance in the workplace, as it does their capacity to respond to change, learn in the workplace, and contribute to the changing character of the workplace.

The status of individuals' employment and their personal standing also determines access to activities and support. Darrah (1997) describes how work tasks undertaken by production workers in a computer manufacturing company were taken for granted. These workers were denied opportunities for structured learning, despite the complexity of their work, whereas those in the design area were the focus of attention, praise and support. Accordingly, discretion, opportunities and support were apportioned asymmetrically across workers depending on perceptions of standing (Milkman, 1997). These findings are consistent with international studies that identify patterns of employer expenditure on employees' training and development. As foreshadowed earlier, these studies suggest a consistent pattern of employer preference for expending training funds on workers who are well educated, young and potentially mobile (Bishop, 1997; Brunello and Medio, 2001), that is, those employed in relatively high status positions within the workplace. These funds are also distributed in ways which seem to favour some cohorts over others, for instance men over women, young over old, native speakers over non-native speakers, and white over people of colour (Bishop, 1997; Leuven and Oosterbeek, 1999). So, beyond the status of their employment, there are also personal factors of individuals' standing which will shape their access to workplace engagement opportunities.

Barley and Orr (1997) report similar asymmetry of opportunities being premised on perceptions of work being categorised as either manual or professional, a legacy of Taylorism. This was very much the case in Darrah's (1996) study of computing manufacture. Part-time workers, as peripheral participants, are also more likely to engage in routine tasks than their full-time counterparts (Forrester et al., 1995) thereby limiting opportunities for their engagement and development. Individuals with low literacy levels, and non-English speakers' literacy and language skills are likely to inhibit their participation. Hull's (1997) study of a manufacturing plant in the US with a significant number of Korean workers noted that there were no Korean supervisors, resulting in the workers of this nationality having difficulty with handling and avoiding being held responsible (i.e. scape-goated) for workplace problems. Language and writing skills can also become the basis for social regulation and control (Whalley and Barley, 1997), with those whose skills are perceived as deficient or who are unable to negotiate in mainstream discourses being marginalised.

Together, individuals' status, the bases of their employment and the standing of their work is influenced by structures within the work practice that have the potential to either invite or inhibit their participation in work activities. Given the interdependency between workers and workplaces in workplace performance and prospects for assisting, influencing, or being disadvantaged by change, the conditions of individuals' engagement with work activities is a key component of work performance. In this way, individuals standing and status needs considered in understanding the requirements of workplace performance and how individuals engage in and perform at work.

3.3.3   Reciprocity of values

Aligned to this issue of interdependency and engagement is that of the degree of confidence between individuals' values and those espoused or practiced within the workplace. Such, a relationship is likely to be central to the degree to which individuals will exercise their full agency in participating in the workplace. One view is that merely by participating in a workplace a greater consonance between the individuals and the organi-sational values is achieved (Lave and Wenger, 1991). That is, identification with the work practice will arise through participation as will learning. However, such participation might generate learning and identity formation that are quite counter to those in the workplace. For instance, Hodges' (1998) decision to dis-identify with a practice in which she had participated and believed is indicative of dissonance in identity and learning that might arise through participation premised on a lack of reciprocity of values. In this way, the values of a workplace may be more or less consistent with those of the individuals who work within them. For instance, not all educators feel sympathetic towards changing policy and goals of educational systems, particularly when they are perceived as compromising their professional practice.

The relatedness (Valsiner, 1994) between workplace goals and individuals' values will influence how individuals interpret and adapt or adopt changes to work practice. Some human resource management commentators give primacy to the congruence and reciprocity of values between employers and employees being associated with the company's survival and development. They propose that in an era of high levels of competitiveness, employees and employers have never needed each more (Rowden, 1995). Similarly, the requirements of 'new workplaces' are characterised by the involvement of workers in decision-making within the enterprise (Davis, 1995) that aims to capture their enthusiasm, commitment and loyalty. However, other views question whether the reciprocity of values is likely to be realised. For instance, part-time bank workers are reported as quitting because they cannot see prospects of promotion in the new structuring of banking work practice (Hughes and Bernhardt, 1999). They perceived a growing disjuncture between the bank's corporate strategy of individual commitment and its procedures for securing that commitment. Workers also react with understandable cynicism when high discretionary and team-based approaches to work are dismantled by management concerned that these approaches are eroding their control (Danford, 1998).

Moreover, there may well be distinct and conflicting values within workplaces that individuals will ascribe to and which will shape their participation. For instance, in the open cut coalmining industry workers' values are likely to be aligned to particular sets of interests depending upon whether they are union affiliates, supervisors or managers (Billett, 2001c; Somerville, 2003). The strong culture of coal miners as epitomised through their demarcations and union representation, is quite contrary to that of the mine site management. Therefore, participation and engagement is likely to be premised upon the degree to which set of values individuals adhere. A coal worker's adherence to union-organised work practices might demonstrate reciprocity of values, which could be seen by mine site management as inconsistent with their values of securing high productivity for low costs.

So whereas it might be seen as desirable for there to be reciprocity of values, between individuals' and the enterprise's desired work practice, this may be quite difficult to achieve. Even if the whole historically, culturally, and situationally derived mess of differences in values between the perspectives of employees and employers, between those of supervisors and those supervised, between old-timers and new comers, and between part-time and full-timers were resolvable, other aspects of the relatedness of values would need to be reconcilable. Also, as argued in Chapter 2, the cultural values of employees may not always be consistent with values within the workplace's social practice. So concurrence between values of the social practice and the individuals who are to act in that social practice are likely to influence how they engage in, commit their loyalty and energy to a particular social practice: their relatedness.

It is this relatedness that likely shapes how workers engage in the daily activity of work and its remaking. Central here are individuals' identity and subjectivity that initiate and exercise their capacities in engaging in work. Beyond the objective requirements for work, are the subjective bases by which individuals were actually perform those work requirements, and how they will contribute to the work practice and be involved in its re-making.

3.3.4   Artefacts/external tools

Interactions with technologies, equipment, tools and the work environment also influence individuals' participation within their work practice. Learning to perform at work may well be bound to these artefacts. For instance, it is not possible to conceptualise hairdressing without considering hairdressers and their hairdressing tools (e.g. combs, scissors) together—a relationship that Wertsch (1998) describes as being irreducible. Performance (knowing and acting) can only be premised on hairdressers and their tools working together. However, more than this, the artefacts can shape the practice itself and engagement in that practice. For instance, there are clearly discernable differences in the use of hairdressing tools between barbers and hairdressers. But there are also differences in tool use between those hairdressing salons that specialise in perm and sets and those that specialise in colour and cuts. Similarly, technologies of different kinds are seen as: (i) reconfiguring workplace tasks, (ii) reconfiguring the division of labour, (iii) providing unanticipated asymmetry to communications (Heath and Nicholls, 1997). Take, for instance, the introduction of information technology to work practice. 'Old-timers' might find their expertise super-seded and displaced by new understandings and 'newcomers' who are competent with these new tasks and their conceptual bases. The 'command and control' organisational practice of police, fire fighters and armed forces is discomforted and confronted by junior ranks having to guide senior officers through computer-based work applications.

Equally, electronic means may open channels of visual, voice and text-based telecommunication that provide instantaneous access to information that cannot readily be controlled by supervisors. Heath and Nicholls (1997) illustrate how real-time interactions mediated by technology (video shots of aircraft docking facilities) in airport work, provide simultaneous visual access to a number of workers whose performance needs to be co-ordinated. Not only does this technology assist performance, but it makes decision-making public and interactive. Technology can also provide broader dis-cretion, enhance work roles and improve access to workplace knowledge. As discussed in the previous chapter, bedside computers in hospitals, for instance, centre the care of patients at the bedside, rather than away from it and provide access to records that enhance nurses' discretion and empower patients thereby transforming nursing practice (Cook-Gumperez and Hanna, 1997). However, technology can also separate workers from the means of production (Zuboff, 1988; Martin and Scribner, 1991; Heath and Nicholls,

1997), thereby potentially restricting their access, de-skilling or, conversely, requiring high levels of symbolic knowledge. So artefacts and tools can be essential for participation, can enhance or restrict access or change significantly the relations within practice.

As illustrated above, the bases of engaging in the social practice of work are varied and problematic. Factors associated with interactions with others, the mode of engagement, reciprocity of values, as well as homogeneity of work tasks, will influence individuals' access to participation, how and what activities they participate in, and the kinds of guidance and support likely to be encountered in their work practice. The structures that determine access are formalised by organisational structures, values, prejudices, concerns about displacement and so on. These structures not only establish rules for practice (e.g. who has access and who does not) but also who is able to violate these norms and whose transgressions are not tolerated. So, on the one hand, there are sets of related interdependencies in work practices that are important for performance, thinking, acting and learning. These interdependencies also afford access to opportunities to learn and develop. Given that work practice is contested and the site of the enactment of power and social relations it follows that access to social practice will not be uniform or uniformly available. However, and importantly, much of this interdependency is mediated by factors that are beyond the individual. Individual workers are subject to many of these interdependencies. Nevertheless, they are able to exercise discretion in how they participate and what they learn from what is afforded to them.

4. DESCRIBING WORK REQUIREMENTS AND EXPERIENCES

In sum, through a consideration of categories of Activities and Inter-dependencies, a framework has been proposed here for describing work requirements and the experience of work. It comprises elements that offer premises for objective and subjective appraisals of work and working life. For the workplace, these categories of activities and interdependencies are those required to support its continuity. Consequently they cannot be excluded from an analysis of skills, because it essentially structures the work and learning that occurs there. Yet, it is also important to include in the analysis of work and work requirements the subjective bases by which individuals construe and engage in their work and its re-making, and develop and pursue their personal work life goals. Together, these are the dualities that are required to understand work and workplace participation: the human experience of work. The lessons to be learnt are that skill requirements are not derived in any simple way in asking workers about the their jobs (or those of others) or observing them at work.

In the next chapter, this is discussed further through the analysis of work conducted by three workers.

Chapter 10

CHANGING WORK PRACTICE AND WORK REQUIREMENTS: CASE STUDIES

The conventional notion of careers was one constructed by employers (referred to as the industrial model by Osterman and Kochan (1990) and has now been replaced by a world in which careers are increasingly constructed by workers as they respond to opportunities either within or outside of their own company. (Grubb, 1996: 235)

This chapter builds upon the contributions of the early chapters to illustrate and illuminate how the requirements for work performance and individuals' conduct of that work are interwoven and how that analysis of work activities and interactions can be applied in understanding work and work life. It provides a way of considering these changes through the perspectives of the activities in workplaces that are directed towards the continuity of the work practice and those continuities that individual workers are attempting to secure through their engagement in work. These are at the heart of workplace participatory practices. These perspectives are elaborated in a study of the work, workplaces and continuity of three workers. It argues that the interdependency between the workplace and these workers plays out in particular ways given the negotiations between the two. Relationships between the continuity of the workplace, how support is afforded and discretion exercised and how individuals participate in, practice and learn, as discussed in Chapters 2 and 3 are elaborated in this account. The different bases for participation in work, as discussed in Chapter 6, are built upon and illustrated as are the changing requirements of work identified in Chapter 7. The framework for describing and analysing work that was developed in Chapters 8 and 9 is used as a platform for the gathering and analysis of data. In this way, much of what has been proposed in earlier chapters is illustrated in the analysis of changing work practice and changing work requirements, albeit through a study of three workers.

1.   ILLUMINATING THREE WORK PRACTICES

In order to trial and refine the framework of activities and interdependencies that were elaborated in the previous two chapters and understand the relationship between changing work and workers, a study was undertaken to elaborate the requirements of work and the workplace participatory practices that shape how individuals engage in work, how changes to that work occur and how individuals respond to those changes. As noted in Chapter 3, these participatory practices are central to the conduct and remaking of work and work practices.

The investigation comprised two interrelated sets of activities. In overview, the first mapped the requirements for three participants' work practice and the second investigated their workplace participatory practices. The first phase described the subjects' work, including their participatory practices. Three individuals were selected for participation in the project. The goal was to identify individuals who engaged in different kinds of work and work practice, including at least one who was a contingent worker (i.e. part-time, contractual or home-based), given the prevalence of this form of work participation as identified in Chapter 6. The participants were: (i) a trade union official; (ii) a grief counsellor at an institute of forensic pathology; and (iii) an information technology (IT) consultant to five primary schools. The work and work practices of each of the workers were quite distinct. The scheme of *Activities* and *Interdependencies* elaborated in the previous chapter are used to describe the three individuals' work practice period through interviews and observations over a six-month period. Direct observation of work and interviews were used over a period of nine months to describe the work practice. Data were gathered and analysed to understand: (i) the requirements for that work practice; (ii) how workplace change arose within the settings and the role of workers in that process; and (iii) the factors assisting or inhibiting participation in work and changing work practices. Tables 10.1 and 10.2 present the schedule of questions that were used in the first phase. This includes all the categories of activities and interdependencies that were identified in the previous two chapters. The categories for describing work have been augmented by the introduction of questions to elicit responses about those categories of work. So, data were gathered about the routineness of work, the discretion that is available to workers, the intensity of the work, the complexity and multiplicity of the work tasks, and the degree to which the knowledge to be learnt is opaque.

The final sets of data gathered relate to the homogeneity of the work to be conducted, the requirements for working with others and artefacts, the basis of engagement in work and the reciprocity of values between the worker and those of the workplace. In this way, the table provides a means to elicit data about work requirements that pertain to both the objective reality of work and also the subjective experience of work and work requirements.

The second phase comprised a six-month investigation of the workplace participatory practices of the three workers. Commencing, progress and sum-mative interviews with the participants were conducted throughout the six-month period, using sets of items designed to map the trajectories of both the work practice and the subjects' participation in their work practice. The interview schedule was used to guide the process of describing the individuals' work activities and participatory practices based on the dual concerns of workplace affordances and individuals' engagement. Initial interviews focused on gathering data about individual's personal history and career trajectory, and personal and professional goals. Then, interviews focused on changing work requirements and activities and processes of engagement in work through these changes. At each progress interview, data and tentative findings from previous interviews were presented to the subject to verify and elaborate specific issues or findings.

2.   WORK PRACTICE AND WORK REQUIREMENTS

The study illuminates and contrasts the three subjects' work practices, requirements for competent work practice and participatory practices. Overall, the analysis identifies and compares the requirements for their work, how they participated in work and the kinds of learning they secured through their work.

The first set of findings relates to workplace requirements that were identified and compared across the three workers using the scheme of activities and interdependencies outlined in Tables 10.1 and 10.2. This analysis is used to describe the work requirements of the three workers and also make comparisons across them. It is this analysis that is used throughout this chapter to identify both work requirements and participative practices and the relationships between two.

Table 10-1. Workplace activities

Activities within work practice can described in terms of their:	
Routineness—the degree to which work practice activities are routine or non-routine thereby requiring robust knowledge	Describe the range of activities you frequently engage in. Which of these are hardest to learn? Why? Describe activities that you engage in less frequently than monthly? Which of these are hardest to learn? Why? Describe any activities that you may be called to engage in but occur only in exceptional circumstances.
Discretion—the degree to which the scope of activities demands a broader or narrower range of decision-making and more or less autonomous practice.	How broad is the scope of decision-making in the workplace and its impact? What are the rules that determine who is permitted discretion?
Intensity—the degree to which the intensity of work tasks demand strategies for managing the work load and undertaking multiple tasks simultaneously	Describe some instances of where your work could be characterized as being intense. What are the attributes that permit you to manage these intense parts of your work?
Multiplicity—the range of activities expected to be undertaken as part of work practice	What is the range of tasks you are expected to conduct in this workplace? Who or what determines how these tasks are to be distributed?
Complexity—the degree to which work task decision-making is complicated by compounding variables and the requirement for negotiation among those variables	Using a recent workplace incident, indicate the complexity of your work and the range of variables that need to be considered in responding to that task. How did you learn to respond to those variables?
Accessibility (opaqueness of knowledge—the degree to which knowledge required for the work practice is either accessible or hidden.	What knowledge do you need to undertake your work that is hard to learn because it is not easy to access in the workplace? What would you be unable to learn by not being fully involved in the work practice

Table 10.2 Workplace interdependencies

Interdependencies within work practice are held to be describable under:	
Homogeneity—the degree to which tasks in the work practice are homogenous. Similarities may provide for greater support (modelling etc.) in development of the ability to perform	In what ways are the tasks in the workplace similar? How does the degree of homogeneity influence how you participate in the work practice?
Working with others (teams, clients)—the ways work activity is premised on interactions with others	In what ways is your workplace performance premised on interacting with other workers? On what bases do these interactions proceed or are inhibited?
Engagement—basis of employment	How is the distribution of work tasks and acknowledgement of performance determined? Employment basis (e.g. full-time, part-time, home worker, shift worker) Standing of the individual (e.g. personal competence, affiliations, membership of cliques etc.) Standing of work role (e.g. high status – low status work)
Status of employment—the standing of the work and whether it attracts support	
Access to participation—attributes that influence participation	
Reciprocity of values—the prospects for shared values	What directs your interest and motivation to perform particular workplace tasks? In what ways do you share the values and norms of the workplace/organization/work team?
Artefacts/external tools—physical artefacts used in work practice upon which performance is predicated	How do the physical environment, workplace tools and equipment shape your work activities? How do they influence your participation in the workplace?

Taking some examples as illustrative of these purposes indicates not only how the framework articulates the requirements of work, but also how these requirements vary across the three individuals' work practice. For instance, the 'routineness of work activities' is quite distinct across the three workers and describes particular qualities of their work. There is little that is routine in Anna's work. She is a project officer within a union. The work is often project based, focuses on emerging or strategic issues, and is often directed by deadlines that are not of the union's making. Much of Jim, the grief counsellor's work is, in contrast, quite routine. That is, contacting or being contacted by the next of kin and engaging in counselling procedures, and interacting with police and staff within the forensic pathology unit. However, although routine, his work is highly demanding and exposes him regularly to traumatic experiences that few would encounter more than once or twice if at all in their lives. So, from a person-dependence perspective, this work has many attributes that question the easy distinctions between routine and easy work. For Aden, the information technology consultant, much of his initial work was also quite routine. However, the routine tasks were performed across five schools with five sets of teachers and administrators to come to know and work with. So, in this way, the category of routineness means quite different things for these workers. The category of 'discretion' also reveals a capacity to understand the scope of discretion and how it is mani-fested in particular instances of work. For instance, Anna's work has high levels of discretion, with a very open-ended job specification that potentially offers far too much discretion in the form of an impossible workload. The category of 'working together' also is helpful in elaborating the requirements for work and contracts across these three workers. For instance, Anna's workplace uses collective and consensual decision making processes that demand the need for a case to be made for particular decisions and that case being discussed by and accepted by others in the workplace.

Given that work practice and fulfilling work requirements also comprise a subjective component, the responses to the reciprocity of values between the worker and the workplace are richly informing. As is elaborated in the discussion below, Anna is highly committed to the collective and social justice values of her work as a unionist, but perhaps less to the political party to which the union is sometimes aligned than a number of her colleagues. This issue pervades some of her workplace interactions and relations. Jim has a solid commitment to counselling particularly counselling that is conducted through a publicly funded agency, with no cost to those in need of it. So, there is a high level of congruence between his personal values and the practices being enacted in the workplace. Part of this arises from his capacity to transform the workplace to his preferred mode of counselling. Aden is comfortable in school environments, shares their values, and enjoys supporting teachers, administrators and students. However, this satisfaction does not constrain his ambitions for more challenging and corporate infor-mation technology work.

Thus, the categories of activities and interdependencies can be used to illustrate the complexity of contemporary work, describe and elaborate parti-cular work requirements, and be used to make comparisons across different kinds of work. The elaborations of these categories provide a way of under-standing and comparing what work performance actually warrants from these individuals. It also offers a basis for comparing different kinds of work, and how these categories of work requirements play out for individuals. That is, they can elaborate both the objective requirements for work and subjective experiences that comprises work.

3.   CONTINUITY OF WORK PRACTICE

The bases for the continuity of each work practice need to be elaborated to understand their goals and the premises for permitting and encouraging participation. The trade union exists to represent the industrial and professional interests of its members. To sustain itself, the union has to be positioned to address members' needs and also to advocate for the public sector and its members' professional standing in that sector. As government policies are central to shaping the public sector's employment practices, the union also seeks to influence government policy. The union is aligned to one major political party (Labor). However, this affiliation is complicated when the party is elected into government and becomes the employer of the majority of the unions' members. This affiliation brings additional internal complications for the union as some of its officers are also affiliated to the party. So there are complex relations between the industrial and professional concerns of its membership and the union's political affiliations. As the union's industry sector is responsive to and services the community, it is also important to be positioned in key debates and discussions about the sector. In addition, the union plays a role in supporting and promoting employee unionism.

Given its focus on working with external agencies and negotiating key agreements, the expertise required within the union is premised on the ability to conduct complex negotiations in industrial commissions, with employers, with governments, and in professional forums. The loss of three senior staff in the months leading up to and during the time in which the investigation occurred tested the capacity of the union to function effectively and strategically. With the departure of these staff, internal contestation, which is so common to workplaces, intensified. Yet as collaborative decision-making is a feature of the workplace, this contestation manifested itself in the actions and power of particular cliques. This meant that positioning for and support of individuals and their participation in the workplace became more complex and demanding. For instance, a campaign to raise community awareness about the role of the union members work and members' workloads was proposed by Anna (our informant) as a highly strategic move. However, this proposal was undermined by colleagues through affiliation support, rather than on its merits. So the changing workplace environment, including the interests of particular cohorts, shapes how Anna is permitted to participate in the workplace.

The forensic pathology centre, where Jim works as a counsellor, has quite different bases for its continuity. The coronial autopsies the centre performs are a legislated requirement. This means the work it conducts is not under direct threat unless the legislation under which they occur is revoked. As long as the state wants coronial autopsies, this work will need to be done. Nevertheless, like any other government body, the centre needs to be seen to be performing effectively to maintain its current level of funding and to secure growth funding (e.g. for an adequate provision of counsellors). However, there are emerging threats to the centre's continuity in the form of potential privatisation of the forensic pathology function and also the issue of malpractice in other centres. In a climate of outsourcing and cost-cutting, the possibility of privatising the centre's functions has been canvassed. Another threat to the continuity of the workplace has arisen from earlier practices in other institutes of forensic pathology involving the unauthorised access to body parts and their retention without consent. This issue, and non-consented retention of human tissue in hospitals, raised widespread concerns in the community, upon which governments in a number of Australian states as well as those overseas have acted.

The centre's recently established counselling section plays an important role in addressing matters associated with the identification of the deceased, processes associated with gathering coronial evidence and assisting those who are grieving as a result of a relative's traumatic death. Although not explicitly intended, the counselling service also plays an important role in managing client relations externally. For instance, the counsellors took the lead role in responding to governmental inquiries and community concerns about the retention of human tissue for coronial and scientific purposes. Internally, along with an institutional ethics committee, the counsellors' work to make scientific staff aware of the need to consider their respon-siveness to changing community expectations. This situation has resulted in the counsellors being afforded autonomy to practise. However, if these practices threaten to disrupt other interests in the workplace, the relations that permit that autonomy could be transformed.

The five state-funded primary schools, in which the information technology consultant (Aden) works one day each a week, play an ongoing role in the community, educating young children. Like other public institutions, the schools have been subject to changes in their work goals and activities. These changes include the requirement for each school to adopt wider administrative responsibilities and be responsive to innovative practices, such as the use of information technology (IT) for both administrative and educational purposes. Responsiveness to departmental initiatives, such as the use of information technology, has become an important performance measure for these schools. As primary school staff lacked appropriate computing expertise, the five schools collectively employed Aden to provide these services. Much of Aden's initial work was to assist teachers with routine breakdown and maintenance tasks. So, early in his employment at these schools, his tenure as a casual employee was dependent upon working effectively with teachers and their approval of the quality of his assistance with technology for educational purposes.

However, departmental directives about the implementation of the Standard Operating System (SOS) caused a change in the schools' priorities. As an effectively functioning IT administrative system became a key departmental goal, there was a reduced emphasis on IT support for educational purposes. The requirement for the establishment and maintenance of this system took precedence over providing IT support for teachers in the schools. In this way, the continuity of the schools is premised, in part, on being responsive to meet departmental requirements for the use of technology in schools for teaching and administrative purposes.

In these ways, the complex of work activities and interactions directed towards the continuity of the workplace go beyond the mere exercise of workplace activities, as they extend to interactions and the activities of those engaged in work and how they elect to participate. Indeed, in order to understand how work changes and is remade, it is necessary to identify the bases on which individuals engage in the workplace, that is, what motivates and drives their work practices including new practices.

4. CONTINUITY OF INDIVIDUALS' PRACTICE

Anna's reasons for working in the union are highly consonant with the union's goals and bases of its continuity. She has a deep and long-founded concern with equity and social justice and comes from a family with a tradition of public service, so she enjoys a high level of relatedness with most, but not all, of the work practice's core values. An exception is her growing disaffection with party politics and the union's associations with the Labor party of which she was once, but is no longer, an active member. Her concerns about being closely affiliated with one political party are not shared by many of her colleagues, some of whom are active members of that party's factions. In a work practice where factional support and numbers can be very potent in the decision making process, this complicates her standing in her workplace, as she is unaffiliated. Also, some union officials are interested in being pre-selected for winnable seats in the legislative assembly through their affiliation to the Labor Party. Therefore, their relationships and loyalties are at times ambiguous and different from those of Anna's. Her concerns about the union's close association with the party complicate her interactions with others in her workplace, because of divergent premises for the continuity of career paths and personal beliefs. Also, given her strong professional and social justice interests (and now disaffection with party politics), her commitment to some of her colleagues' values is further challenged, when factional politics are used for what she perceives to be short-term pragmatic and selective goals.

Nevertheless, Anna is skilled in developing and arguing her case through the union's systems of decision-making forums. Her capacities to read, write and effectively present cases are well aligned to the procedures for advancing policies in the union. Through her position, she is able to exercise her interests in social justice issues and commitment to the public sector. Given the high level of congruence between Anna's personal values and subjectivities, and the union's goals for its existence and continuity, it is not surprising that she has not looked elsewhere for work.

Yet, she commented that the breakdown of personal relations in the workplace would be the cause for her to consider looking elsewhere. More than the volume, intensity and complexity of her work, the deterioration of workplace relations (i.e. its affordances) presents the key threat to the continuity to her vocational practice. For instance, she refers to the frustrations about not getting enough support for a campaign to raise public awareness about members' work conditions. Having stated that it is not so much about being undermined, she continued, "It's not a personal investment in it. It's the fact that … if you listen to any of the organisers and just how bad it is out there and it's the fact that we have an obligation, that's what we're here for. We have an obligation to do something for our members."

So here the tension between Anna's own vocational concerns and directions and how these are frustrated by workplace factors that may inhibit the realization of responses to address these concerns. She is also concerned that other staff associated with her may become subjected to workplace contestation through that affiliation. Anna works closely with some junior staff whom she believes make significant contributions and will do more so in the future as they grow in expertise. However, she believes that in the—at times—intensely contested work environment, these newer workers may be targeted or marginalised because of their associations with her. In terms of her participatory practice, the work pressure and the shifts in affiliations have meant Anna has to "make more of an effort to contribute more". Despite her growing workload outside the union workplace and her need to address key policy matters, she needs to maintain her standing and engage closely within the workplace. This has required her to direct energy and time to engage more fully in the on-going negotiations in the workplace to maintain her standing.

Jim, the grief counsellor, is engaged in work he is well prepared for, experienced in and finds interesting, challenging and, at times, rewarding. His interest in working directly with clients and providing a public (free) service is central to his beliefs about grief counselling. He has a strong commitment to the public provision of counselling services and the obligation for government to fulfill its social obligations. He studied and engaged in social work after several different kinds of employment that followed the completion of his undergraduate degree. Nevertheless, despite his commitment, he remains skeptical about it and adopts a critical attitude towards his counselling practice. He claims to be open to questioning its processes and values.

These qualities contrast with the professional medico-scientific values and discourses that are the most influential in the forensic pathology centre. At the commencement of the project, Jim was a casual employee. However, during the period of the project, he secured a newly created permanent position. This permanency permitted him to enact goals for realising a mode of counselling that is more consonant with his personal and professional beliefs. This included extending the counselling service to include more face-to-face grief counselling and to a wider clientele. In essence, he has transformed the counselling practice through his agency and work. In considering the (as yet remote) prospect of privatisation, Jim is adamant that he would not work as a counsellor for a private company because this is inconsistent with his values about public practice. He suggests that continuity of his practice would be so constrained by such developments as to make it very difficult for him to continue his practice under those circumstances.

For Aden, the schools in which he works are familiar environments. His parents both work in primary education (as a principal and teacher). Most of his life, he has been involved in family discussions about and lived in close physical proximity to primary schools. His interest in and competence with computers and information technology arose initially through having access to a computer at home. While still at school, he undertook a period of work experience that permitted him to extend and demonstrate his computing competence. His academic performance at school was not strong. After he left school his father encouraged his interest in computing through a course in a vocational college. His father advised him of the widespread use of computers in schools and potential growth of employment in this field. His mother secured his first job in a nearby school, which subsequently led to employment in four others.

Initially, he viewed this kind of employment as paid work experience, but it has since grown to full-time employment. Aden remains concerned that working in schools as a consultant will exclude him from more interesting, prestigious and highly remunerated work in the corporate world. Yet, his current work suits his familiarity with primary schools and presents an environment in which he is comfortable and effective. So although quite content with the work in schools, he could be tempted by an offer from elsewhere, but is not actively seeking such opportunities.

However, in later interviews, for reasons elaborated above, he states that his work is now a 'proper job'. It has transformed from being a casual appointment into one that is central to the maintenance of the schools' information system. His job has now been classified within the education system (i.e. a Technology Officer), is included in staff phone listings and he now has his superannuation paid for by the department. Therefore, although still a contingent worker, the workplace has come to invite his participation and involvement more strongly because it needed his expertise. However, these workplace changes and elevation in status and conditions are quite consistent with his personal goals.

The three individuals' working life directions and how they engage and confront change in work requirements and participate in work are linked with their subjectivities. They are also engaged in remaking their work. There were some identifiable bases associated with individual subjectivity that shaped their participation in work activities, and directed their energy and agency in their learning and the remaking of their work practice. Whereas Anna had never sought out alternative employment, and Jim would not consider working for a private sector company in a counselling role, Aden could be tempted by an offer to engage in the kind of corporate work he cherishes, however he's not looking. In order to illuminate the reciprocal process that were elaborated in Chapter 3 and are being enacted through the three subjects' participation in work, and their responses to changes, comparisons across their practices are now elaborated to reveal the diversity and transformative qualities.

5.   WORKPLACE PARTICIPATORY PRACTICES

Instances of diverse kinds of participatory practices were identified from the three informants' data and through observations of their workplaces. These practices had consequences for the conduct of their work and also the work of others.

In the highly demarcated professional work environment of a forensic pathology centre, the counsellor was permitted to exercise considerable discretion in his work activities, without the need to consult or seek permission, because his professional practice afforded him this opportunity. The centre has a number of work areas where quite distinct forms of work are conducted (e.g. dissection rooms where the pathologists and mortuary attendants work, laboratories where scientific testing and analysis are undertaken, storage areas for cadavers and others for samples, counselling facilities, police facilities for investigation and administrative purposes). Functionally, the workplace is characterised by distinct divisions of labour premised on particular specialist forms of knowledge. Professional autonomy is prized and accepted in this workplace. Staff designated as professionals enjoy discretion within their demarcated area of work. However, the administrative staff and mortuary attendants are not granted the same levels of discretion. Given the relative standing of counselling work, Jim was able to control and direct his work. Much of his work might be described as routine (e.g. only the conduct of a few standard functions—identification of cadavers, counselling, assisting with coronial processes). Yet, given the emotionally demanding and distinct character of each event, its requirements go beyond the mere repetition of frequently performed tasks. It also involves his interacting with other staff in order to perform his work functions. This includes the mortuary attendants who provide information and make the cadavers ready for viewing and the pathologists. They also assist police in interviewing the next of kin or relatives about the deceased. Yet, despite this discretion, there is little boundary crossing because the work functions are so discrete and demarcated. One incident of boundary crossing did occur. Two groups of the mortuary staff sought Jim's advice about a workplace grievance against each other. Jim advised them, even though this was not part of his job description. Later, it came to the attention of a workplace counsellor who objected to Jim's intercession.

The union officer's workplace is more homogenous in terms of activities undertaken, but it is characterised by complex workplace decision-making premised on negotiations, collaborations and consultations. Consensual and collective processes of workplace decision-making are used. However, as noted, there are also cliques and affiliations that sometimes use these negotiations to secure their positions or interests. Hence, unlike Jim's, Anna's standing and capacity to make decisions are constrained by tightly interrelated and constantly renegotiated workplace relations and affiliations as well as decision-making processes that are open to contestation. Although her work encompasses a broad range of tasks and discretion, ultimately her authority is limited by the executive role of the union Secretary's position. So, while Anna enjoys wide discretion in her work, she is denied a commensurate level of authority. This authority is embedded in negotiated and consensual arrangements, at one level, and highly centralised executive authority of the union Secretary, at another. In these ways, Anna's capacity to take relatively unilateral actions is quite distinct from Jim's.

The work requirements of Aden, the IT consultant, are constructed through the interactions with the five schools he serves weekly. As a contingent worker, he has been required to maintain positive working relationships with administrators and teachers in the five schools. However, over the duration of the project, the focus and standing of his work changed, which transformed the basis upon which his tenure was premised. As the five schools converted to a departmentally mandated standard system of computer operation and interface, his work became more focussed on setting up and maintaining that system. As the implementation of this system became a key strategic goal for the schools, it also became the source of Aden's tenure. He became less dependent upon maintaining his tenure through teachers' appraisal of his performance and more focussed on his capacity to establish and maintain the SOS in the school. As the goals have changed, so too have the participatory practices and range of tasks he participates in.

Differences in and transformations of these participatory practices are explainable by changes in the requirements for work performance and also those brought about by individuals' agencies. Over the duration of the project, each participant was afforded the opportunity to exercise and extend his or her vocation in different ways. However, there were different bases by which they are able to exercise their participation. Over the duration of this study, both Jim and Aden experienced expansion in their affordances that permitted them to extend the scope of their practice and their discretion within those practices. Anna, on the other hand, although enjoying wide discretion, did not experience an extension of her practices. Instead, she felt the need to give extra time to manage workplace relations, despite her growing workload. That is, the workplace became less invitational. Taking account of the changes in work requirements and participatory practices is necessary to help understand participation and learning through work.

So, here illustrative examples of the changing character of workplace performance requirements and the relations that constitute them are provided. To explicitly capture and illuminate their dynamic qualities and identify consequences for participation in and learning through work these changes can be understood through consideration of both the social suggestion that is encountered in the workplace and individuals' engagement with that suggestion: the interplay between affordances and engagement that constitute workplace participatory practices (Billett, 2002a).

The next section attempts to map changes arising from each of the three participants' workplace participatory practices. This is achieved using instances of change in each of their practices.

6.   CHANGES TO WORK AND PARTICIPATION

Over the six-month period that comprised the duration of the investigation, each of the three subjects' work changed. In each instance, there were changes in the workplace's participatory practices. There is evidence of changes in the complex interactions between the affordances of the workplace and individuals' agentic actions, albeit marked by different degrees of contribution of one or the other. These are intended as a way of representing the interrelationships between the two trajectories. Key changes and consequences for others are also evident in these relations.

On gaining permanency of employment, Jim transformed the conduct of the counselling practice to be more aligned with his values and beliefs about counselling. The counselling practice was transformed by the introduction of more face-to-face counselling, thereby reflecting Jim's preferences and goals. Yet, the introduction of this approach to grief counselling brought about change to others' work practice. Administrative staff had to learn to handle tasks previously undertaken by the grief counsellors (e.g. initial contacts with clients). because the counsellors were no longer available to take calls—they were in counselling sessions with grieving next of kin. These staff often found it difficult and distressing to be the first point of contact with recently bereaved clients. Sometimes the staff responded inappropriately through an (understandable) inclination to want to assist a distressed person on the telephone. This required Jim to explain to them the procedures for making this contact and of his commitments to return the clients' call as soon as possible. He also had to discuss and make more transparent his appointment schedule so that administrative staff could advise clients about his availability. In addition, Jim had to spend time with these staff as well as others for whom interdependencies are essential. In these ways, he made his own and their work practice.

There were other changes arising for workers as a consequence to engage in more face-to-face counselling. Firstly, there was an increased presence of grieving clients in the workplace. This meant that other workers had to behave appropriately in their presence. In the mortuary, humour is deployed as a strategy to manage the demands of what is often gruesome and confronting work. Yet, the presence of grieving relatives requires sensitivity in the timing and volume of humour, thereby having an impact upon how mortuary attendants conduct their work practice. Secondly, Jim routinely advised his clients of their right to appeal the conduct of a post-mortem on their next of kin. This could lead to an increased incidence of appeals with consequences for others' work (e.g. forensic pathologists). He believed these changes were about performing counselling in a way consistent with his values and previous successful practice. Although aware of the consequences for other staff, Jim was quite unapologetic about the consequences of his changed practice, a result of his strong commitment to and beliefs about counselling, including the rights of his clients and his obligations to those clients.

Building relations with teachers and gaining their confidence were initially important for Aden's work and his standing in the five schools. However, later, when he was given a more strategic role in each of the five schools, his relations with the teachers changed. Both his participation and engagement changed, as did his status. His line of accountability shifted from the teachers to the administration and his task became directly aligned to assisting the school's new strategic direction. There was something of a parallel path and accommodation between the trajectories of the workplace and Aden's professional path. The schools' need for the administrative system and Aden's need for more 'corporate work' reflect reciprocity and mutuality at this point in time.

The intensity and direction of work, periods of absence to participate in an election campaign and changing workplace relations have required Anna to interact and communicate more in the workplace. Her critique of the existing industrial processes has led to intense interactions with some colleagues and she has had to direct additional effort to workplace political processes. Given the collective and negotiated bases for decision-making in this workplace, processes of engagement and interaction are important. Anna has argued that the current industrial processes are unable to address many issues associated with the status and conditions of their members. Consequently, she has proposed a broader campaign to raise awareness in the wider community about the conditions of these public sector workers and how successive government policies are eroding the crucial public service provided by these workers. Through such a process she hopes to secure broader goals for the membership. However, some colleagues see this approach as being extra-industrial and marginalising the industrial processes in which their expertise and standing resides. This dissonance has led to periods of intense debate within her workplace. With the recent loss of supportive colleagues, Anna is concerned about her capacity to realise these changes to practice. Over the duration of the study, the direction of the union's pathway to continuity seemed to shift away from where Anna's goals reside.

So, there are dynamic qualities to workplace activities and participatory practices evident across these three workplaces. Jim is able to exercise agency, while the changes to his practice and that of the counselling service have become closely aligned. Aden's bases of accountability and continuity have changed and firmed as well. He has clear goals and lines of authority, and his vocational interests and the requirements of the workplace have become more aligned. Anna's participation continues to develop as staff change and affiliations of interest transform in her workplace. This evidence of associations between changes in work and participatory practices illustrates the dynamic social ecology of workplaces and what shapes engagement, participation and learning.

6.1   Learning and remaking of practice

As proposed in Chapter 3, there is little or no separation between engagement in work activities and between ongoing processes of learning through work and the remaking of work practices. Some changes merely reinforce, while others refine and some extend knowledge and transform practice. Through their engagement in work activities and how they engage in these activities associations with learning for the three subjects can be identified. These opportunities were shaped by the reciprocal participatory practices.

Through introducing his preferred face-to-face counselling, Jim remade the work practices within this workplace. Moreover, he learnt more about the probable client base he will encounter in this workplace. For instance, he has fewer Muslim, but more indigenous clients in this work setting than in his previous position. The latter typically do not want counselling, being primarily concerned with the prompt return of the deceased. So his practice is being refined through his day-to-day work. He also had a positive professional experience with counselling next of kin after an aeroplane crash. This was in contrast to his earlier involvement with on-scene counselling in other disasters, which he concluded had not been effective. This earlier experience had provided the opportunity for him to reflect upon that incident and identify ways in which such interventions could be helpful (i.e. being able to quickly access next of kin, collaborative working relations with police). Jim's consideration of procedures associated with an anthrax scare that was a global concern during the period of the research had extended his consideration of counselling at the centre and how they would handle interactions with next of kin and the management of mass fatalities. So, as his learning increased, he was able to contribute to the remaking of the work practice that included more intimate interactions with the community it serves, and being prepared for the counsellor's role in the event of mass chemical warfare and potential terrorists attack.

For Anna, there was evidence of significant new learning in the refinement and elaboration of earlier concerns about how her members' interests were being addressed through industrial processes. It comprised a process of remaking practice through negotiating new workplace participatory practices with the change in existing staff. This learning was consolidated through the opportunity to prepare papers on these issues for workplace meetings. She has also learnt new knowledge from her participation in a committee that manages retirement funds for employees in the industry sector. Although she has worked hard to understand the complexities of appropriately managing these funds, Anna still feels a novice who does not fully understand the consequences of the decisions she makes. However, one of the roles of the fund's board is to act as a custodian for disputed cases, such as those occurring between competing kinsfolk in the case of an unexpected death. Here, she has found herself able to make a significant contribution, building on the kinds of well-developed advocacy skills she possesses. So she learnt new knowledge, reinforced other knowledge and learnt to apply her advocacy skills in another context.

Aden's work provided learning opportunities mainly in the form of reinforcing how he goes about troubleshooting in the schools and in remaking the work practices within schools. Week in and week out, he was faced with similar tasks and problems, which assist his capacity to be effective in responding to these. His own knowledge has evolved, as he is using strategies to efficiently address many of the routine tasks required to be performed in IT assistance. Aden's opportunity for new learning arose from the need to learn how to implement the SOS. This required attendance at a workshop and interactions with staff whose responsibility it was to implement this system. In learning about this system, Aden's role in the schools was more firmly established.

New activities for all three participants (e.g. involvement in an on-scene disaster response, involvement in decision making about retirement funds, implementing the SOS) reportedly led to significant new learning and constituted the remaking of work practices. These opportunities arose from events that were structured by workplace practices. They were not ad hoc or incidental; they were central to the workplace's practice and were afforded by workplace circumstances. Along the way, each of the three subjects elaborated on and refined their knowledge about work through engagement in everyday work activities.

Learning and the remaking of practice arising from changes in workplace tasks provided different bases for participation. Aden developed valued expertise possessed by nobody else in the schools; Jim exercised his preferred mode of conducting his practice; and Anna was able to position the debate (direction) of the union by questioning some of its key emphases. Central to the learning was the relationship between what was afforded by the workplace and how the three individuals selectively engaged in ways that sought to address their interests and vocational direction. At the same time the work practices changed through this period.

7. CHANGING WORK PRACTICE AND WORK REQUIREMENTS

The data presented and discussed here are used to illuminate how work-places' micro-social practices reciprocally shape participation and learning in work and the remaking of work practices. These findings elaborated the contention that participation and learning are premised on deliberate individual and situational intentions. This intentionality arises from the kinds of micro-social processes identified in Chapters 2 and 3. Corresponding with the intentionality of the workplace (i.e. its affordances) are individuals' decisions about how they elect to engage in the workplaces. For example, the decision of a grief counsellor to conduct face-to-face, rather than phone-based, grief counselling was a product of his earlier practice. This decision transformed and remade both the counselling work and the work of administrative staff and mortuary attendants. Significantly, the counsellor's change in work practice coincided with his movement from temporary to permanent employment, indicating the potential provided by different forms of workplace participation as discussed in Chapter 6. So, this change in practice was premised on a complex of factors comprising the enactment of the individuals' agency, buttressed by the capacity for relative autonomous practice that arose from employment status (i.e. a workplace affordance), yet which was not afforded to other workers. In all, this single change transformed work practices, bases of participation and requirements for performance (as discussed in Chapters 7 and 8). This example of workplace participatory practices illustrates how opportunities for change, learning and development are distributed across the workplace. For instance, workers with less discretion (e.g. the mortuary and administrative staff) may be subject to the changes of others and not be able to intentionally transform their participatory practices and learning, as others in that workplace were able. So, just as the teachers in the schools experienced a reduced level of technical support when the schools' priorities for information technology changed, the administration in the forensic pathology centre had to learn to accommodate Jim's changed schedule. These examples indicate different bases for the remaking and continuity of the practice as exercised through participatory practices, as outlines in Chapters 2 and 3.

In all three cases, there was evidence of the exercise of individuals' agency in shaping the organisation of their work. This agency was associated with their preferences, beliefs and values—the participants' subjectivities and identities, and how they viewed themselves in relation to the workplace's activities and tasks. The exercise of personal agency varied over time and circumstances, and more so for some of the participants than others. In these ways, the study illustrates just some of the complexity of the inter-psychological processes occurring through work and the micro-social processes that support their learning. Given that micro-social practices play such a salient role in this analysis, it is timely to consider afresh the social ecology of workplaces including the agency of individuals in their engagement and negotiation with the social world. As in Somerville and Bernoth's (2001) study, individuals' subjectivity provides an explanatory principle for the direction and shaping of individuals' agency. This agency was most exercised when there were threats to their subjectivity and identity, brought about by changes in the workplace or where the individual had the opportunity to exercise their agency.

Through using a framework that offers a comprehensive account of both the enactment of the social suggestion that comprises workplace affordances and individuals' subjective account of work the experience of work, it's enactment and remaking can be apprehended.

Chapter 11

WORK, LEARNING AND IDENTITY

The final chapter revisits and synthesises the key premises and propositions raised in this book and rehearses the case for a relational consideration of what constitutes work, learning and work identity. This relational basis comprises the associations between the historically and culturally derived and situationally manifested objective basis of what constitutes work, on the one hand, and a personally subjective view of what constitutes work, worthwhile work and individuals' engagement in work, on the other. Without such a basis of understanding how individuals might best engage in work, progress through working life and develop, sustain and transform their work identities, considerations of work will likely remain captive to views premised in either the social or individual contribution not in the complex of relational interdependence between the two. It is through consideration of these relationships that a more comprehensive view of individuals' work and their working life can be sustained, and the process of remaking work as well as lifelong learning can be understood more fully. The chapter concludes with some considerations for maintaining competence throughout working life

1. KEY PREMISES AND PROPOSITIONS

The key premises and propositions advanced in this book are that work and working life are changing, and are likely to change in the future. Moreover, there are impacts in terms of the kinds of work that are available, how people participate in work, who is participating in work and what kind of capacities are required for effective workplace practice. However, the impacts of these changes will be experienced in different ways across countries, industries, locations, cohorts of workers and individuals within all of the proceeding. It is important to understand the variations of these impacts and the factors that underpin them to appraise the kinds and sources of these impacts. It is suggested that principally there are both social and individual factors that play out in different degrees and with different levels of potency across the differences in both change and impacts of change. Therefore, more than understanding the social experience or institutional facts that shape working life, it is necessary to consider individual, albeit socially derived construals and constructions of what is experienced within working life and how, then, individuals engage with working life. Central to the process is the negotiation between individual and social contributions. It is the relational nature of these contributions and negotiations that occur as individuals engage in work, make strategic decisions, decide how do exercise their intentionality and agency that is central to the conception of working life.

1.1   Work and working life is changing

There are widely held views that there have been and continue to be considerable changes in the kinds of work available, how it is practised and who engages in that work. Moreover, the capacities required for effective workplace performance are different from an earlier time and are likely to continue to change in the future. This suggests that while the actual capacities or knowledge required for individuals to engage in work is changing (i.e. the act of paid work), so are other dimensions of engaging in work activities and working life more broadly. A common claim is that a continuous and logically coherent working life is now less available, thereby making continuity of work skills and identity problematic. Many new jobs are held to be contingent—fixed term and part-time (Carnoy, 1999), making working life insecure and insufficient, both financially and personally. Beyond the unpredictability of what constitutes many contemporary paid work tasks is the claim that the kinds of work we engage in are increasingly subject to change, and will do so increasingly frequently within individuals' working lives. It is often popularly claimed that individuals will need to engage in multiple careers and will be required to reinvent their occupational identity a number of times throughout their working lives. This claim will be more or less true for some workers than for others. Some will be in forms of work that are less subject to change, while for others changes throughout working life will comprise the incremental transformation of their work. Nevertheless, all this fuels the notion that paid work which provides adequate and consistent remuneration, personal fulfilment, and pathways to self-identity and sense of self is becoming less likely, and that jobs which are both secure and well regarded are becoming less available (Bauman, 1998). Yet, because such claims are premised in theoretical accounts rather than empirical work they warrant further analysis. Consequently, the attempt here is to engage in discussion about these kinds of assumptions and premises.

1.2   Impact of changing work

Certainly, it seems that for some, perhaps many, cohorts of workers and individuals the predictions about work becoming less secure, attractive and worthwhile are upheld. That is, the changing availability of employment in particular occupations, the means of working across a range of occupations and the requirements for effective work performance are changing in particular ways. Yet, this impact is partial, selective and relational. Particular kinds of occupations are more prone to be shifted from one location to another, even across national boundaries. For instance, those working in occupations which require highly specialised or face-to-face encounters (e.g. doctors, nurses, accountants, electricians, builders) are less likely to be exported elsewhere and overseas than those occupations that can be relocated, particularly to lower cost locales. Technological innovations have had a greater impact upon some occupations than others. For instance, managerial, professional and technical occupations have generally thrived with the advent of electronic forms of information processing and communication. Also, some of those that are premised on face-to-face interactions seem to be stable. However, administrative and process workers are more prone to be disadvantaged by such arrangements, because some of their jobs are able to be exported. So, while all forms of work have likely being influenced by these kinds of changes, the distribution of both positive and negative impacts has not been equal.

For instance, it seems that the major occupations (i.e. medicine, law, accountancy), which have long enjoyed high status and high benefits, are of the kind that are least likely to be affected by the negative impacts of these changes. Conversely, the less educated, those without skills that are privileged, or those engaged in work which cannot easily be rationalised, exported or restructured and which are not well regarded in the community will likely have suffered the most. Yet, the impacts of these changes are also relative. That is, they play out in particular ways for particular groups of individuals and individuals themselves. While acknowledging that the material circumstances comprising the working lives of many workers remain unsatisfactory, turbulent and poorly remunerated, it would be wrong to concur with those proposing that changes to work are inevitably disempowering and unhelpful to those employed in work. Mediating such a judgement is that not all changes are inevitably disempowering and unhelpful to individuals (Billett and Pavlova 2005), but also that individuals' perception cannot be comprehended through dis-embodied analyses of the changing character of work. Instead, what these changes mean to individuals is central to how they can be classified as either liberating or disempowering, de-professionalising or opening up new opportunities, transformative or just about inevitable change.

Part of the questioning of such assumptions is to suggest that change in the kinds of work available and how that work is undertaken and by whom has always occurred. Moreover with paid work being a product of changing cultural needs, it will continue to be subject to constant change. As well, those forms of changes that are not inherently intended to disempower, might yet be orchestrated and organised to do so. Yet, even then, the extent to which change impacts upon individuals is subject to their previous experiences and expectations.

Yet, rather than viewing changes to work as being inherently against the personal interest and destabilising, the impact of these changes can be seen as dependent upon:

- individuals' construal and construction of these changes;
- their readiness for and capacity to change;
- their needs to engage in paid work;
- the scope of the changes required; and
- the degree to which they are supported in making those changes.

Also, beyond these changes are others associated with the overall impact of the changing:

- availability of particular occupations;
- ways of working;
- compositions of workforces; and
- requirements for work performance.

Consequently, given the important personal dimension, as discussed throughout this book, there is a need to understand work not only from the perspective of its material components and benefits but also from the perspective of those engaged in work. That is, work and working life are enacted by individuals who have particular bases by which they come to value their work, working life and its benefits for them. This is also important to understand the role that individuals have in both their own learning and the remaking of the work and work practices in which the engage. While being cautious not to over emphasise positive accounts of change and personal empowerment, such as those encountered in empirical work (Billett et al., 2004; Billett and Somerville, 2004; Billett and Pavlova, 2005; Billett et al., 2005), there is evidence that individuals are able to negotiate change in work and work lives in ways that meet their needs. Moreover, this perspective also permits consideration of those for whom work has not led to positive outcomes. Further, in considering individuals' negotiations with work and working life it is necessary to go beyond simple accommodations to changing workplace norms and practices. Instead, it constitutes their ability to exercise their agency and intentionality in constructing work lives that are personally meaningful for them. This exercise of personal agency warrants greater attention because work is important to individuals in different ways (Pusey, 2003). That is, more than trading time and labour for remuneration, work also has important individual, personal and social salience for those who engage in it.

This view is not to deny the important role of social institutions (e.g. governments, workplaces) and cultural practices (e.g. the privileging of kinds of work, and their standing), but to acknowledge and emphasise:

1. the centrality of the individuals who conduct the work in consideration of work life (and its salience to their sense of self and identity) and
2. their role in negotiating with social forms and press (i.e. those of social institutions and practices).

1.3   Negotiations and the remaking of work and working life

As proposed throughout this book, the negotiation between individuals and the social world is essential for and central to the evolution of work and working life. Through that negotiation, not only do individuals learn, but they also are engaged in the ongoing process of remaking work practices and working life. Without this active engagement, individuals would not continue to learn the requirement needed for evolving work practice. Consequently, the ongoing process of remaking work, work, work activities and work life would remain moribund and unfulfilled without the engagement of individuals in the active process of remaking these practices. It their engagement at particular points in time, in particular circumstances and in response to the factors that constitute the situation in which they are engaged with and are responding to that leads to the evolution of the practices of work. Instead, the necessary and ongoing processes of individuals making sense of and construing and constructing their everyday work experiences necessarily passes them into the active process of remaking and transforming work and work practices. However, these processes of learning and remaking work practice, while inevitable and necessary, need to be understood as the relational engagement of two sets of concerns: the agency of the social world and the agency of individuals both alone and collectively. It is the working through of how these two sets of sometimes conflicting interests plays out which shapes how work and working life progresses. This negotiation does not of itself guarantee a 'better' working life or better ways of working.

Instead, it reflects the logic of relational negotiations between social forms and practices and individuals' engagement with those practices.

Moreover, these negotiations are likely to be quite diverse and un-predictable. This is because, firstly, work practices themselves are highly diverse in terms of their performance requirements, norms and practices. Secondly, individuals who comprise workers, even when categorised in particular ways (e.g. professionals, low skilled, women, disabled etc.) are heterogeneous, rather than homogeneous in terms of their readiness, needs and desires. Thirdly, the scope, direction and intensity of the negotiations between individuals and workplaces will be as diverse as that range of factors that contributes to them. So, while theorists offering general descriptions about how social circumstances play out for workers per se or cohorts of workers are useful, they offer a level of analysis which requires further differentiation and elaboration in order to understand individuals' experience of working life more comprehensively and effectively.

2.   SOCIAL AND INDIVIDUAL CONTRIBUTIONS TO KNOWING AND KNOWLEDGE

The ideas above can be both understood and elaborated within theoretical conceptions associated with the social origins of the knowledge required for and deployed when engaging in work and its construction by those individuals who engage with it. In Chapter 2, some attention is given to the social geneses of working knowledge and its transformation. It is proposed that there are historical, cultural and situational contributions to that knowledge that exist as institutional facts. That is, they are generated by human endeavour and cannot be wished away, to use Searle's (1995) term. However, as is elaborated in Chapter 2, the situational contributions include the actions and agency of individuals who comprise the situation. It is through their engagement that not only does the work practice change but so do the individuals. Just as situations such as workplaces need to account for the individuals participating in them, the legacies of individuals' engagement likely include situational contributions. This interdependency is elaborated in Chapter 3, which also argues for bringing individuals once more to centre stage. Rather than weakening the social and cultural account of human development and activities, it is claimed that only through understanding the unique set of social experiences that individuals encounter and the diverse social legacies arising from those experiences will be the range and extent of contributions of the social world be fully understood. That is, rather than seeing individuals as asocial, they represent the epitome of the social.

Nevertheless, work and working life cannot be satisfactorily explained by accounts which refer only to objective measures and impacts of what constitutes work and working life. Instead, it is necessary to understand how individuals construe and construct what they experience in their working life. Moreover, individuals' engagement is central to their learning about work and how to stay effective in the workplace as well as the making, remaking and transformation of their work. What is important is to articulate not only the interdependence between humans and the social world, but also the relational bases of that interdependence because of its situational and personal dualities.

2.1   Relational accounts of work

This relational way of considering work is exemplified in considerations of the worth of work (Chapter 4). Much of the literature on the worth of work focuses on its societal value and objective features and benefits. This is of course important. The standing of particular occupations does much to justify the price the community pays for those occupations and the demands for being committed to practice those occupations. At a more general level, the kinds of benefits which accrue from particular kinds of and means of comparing those benefits against different kinds of work are useful to consider and to contest premises about levels of remuneration and other benefits. Certainly, there are well-established hierarchies associated with certain occupations and members of different kinds of occupations. These have acquired particular levels of expectations and rewards, regardless of whether these are warranted through a considered analysis of what comprises their work practice and its importance to the community. Yet beyond these broader societal perspectives, there are the purposes and needs of individuals who engage in work. These likely have greater significance to individuals than is represented in current accounts of the worth of work. If only those engaged in all work at the top of the hierarchies were accepted as identifying with worthwhile work and the vast majority of workers would be rendered as engaged in worthless pursuits for only material gains. However, this is clearly not the case.

Nor is the only key driving sentiment and bases for making judgements about the worth of their work engagement in work that is highly prized and societally well-regarded. Instead, individuals find purpose and meaning in their work as something important to them at a particular moment in time or for their local community, for instance. It is most likely individuals' sense of self and their goals, albeit constructed in diverse ways, that are the key drivers for their effortful and intelligent engagement in working life. To dismiss workers engaged in forms of employment which are not highly regarded in society as being engaged in activities of low worth and to easily categorised them as 'subjugated workers' again over-emphasises the objective accounts of work and their valuing at a societal, rather than a personal level. This is not to deny that there are workers engaged in work that are poorly remunerated, that is, in bad jobs. For instance, much part-time employment is involuntary in its engagement. However, this is not a judgement that can be made without accounting for individuals' subjective experience, construal and construction of that work. As elaborated within earlier chapters, individuals find meaning and purpose and exercise their agency within forms of work which are not highly regarded.

This relational premise, used above to consider the worth of work can be drawn upon elsewhere. In the reviews of the changing availability of occupations, the changing ways of participating in work, those who now comprise contemporary workforces and the contemporary and emerging requirements for workplace performance, this same premise can be deployed. Changes in the availability of different kinds of work and the changing means of participating in work are not distributed evenly across populations. Moreover, the opportunities for individuals to engage in work and ways of working which suit their purposes are relational depending upon individuals' circumstances, age, skills, capacities and social circumstances. There are some salient social patternings that cannot be ignored. Certainly, the prospects for continuity of paid employment are aligned to particular occupations and the level of skills and capacities within those occupations. These stand as institutional facts. However, they are not constant nor without variations across countries, industries and workplaces as has been elaborated in earlier chapters. So, as argued throughout, there appears to be a growing polarisation between workers on the basis of their skills and pay. Yet, the requirements for individuals to realise high skill work that attracts high pay are distributed not only on the basis of individuals' human capital but also on measures such as age, ethnicity and ableness.

At a workplace level, these factors are evident in the workplace's participatory practices that constitute, on the one hand, the affordances of the workplace (e.g. support, its invitations to participate, the distribution of prized work and opportunities for advancement) and, on the other hand, the ways in which individuals will engage with what the workplace affords. So, just as the workplace is selective in distributing its affordances, individuals may also be selective and strategic in how they engage in the workplace and for what purposes. At the heart of these two forms of participation is the negotiation between the affordances of the workplace and individuals' agency and intentionality. Again, there will be a diversity of affordances that will be distributed in different ways by workplaces according to their norms and practices, and quite diverse ways in which individuals will elect to participate in the workplace.

Sitting within these capacities and means of construing and constructing what the workplace affords are the previous experiences of individuals and the relationship between those and the new forms of work they seek to engage in. The capacities to successfully utilise technology and collective ways of working may not always be aided by individuals' previous experience or cultural heritage. So, the changing requirements of work, diverse and varied though they will undoubtedly be, do not represent some level playing field upon which all individuals are equally able to engage and participate. Again, the dark side of the relations between individual and social play out in particular ways here.

Consistent with the case being made here, there have been considerable changes in the composition of workforces for many nations. Principal among these changes is the increase in women's engagement in working life. However, this increased participation has not led to positive outcomes for all women. While some women have secured highly paid and high skilled work and are able to enjoy significant benefits and security of employment, for many others working life is in the service and administrative sectors featuring insecure forms of employment that is often poorly remunerated. Also, and consistent with the point made above, because of past experiences and opportunities, many women lack the human capital required to best exploit changing employment circumstances. Moreover, as nations such as Britain and Australia increasingly move into eras when the social welfare provisions will become meagre, those women without a long work history and superannuated partner face a potentially bleak and relatively poor life beyond work. Consequently, women's needs to engage in paid work and for what duration are likely to be quite diverse, however their prospects are likely to be shaped quite differently depending upon their capacities and the kinds of support afforded them.

2.2 Relational interdependence at work

Much of what has been argued above refers to the relational and relative interdependence between the social lived world consisting of paid work and individuals' personal agency that is itself shaped by socially derived subjectivities and practices (i.e. social agency). This comprises the complex and constructed relations between individual intentionality (i.e. their agentic actions) and the social subjectivities, practices and norms that arise from social and cultural practices, such as paid work and what occurs in work-places. This is what Giddens (1991) refers to as the reflexive negotiation of the self as individuals come to terms with transforming communities and societies and practices, such as those in workplaces. Whereas the relations between individuals and social practices are not always engaged in nor intensely negotiated, work and working life likely represent an instance where the engagement and negotiation that constitute the relative relational interdependence are likely to be intense. This is because of the salience of identity, intentionality and subjectivity of individuals as workers (Pusey, 2003) and the centrality of the culturally and situationally constituted practice of work activities to workplaces. For some workers, this agentic action and their intentionality will be driven by the need to engage in work that is held in high esteem within the community (e.g. Grey, 1994). The Russian émigré Lev referred to deliberately striving for the goal of being accepted and secure in a good middle class job that is categorised as being professional (Billett and Pavlova, 2005). So, for some workers, the status of their work is what drives and directs their intentionality. Yet, for other workers the status of their occupations is less important than how it meets their personal needs. For instance, in the same study, Ken, the manager of the information technology unit within a government department, was primarily concerned about this job providing him with security in a well-paid and superannuated position through which he could support his family and contribute financially to his church community. Similarly, Karen the single mother employed in a part-time job in the fruit and vegetable market was looking to her work to form an identity outside of the home and a better standard of living for herself and her children. Although able to establish his own insurance brokerage business, Carl felt obliged to continue to work for a large company that had provided him with an opportunity to learn about and engage in insurance brokerage.

All this suggests that policies and practices by both governments and employers need to take a greater account of, acknowledge and privilege individuals' intentionality and subjectivity. These factors are important when considering how to engage workers in effective work practices, to develop their capacities to the fullest, to engage them in learning and developing their vocational capacities throughout their working lives. However, current lifelong learning policies focus upon a particular kind of worker identity; the enterprising worker (Du Gay, 1996) that is willing to manipulate and connive to meet the employers wishes. As Edwards and Boreham (2003) argue this focus is misplaced and inappropriate as it is directed at goals that are based on assumptions about the self as being compliant to de-contextualised and abstracted societal goals (i.e. governmental objectives for economic performance and societal cohesion), rather than those reflecting localised and individualised subjectivities of the kind that direct individuals efforts and intentionalities.

Highlighting this mismatch between policy focus and localised and individualised goals is important for two key reasons. Individuals' learning and development will likely arise most strongly when the focus for the demanding process of development is related in some way to their interests, concerns or identity. As argued above, individuals are more likely to deploy their energies and conscious thought in a directed and sustained way when issues of importance are the focus of their thinking and acting. Similarly, there are clear links between engagement in conscious thought and learning. This learning is, however, a product of the reciprocal interaction between individuals and the social experience. What learning will occur cannot be predetermined; this is a product of negotiation, circumstances, individuals' dispositions and interests, and just plain energy. The learning arising through workplace experiences may be quite different from what was intended or afforded by the workplace. Therefore, focuses on issues, interests or situations that are central to the individual will more likely lead to richer learning outcomes than those which do not entertain the individual.

Secondly, whether considering the initial or ongoing vocational education provisions or lifelong learning policies, much of the emphasis is on a particular view of the self. The key focus is on the needs and interests of industry, government, employers and unions in vocational education. Moreover, lifelong learning policies are being increasingly directed towards the individuals' development also in terms of workplace performance (Organisation for Economic Cooperation and Development, 1998; 2000), rather than their needs and intentionalities (Edwards, 2002). While the learning of skills and skilfulness is just one part of developing successful economies it may not be possible to easily separate out transformation of the development of these skills from transformations in their identities and subjectivities. Therefore, in order to secure a better balance, considerations for policy might want to focus more on individuals' identity, subjectivity and intentionality. This is not just to provide a focus that is a more appropriate consideration of learning and transformation, it is also to humanise the goals and processes of lifelong learning.

2.3 A focus on individuals' subjectivities and identities

Lifelong learning needs to be understood as something that is constituted by the self, albeit socially mediated. A policy prescription is just that. Individuals will likely work to construct the direction, focus and intensity of their ongoing learning—their enterprising self—for work, based upon their interests and intentionalities. All this is well captured by the expansive Deweyian notion of vocation (Dewey, 1916). Just as curriculum prescriptions are intents, that may or may not be realised, the learners are ultimately the construction of the curriculum; regardless of what is enacted.

Much of the effort associated with attempts to organise learning is directed towards achieving intersubjectivity—shared understanding. This goal of shared understanding is normally premised on the assumption that the less experienced partner (e.g. the novice, the student) will come to share the understandings and practices of the more experienced partner (teacher, workplace expert). This assumption, however, has some flaws in it. The goal of securing intersubjectivity may fail to fully account for the process of knowledge construction that is in many ways unique to individuals (Gergen, 1994), rather than being common. Even with an objectified entity such as an occupational practice, there is unlikely to be commonality or much shared understanding. Partners who have worked or cohabited together may come to share many understandings. However, there will likely have quite different conceptions outside of those that are regularly the focus of intersubjective constituting activities. All this suggests that a focus on the self is not about being selfish, individual or singular. It reflects the brute fact (Searle 1995) that individuals' thinking and acting have their geneses in unique personal histories. Like institutional facts, these cannot be wished away. So learning for work and changing work requirements might best be focused not at securing intersubjectivity as a single goal, but enriching individuals' constructions of their vocational practice as it comes to confront new challenges. Interests, subjectivities and intentionalities that are socially structured yet unique to individuals as they confront situations and circumstances are socially structured yet unique in localised manifestations. While such goals may be at odds with uniform program goals, they appear to reflect more closely the evolving needs of vocational practice and the processes of agentically derived learning. This is not to suggest an abandonment of goals derived elsewhere (e.g. safer working practices) but that these goals need to be achieved in ways that include consideration of the learners and their engagement in directing that learning. It is about engaging the enterprising self in ways that meet both the localised requirements of particular workplaces and the individualised requirements of the self.

2.4   Inviting individuals to participate in transforming practice

Technical and societal change occurs through a process that may be driven by social factors (Leontyev, 1981; Rogoff, 1995), but its construction and enactment is also in part a product of individuals engaging with tasks and goals and reinventing and transforming them (Leontyev, 1981). Change is therefore not a uniform or deterministic process, (i.e. like some tidal wave or behavioural response to specific stimuli). Instead, it is given meaning in particular circumstances as the requirement for change is shaped both by the circumstances and by the actors engaged. Its various manifestations are mediated by individuals' construction of it. At a particular moment in history, each generation is involved in this transformative process of enacting change. When changes are required because the existing practices are inadequate, it is individuals' engagement with and transformation of the existing practices that constitute change. Individuals are often at the vanguard of change because they have to make sense of, respond to or monitor responses to changing structures and practices. Therefore, rather than conceptualising individuals as being mere implementers of change processes, individuals should be invited to contribute to those transformations, that is, to exercise existing and emerging ideas in the context in which they think and act in practice. It is only through the uptake of a commitment to change by individuals that it can be sustained.

It follows then that individuals are active participants in remaking culture (e.g. work practices, technical innovations and values associated with work), albeit in a relational and relative sense. Therefore, instead of top-down implementation strategies, ongoing development for work and learning through-out working life should be seen as being more reciprocal, with individuals invited to assist in the transformation of existing practices. That invitation serves to legitimise their participation in the thinking, acting and learning associated with change. So the issue of work, identity and learning are not novel or restricted to current times and transformations of work and working life. They represent, however, perhaps an under-appreciated and neglected focus for research, policy and practice in adult learning.

3. DESCRIBING WORK AND ILLUMINATING CHANGING WORK LIFE

A key tool to understand and illuminate the changing nature of work and work life is a capacity to describe work comprehensively and capture both the objectives and subjective contributions to what constitutes paid work and working life. A framework for describing the experience of work comprising categories of *Activities* and *Interdependencies* was generated to find a way of capturing the comprehensive of work and the requirements for work performance. The development of this framework can be found in Chapters 5, 6, 7 and 8. It is articulated in Chapter 9 and illustrated in Chapter 10. In summary, these categories of *activities* and *interdependencies* are as follows.

Activities within work can be described in terms of their:

- *Routineness*—the degree to which work practice activities are routine or non-routine thereby requiring robust knowledge
- *Homogeneity of tasks*—the degree to which tasks in the work practice are homogenous. Similarities may provide for greater support (modelling etc.) in development of the ability to perform.
- *Discretion*—the degree to which the scope of activities demands a broader or narrower range of decision-making and more or less autonomous practice
- *Intensity*—the degree to which work is complicated by having to perform multiple tasks simultaneously, thereby requiring high levels of managing, monitoring and prioritizing work activities
- *Multiplicity*—the range of activities expected to be undertaken as part of work practice
- *Complexity*—the degree to which decision-making is complicated by compounding variables and resolution of tasks requiring negotiation among those variables
- *Accessibility* (opaqueness of knowledge)—the degree to which knowledge required for the work practice is either accessible or hidden.

Interdependence within work practice can be described in terms of:

- *Working with others* (teams, clients)—the ways work activity is premised on interactions with others
- *Engagement*—the basis of employment
- *Status of employment*—the standing of the work, its perceived value and whether it attracts support
- *Access to participation*—the attributes that influence participation
- *Reciprocity of values*—the prospects for shared values
- *Artefacts/external tools*—physical artefacts used in work practice upon which performance is predicated.

Through this framework, both the objective and subjective components of what constitutes paid work can be elicited within each category of activities and interdependencies. These categories can be used to understand and describe the requirements of particular work, monitor ways in which they are subject to change and identify the attributes that are privileged in particular workplace settings. It attempts to offer a comprehensive basis to understand the requirements of work and working life. Such understandings are likely to be helpful for the development of individual skills throughout working life. As argued elsewhere (Billett, 2003c), much of curriculum development for vocational education is premised upon national prescriptions of what comprises an occupation, its expectations and requirements. However, ultimately workplace performance needs to be understood in the context in which it is enacted: a particular workplace or work setting. In this way, the framework provided here not only offers the potential to understand the requirements for paid work that account for situational factors, but also stands to provide a mechanism to understand the variations of work requirements across workplaces, even when the same vocational practices are being enacted.

Moreover, as argued earlier (Billett, 2001b) such a framework will assist to elaborate what constitutes expertise in particular workplaces, therefore elaborating and detailing the goals for educational programs that are aiming to develop that expertise. Furthermore, such a framework offers a basis to make more informed judgements about the kinds of work that are undertaken by different workers. For instance, as Darrah (1996) proposed, it would identify the complexity of the work undertaken by production and design staff thereby offering a more informed analysis of the demands of both kinds of work. This may help overcome the valuing of work premised on assumptions and historical premises. It provides, instead, a means to understand the qualities of different kinds of work through elaborating their characteristics and qualities. Assumptions about the complexity of particular kinds of work are thereby supported or challenged, ultimately questioning work hierarchies premised on the inherent social regard of particular kinds of work. In this way, the framework stands as a means to enrich accounts of work and the complexity of paid work.

It follows from this discussion that there are a set of consequences for the development of vocational capacities that arise through the changes to work which have been identified within this volume. The next sections conclude the book by identifying some of the key consequences for developing work and vocational practices that have emerged throughout.

4.   CONSEQUENCES FOR WORK PRACTICE AND VOCATIONAL DEVELOPMENT

In the previous chapters, attempts have been made to identify the requirements for contemporary and emerging work and also how these requirements are changing, yet diversely deployed across different kinds of work and workplaces. The requirements for work performance also warrant a consideration of their development throughout individuals' working lives. Clearly, given the diversity and person-dependent bases elaborated earlier, there are no simple generalizations or set solutions. There are different requirements for different workplaces (e.g. those continuing with long production runs might best profit from set and standard approaches, whereas those with short runs require more flexible approaches) (Bailey, 1993).

Moreover, the case and direction of changes in requirements in workplaces will not be uniform. Nevertheless, from the factors identified above three consequences for learning these requirements are discernible. These are:

- increased demands for work (i.e. intellectual, effortful, currency)
- an on-going commitment to currency of skilful knowledge (life-long learning—constant change)
- situational-occupational bases for workplace performance

4.1   Increased demands for work

The educational implications for the changes and diversity in workplace performance requirements identified above are themselves subject to diverse views, particularly about whether contemporary and emerging work is becoming more or less demanding. The up-skilling thesis—that work is getting more demanding to learn about and maintain competence within— suggests the need for a more fulsome preparation and, in particular, a solid grounding in foundational or canonical work knowledge as these might sustain individuals through periods of constant change. It is these very basic skills which have been manifested in key employment competences or capacities that are often favoured by government as an educational device to secure effective workplace performance. The contrary position—the de-skilling thesis—suggests that investment in educational provisions is unnecessary because work requirements are being eased and reduced through the 'dumbing down' of workplace requirements. Yet, given the diverse range of work requirements proposed above and also the frequency and scope of change likely to be encountered in and needing to be addressed in work and working life, it seems reasonable to suggest that the preparation for and ongoing development to maintain vocational currency will become more thorough and more demanding. A review of studies of workplace change (Berryman, 1993) across a range of industries (e.g. insurance, banking, textiles, apparel, automobile, business services) reveal similar patterns (i.e. intensified international competition, proliferation of products, accelerated production cycles, faster pace of change in production technologies and a generally heightened level of uncertainty) are altering the nature of work and the skills required for frontline workers, managers and professionals. It seems predictions in the early 1990s are often upheld in the contemporary experience of work: "Employees need more formal education, a broader understanding of the context in which they work and the ability to make sound judgements in an environment of less direct supervision" (Berryman, 1993: 358).

The issue of change and its scope and impact must be assumed to impact most people through their working lives, because even in most forms of work (e.g. occupations that stand privileged in some ways) there will be changes to the composition of workforces and the means of engaging with and conducting work. Much earlier, it was predicted that with the shift from industry to service functions, which place more importance on tasks like information-handling, there is a requirement for higher levels of education (Bell, 1974). In contrast to the de-skilling thesis proposed by Braverman (1974), it is possible that the nature of work is becoming more demanding and skilful, because of the frequency and scope of changes that impact upon work tasks and working life. So even attempts to de-skill work and workers bring with them change and new learning and negotiations. While Braverman and other may have been correct in terms of intent, the subjective experience of those who work would have been a lightening of the load that comprises work. However, the increase in change, the breadth of likely applications, the use of technology and so on lead to the view that against these intentions the demands of many contemporary and emerging forms of work are complex, and require a thorough preparation. As is discussed in the next section, even the means of participation in the workplace have made engagement with work tasks more demanding for many workers, particularly those who are made contingent through their employment conditions. Hence, preparation for work is likely to become more demanding, as will be the requirement to maintain currency. This perspective—to suggest that learning is seen as internalisation—makes unconscious much of what is done in the conduct of skilful activity. However, as foreshadowed, the constantly changing and turbulent nature of workplace requirements may act against the easy achievement of the kinds of tacit knowledge required for work performance. For instance, in the study of automobile mechanics (Billett and Pavlova, 2005) the more rapid the transformation in models of cars, the greater the difficulty in developing richly nuanced understandings that comprise tacit knowledge. So the capacities required for effective workplace performance in contemporary and emerging forms of work will likely become more demanding and requiring of more than the initial preparation and continued ongoing development throughout working life, if for no other reason than the requirements for work will become less routine.

4.2   On-going commitment to currency of skilful knowledge

As foreshadowed above, the possibly unique situational requirements of workplaces, the constant changes in vocational practice and the evolution of technologies (of whatever kind) and work more generally emphasise that initial vocational preparation and learning is unlikely to be sufficient for a working life. For a working life that may involve employment in different manifestations of occupational tasks, if not different occupations, and a variety of work and workplaces, ongoing commitment by the individuals and their potential employers is likely to be required to develop skills throughout a life of work. Yet, against views that this learning will inevitably involve constant wholesale transformation, much of it will be premised on the continuity of what is already known and deployed, the incremental trans-formation of existing practices in response to changing demands and requirements. Against the claims of needing to change occupations a number of times during one's working life, is perhaps the more realistic view that such changes will only come out when there is significant technical and organizational change in work or its availability, and when individuals elect to change their work comprehensively. Yes, there will be significant transformation for workers who are displaced by technical innovations, for instance those that occurred in the printing, information servicing and agricultural sectors.

As well, when work becomes unavailable because it has been exported to other countries or places, then workers are confronted with the need to develop their occupational skills largely afresh. However, there will also likely be more examples of work that incrementally transforms overtime and requires keeping pace with these changes and reshaping practice accordingly. So the task of maintaining competence throughout a working life might not be to develop distinct vocational skills and vocational identity numerous times throughout an increasingly long working life. Instead, it is more likely to be about ongoing learning and development. Aside from changes that come uninvited, are those which individuals elect to pursue for their own vocational purposes (Fenwick 2004). It is those changes that individuals will want to pursue throughout their working life that will be guided by their evolving personal and professional (vocational) needs.

Regardless of the motivation, whether from within the individual or from outside or some combination of both, it seems that both support and afford-ances from social institutions such as workplaces and education institutions will be required through working life to meet the requirements for performance brought about by these changes. However, these affordances will also need to be complemented by the engagement and agency of individuals themselves. That is, these changes must be those that individuals wish to engage with and exercise their interest and intentionality effortfully for rich and new learning to occur. It is the coming together of these two contributions that are likely to sustain individuals learning throughout their working life. It is ironic that, at the very time when individual employers seem to be withdrawing from commitment to their employees' development in many Western-style countries, it is becoming apparent exactly how much ongoing development is required for both the individual workers' and also the workplace's continuity. For instance, Lazonick (1990) attributes

Japanese success to its superiority in producing a variety of high quality goods and generating continuous improvement. This success is attributed to skilled and well educated shop floor workers in the leading firms who are fully engaged in their work and are given 'membership' in their firms (Billett, 1993). Their interests implicitly are tied to the long-term interests of the firm. Despite governments supporting and championing vocational development throughout working lives, there seems to be a growing gap between their goals and employer commitment. This commitment seems to be most evident with select workers (high skilled, educated or younger workers) rather than addressing the needs of all workers' lifelong learning needs. So workers will need support for learning throughout their working lives, perhaps never more so than in their last few decades of working life. Yet it is unclear from where this learning support will be afforded. Perhaps, workers might well adopt an approach based on personal epistemologies and self-direction in learning, rather than risk relying on governments and employers.

4.3 Situational-occupational bases for workplace performance

Certainly there is no end of educational challenges here. A central challenge is to what degree should learning processes and outcomes be focused on highly situated performance, rather than canonical occupational knowledge. Traditionally, this has been an anathema to educational provisions because such learning processes and outcomes are seen to be inherently limited. Yet, opposing such a view is the overwhelming evidence that learning is in some ways highly situational, and transfer of learning from one situation to another highly complex and problematic. For instance, in her study of dairy workers Scribner (1997: 378) showed that:

> Modes of solution came into being around means of solution…on many dairy tasks the environment was more than an external "context" in which problem-solving occurred; it was an integral component of the intellectual activity itself.

This suggests that effective learning processes are required to be functional and situated in some kind of practice. Such a suggestion seems suited to considerations of how individuals learn. For instance, Neisser (1976: 183) has argued that, because perception and action occur in continuous dependence on the environment "they cannot be understood without an understanding of the environment itself". Hence, there is a need to consider learning as a process arising from participation in social practices that afford the kinds of contributions that permit such situated dialogue to proceed and foster effective learning. Nevertheless, while this approach might best stand as an effective learning strategy, it may not readily address the issue of the constant change and capacity to address the novel circumstances and tasks that will likely stand as requirements for effective work practice. Certainly, and as noted earlier, recent accounts of learning emphasise the situated and social contributions to individual learning. These seem particularly applicable to individuals' learning about work practices that have their genesis in historically derived practices, cultural practices that arise from community need and particular situational factors that shape how work requirements are manifested in practice.

Raising issues about individuals' roles in these learning processes tends to attract criticism in that the learner is being seen as an isolated cognitive entity rather than being embedded, engaging with or entwined within a social practice. Yet, it seems that in quite rightly discarding the earlier cognitive claims about transfer as equated to cleverness, the role of the individual within adaptability may have been overly censored. Given that transfer or adaptability, and therefore the capacity to apply knowledge to new work situations and requirements, is in some way dependent upon individuals' capacities and agency it seems important to consider not only the social contributions, and the individuals capacities and agency, but perhaps most importantly the relationship between the two.

In understanding how best to navigate the complex and sometimes contradictory requirements for developing and maintaining individuals' capacity to be effective in working the face of changing and diverse practice acquirements, it would be sensible to turn to appropriate research to inform practice about how these efforts might best be directed. However, there is some space for pessimism here.

> Despite an increasing interest in preparing people well for the jobs of the future, and an ever present concern about workers' skills or the lack thereof, the public discourse on skills and work is rarely informed by research which actually attempts to describe the knowledge and know how required in today's workplaces, including the ways in which language and literacy-related activities are embedded in work. Nor do we often document in helpful detail the successes and failures of education and training programs designed to prepare or repair workers, or to explore the intersection of the desire to acquire skills with the opportunity to acquire and use them in the workplace. (Hull, 1997: xiv)

If understanding work and its development throughout working life is to be advanced, there remain important issues about how education provisions might best address the maintenance and development of individuals' capacities to engage effectively in turbulent and diverse forms of working life. Among these are the means by which it is possible to achieve an ongoing commitment to the currency of workers' knowledge in the face of changing and diverse work requirements.

5.   WORK, LEARNING AND IDENTITY

This book proposes a position about and hopefully a fresh and useful perspective on the changing requirements of work which go beyond those provided through sociological and cognitive accounts. It aims to offer an account premised on the contributions of both the social world and the individual that comprise the conduct of work by humans who have their own motives, construals and intentions. Clearly, some will reject the views put forward here, from both perspectives, and others may suggest that the relational factors are not elaborated sufficiently or fully, or for some, are over-emphasised. Nevertheless, it is hoped that the position advanced here has sufficient coherence and provides a broadly based perspective on how the experience of work and work life can be understood.

References

Alexander, P.A., & Judy, J.E. (1988). The interaction of domain specific and strategic knowledge in academic performance. *Review of Educational Research, 58*(4), 375–404.

Anderson, J.R. (1982). Acquisition of cognitive skill. *Psychological Review, 89* (4), 369–406.

Anderson, J.R. (1993). Problem solving and learning. *American Psychologist, 48*(1), 35–44.

Anzai, Y., & Simon, H.E. (1979). The theory of learning by doing. *Psychological Review, 86,* 124–140.

Appelbaum, E. (1993). *High performance work systems: American models of workplace transformation.* Washington: Economic Policy Institute.

Archer, M.S. (2000). *Being human: The problem of agency.* Cambridge: Cambridge University Press.

Australian Bureau of Statistics. (2002). *Training and Education Experience Australia, 2001.* Canberra: AGPS.

Australian Bureau of Statistics. (2003). *Employer Training Expenditure and Practices, Australia.* Canberra: AGPS.

Australian Bureau of Statistics. (2004). *Characteristics of Small Business, Australia,* (No.8127.0 2003).

Australian Bureau of Statistics. (2005). *Australian Labour Market Statistics* (No.6105.0). Canberra: AGPS.

Bailey, T. (1993). Organizational innovation in the apparel industry. *Industrial Relations, 32*(1), 30–48.

Baldwin, J.M. (1894). Personality-suggestion. *Psychological Review, 1,* 274–279.

Baldwin, J.M. (1898). On selective thinking. *The Psychological Review, V*(1), 1–24.

Baltes, P.B., & Staudinger, U.M. (1996). Interactive minds in a life-span perspective. In P.B. Baltes & U.M. Staudinger (Eds.), *Interactive minds: Life-span perspectives on the social foundations of cognition* (pp. 1–34). Cambridge: Cambridge University Press.

Barley, S. (1996). Technicians in the workplace: Ethnographic evidence for bringing work into organisational studies. *Administrative Science Quarterly, 41,* 404–441.

Barley, S., & Batt, R. (1995). *The new crafts: The rise of the technical labour force and it implication for the organisation of work.* Philadelphia, PA: University of Philadelphia, National Center on the Education Quality of the Workforce.

279

Barley, S.R., & Orr, J.E. (1997). Introduction: The neglected workforce. In S.R. Barley & J.E. Orr (Eds.), *Between Craft and Science: Technical Work in US settings* (pp. 1–19). Ithaca, NY: Cornell University Press.

Bartel, A.P., & Lichtenberg, F.R. (1987). The comparative advantage of educated workers in implementing new technology. *Review of Economics and Statistics, 64,* 1–11.

Bartel, A.P., & Lichtenberg, F.R. (1991). The age of technology and its impact on employee wages. *Economics of Innovation and New Technology, 1,* 215–231. Cher, UK: Harwood Academic Publishers.

Bartlett, F.C. (1958). *Thinking: An experimental and social study.* New York: Basic Books.

Bauer, J., Festner, D., Gruber, H., Harteis, C., & Heid, H. (2004). The effects of epistemological beliefs on workplace learning. *Journal of Workplace Learning, 16*(5), 284–292.

Bauman, Z. (1998). *Work, consumerism and the new poor.* Buckingham: Open University Press.

Beck, U. (1992). *Risk society: Towards a new modernity* (M. Ritter, Trans.). London: Sage.

Bell, D. (1974). *The cultural contradiction of capitalism.* London: Hieinemann.

Berger, P.L., & Luckman, T. (1966). *The social construction of reality.* Harmondsworth, Middlesex: Penguin.

Best, J.B. (1992). *Cognitive psychology (3rd edition).* New York: West Publishing Co.

Best, F, (Ed.). (1973). *The future of work.* Englewood Cliffs, NJ: Prentice Hall.

Bierema, L.L. (2001). Women, work, and learning. In T. Fenwick (Ed.), *Sociocultural perspectives on learning through work* (pp. 53–62). San Francisco: Jossey Bass/Wiley.

Bernhardt, A. (1999). *The future of low-wage jobs: Case studies in the retail industry.* (Institute on Education and the Economy Working Paper No 10 March 1999).

Berryman, S. (1993). Learning for the workplace. In L. Darling-Hammond (Ed.), *Review of Research in Education, 19* (pp. 343–401). Washington, DC: American Education Research Association.

Bertrand, O., & Noyelle, T. (1988). *Human resources and corporate strategy: Technological change in banks and insurance companies in five OECD countries.* Paris: Organisation for Economic Cooperation and Development.

Beven, F. (1997). *Learning in the workplace: Airline customer service.* Brisbane: Centre for Learning and Work Research, Griffith University.

Bhaskar, R. (1998). *The possibility of naturalism.* London: Routledge.

Billett, S. (1993). Authenticity and a culture of workpractice. *Australian and New Zealand Journal of Vocational Education Research, 2*(1), 1 – 29.

Billett, S. (1994). Situated learning—a workplace experience. *Australian Journal of Adult and Community Education, 34* (2), 112–130.

Billett, S. (1996). Situated learning: Bridging sociocultural and cognitive theorising. *Learning and Instruction, 6*(3), 263–280.

Billett, S. (1997). Dispositions, vocational knowledge and development: Sources and consequences. *Australian and New Zealand Journal of Vocational Education Research, 5*(1), 1–26.

Billett, S. (1998). Ontogeny and participation in communities of practice: A socio-cognitive view of adult development. *Studies in the Education of Adults, 30*(1), 21–34.

Billett, S. (1999). Experts' ways of knowing. *Australian Vocational Education Review, 6*(2), 25–36.

Billett, S. (2000a). Performance at work: Identifying the smart workforce. In R. Gerber & C. Lankshear (Eds.), *Training for a smart workforce* (pp. 123–150). London: Routledge.

Billett, S. (2000b). Defining the demand side of VET: Industry, enterprises, individuals and regions. *Journal of Vocational Education and Training, 50*(1), 5–30.

Billett, S. (2001a). Co-participation at work: Affordance and engagement. In T. Fenwick (Ed.), *Sociocultural perspectives on learning through work.* San Francisco: Jossey Bass/Wiley.

Billett, S. (2001b). Knowing in practice: Re-conceptualising vocational expertise. *Learning and Instruction, 11*(6), 431–452.

Billett, S. (2001c). *Learning in the workplace: Strategies for effective practice.* Sydney: Allen and Unwin.

Billett, S. (2002a). Workplace pedagogic practices: Co-participation and learning. *British Journal of Educational Studies, 50*(4), 457–481.

Billett, S. (2002b). Workplaces, communities and pedagogies: An activity theory view. In M.R. Lea & K. Nicholl (Eds.), *Distributed learning: Social and cultural approaches to practice.* (pp. 83–97). London: Routledge-Falmer.

Billett, S. (2003a). *Individualising the social—socialising the individual: Interdependence between social and individual agency in vocational learning.* Paper presented at the 11th Annual International Conference on Post-compulsory Education and Training: Enriching Learning Cultures, Gold Coast.

Billett, S. (2003b). Sociogeneses, activity and ontogeny. *Culture and Psychology, 9*(2), 133–169.

Billett, S. (2003c). Vocational curriculum and pedagogy: An activity theory perspective. *European Journal of Educational Research, 2*(1), 6–21.

Billett, S. (2004). Co-participation at work: Learning through work and throughout working lives. *Studies in the Education of Adults, 36*(2), 190–205.

Billett, S. (2005). Being competent: The relational interdependence between individual and social agency in working life. In H. Gruber, C. Harteis, R. Mulder & M. Rehrl (Eds.), *Bridging individual, organisational, and cultural perspectives on professional learning* (pp. 113–132). Regensburg, Germany: Roderer.

Billett, S., Barker, M., & Hernon-Tinning, B. (2004). Participatory practices at work. *Pedagogy, Culture and Society, 12*(2), 233–257.

Billett, S. & Boud, D. (2001). Participation in and guided engagement at work: Workplace pedagogic practices. Researching Work and Learning: Second International Conference, July 26–28, Faculty of Continuing Education, University of Calgary, Alberta. (321–328).

Billett, S., Ehrich, L., & Hernon-Tinning, B. (2003). Small business pedagogic practices. *Journal of Vocational Education and Training, 55*(2), 149–167.

Billett, S., & Ovens, C. (2005). *Co-opting school students' experience of paid part-time work.* Paper presented at the 13th Annual International Conference on Post-compulsory Education and Training, 4–7th December, Gold Coast.

Billett, S., & Pavolva, M. (2005). Learning through working life: Self and individuals' agentic action. *International Journal of Lifelong Education, 24*(3), 195–211.

Billett, S., Smith, R., & Barker, M. (2005). Understanding work, learning and the remaking of cultural practices. *Studies in Continuing Education, 27*(3), 219–237.

Bloomer, M., & Hodkinson, P. (2000). Learning careers: Continuity and change in young people's dispositions to learning. *British Education Research Journal, 26*(5), 583–598.

Billett, S., & Somerville, M. (2004). Transformations at work: Identity and learning. *Studies in Continuing Education, 26*(2), 309–326.

Bishop, J.H. (1997). What we know about employer provided training: A review of the literature. *Research in Labour Economics, 16*, 19–87.

Blossfeld, H.P., & Hakim, C. (Eds.). (1997). *Between equalisation and marginalisation: Women working part-time in Europe and the United States of America.* Oxford: Oxford University Press.

Bolle, P. (2001). Part-time work: Solution or trap? In M. F. Loutfi (Ed.), *Women, gender and work* (pp. 215–238). Geneva: International Labour Organisation.

Bonazzi, G. (1998). Between shock absorption and continuous improvement: Supervisors and technicians in Fiat 'Integrated Factory' *Work, Employment & Society, 12,* 219–243.

Borgir, H., & Peltzer, R. (1999). Lifelong learning and vocational education and training: A teachers and trade union view. In M Singh (Ed.). *Adult learning and the future of work* (51–62). Hamburg: UNESCO Institute for Education.

Bosch, G., Dawkins, P., & Michan, F. (1994). *Times are changing: Working time in 14 industrialised countries.* Geneva: International Labour Organisation.

Bourdieu, P. (1991). *Language and symbolic power.* (Edited by J.B. Thompson). Cambridge: Polity Press.

Braverman, H. (1974). *Labour and monopoly capital: The degradation of work in the twentieth century.* New York: Monthly Review Press.

Bresnahan, T.F., Brynjolsson, E., & Hitt, L. (2002). Information technology, workplace organisation and the demand for labor: Firm-level evidence. *Quarterly Journal of Economics, 117*(1), 339–376.

Brown, J.S., Collins, A., & Duguid, P. (1989). Situated cognition and the culture of learning. *Educational Researcher, 18*(1), 32–34.

Brunello, G., & Medio, A. (2001). An explanation of international differences in education and workplace training. *European Economic Review, 45*(2), 307–322.

Brunello, G. (2001). *On the complementarity between education and training in Europe.* (IZA discussion paper 309. Forschungsinstitut zur Zukunft der Arbeit- IZA. (Institute for the Study of Labour)).

Bruner, J.S. (1966). On cognitive growth II. In J.S. Bruner, R.R. Oliver, & P. M. Greenfield (Eds.), *Studies in cognitive growth* (pp. 30–67). New York: Wiley.

Bruner, J. (2001). Foreword. In B.F. Malle, L.J. Moses, & D.A. Baldwin (Eds.), *Intentions and intentionality: Foundations of social cognition* (ix – xii). Cambridge, MA: The MIT Press.

Budd, J.W., & McCall, B.P. (2001). The grocery stores wage distribution: A semi parametric analysis of the role of retailing and labour market institutions. *Industrial and Labour Relations Review, 54*(2a), 484–501.

Carnevale, A.P. (1995). Enhancing skills in the new economy. In Howard, A. (Ed.), *The Changing Nature of Work.* San Francisco: Jossey-Bass Publishers.

Carnoy, M. (1999). The Great work dilemma. In J. Ahier & G. Esland (Eds.), *Education, training and the future of work 1.* London: Routledge.

Carnoy, M. (2001). The family, flexible work and social cohesion at risk. In M.F. Loutfi (Ed.), *Women, gender and work* (305–325). Geneva: International Labour Organisation.

Charness, N. (1989). Expertise in chess and bridge. In D. Klahr & K. Kotowsky (Eds.), *Complex information processing: The impact of Herbert A. Simon.* (pp. 183–204). Hillsdale, NJ: Erlbaum.

Chi, M. T. H., Glaser, R., & Rees, E. (1982). Problem-solving ability. In R.J. Sternberg (Ed.), *Advances in the psychology of human intelligence (Vol. 1).* (pp. 7–76). Hillsdale NJ: Erlbaum.

Chi, M.T.H., Glaser, R., & Farr, M.J. (1982). *The nature of expertise.* Hillsdale, NJ: Erlbaum.

Chi, M.T.H., Feltovich, P.J., & Glaser, R. (1981). Categorisation and representation of physics problems by experts and novices. *Cognitive Science, 5,* 121–152.

Cho, M.K., & Apple, M. (1998). Schooling, work and subjectivity. *British Journal of Sociology of Education, 19*(3), 269–291.

Church, K. (2004). *Dancing lessons: A choreography of disability in corporate culture.* Paper presented at the WALL Annual Meeting, Toronto.

Cobb, P. (1998). Learning from distributed theories of intelligence. *Mind, Culture, and Activity 5* (3), 187–204.

Cohn, E., & Addison. J.T. (1998). The economic returns to lifelong learning in OECD countries. *Education Economics, 6* (3), 253–307.

Cole, M. (1985). The zone of proximal development where culture and cognition create each other. In J. V. Wertsch (Ed.), *Culture, communication and cognition: Vygotskian perspectives* (pp. 146–161). Cambridge, UK: Cambridge University Press.

Cole, M. (1998). Can cultural psychology help us think about diversity? *Mind, Culture and Activity, 5*(4), 291–304.

Cole, M. (2002). *Building centers of strength in cultural historical research.* Paper presented at the Annual Meeting of the American Education Research Association, New Orleans.

Cook-Gumperez, J., & Hanna, K. (1997). Some recent issues of professional literacy and practice. In G. Hull (Ed.). *Changing work, changing workers: Critical perspectives on language, literacy and skills* (pp. 316–334). New York: State University of New York Press.

Collins, A., Brown J.S., & Newman, S.E. (1989). Cognitive apprenticeship: Teaching the crafts of reading, writing and mathematics. In L.B. Resnick, (Ed.), *Knowledge, learning and instruction, essays in honour of Robert Glaser.* (pp. 453–494). Hillsdale, NJ: Erlbaum & Associates.

Danford, A. (1998). Teamworking and labour regulation in the autocomponents industry. *Work, Employment & Society, 12*(3), 409–431.

Darrah, C.N. (1996). *Learning and work: An exploration in industrial ethnography.* New York: Garland Publishing.

Darrah, C.N. (1997). Complicating the concept of skill requirements: Scenes from a workplace. In G. Hull (Ed.), *Changing work, changing workers: Critical perspectives on language, literacy and skills* (pp. 249–272). New York: CUNY Press.

Davies, B. (2000). *A body of writing 1990-1999.* New York: Altamira Press.

Davis, D.D. (1995). Form, function and strategy in boundaryless organizations. In A. Howard (Ed.), *The changing nature of work.* San Francisco: Jossey-Bass Publishers.

Department of Labor. (2005). *What jobs do American women and men have?* Retrieved 11 January 2005, from www.prb.org.

Department of Labor. (2005). *Record number of women in U.S. Labor Force.* Retrieved 11 January 2005, from www.prb.org.

Dertouzos, M., Lester, R.K., &. Solow, R.M. (1989). *Made in America: Regaining the competitive edge.* Cambridge, MA: MIT Press

Dewey, J. (1916). *Democracy and education. .* New York: The Free Press.

Du Gay, P. (1996). *Consumption and identity at work.* London: Sage.

Drucker, P. (1973). Evolution of the knowledge worker. In F.Best (Ed.), *The future of work.* Englewood Cliffs, NJ: Prentice Hall.

Edwards, R. (2002). Mobilizing lifelong learning: Governmentality in educational practices. *Journal of Educational Policy, 17*(3), 353–365.

Edwards, R., & Boreham, N. (2003). 'The centre cannot hold': Complexity and difference in European Union policy towards a learning society. *Journal of Educational Policy, 18*(4), 407–421.

Ellström. P.E. (1998). The meaning of occupational competence and qualification. In W.J. Nijhof & J.N. Streumer (Eds.), *Key qualifications in work and education*. Dordrecht: Kluwer Academic Publishers.

Employment Policy Foundation. (2003). *An economic primer to white collar reform*. Washington: Employment Policy Foundation.

Engeström, Y. (1993). Development studies of work as a testbench of activity theory: The case of primary care medical practice. In S. Chaiklin & J. Lave (Eds.), *Understanding practice: Perspectives on activity and context*. (pp. 64–103). Cambridge, U.K.:Cambridge University Press.

Engeström, Y., & Middleton, D. (1996). Introduction: Studying work as mindful practice. In Y. Engeström & D. Middleton (Eds.), *Cognition and communication at work* (pp. 1–15). Cambridge, UK: Cambridge University Press.

Ericsson, K.A., & Lehmann, A.C. (1996). Expert and exceptional performance: Evidence of maximal adaptation to task constraints. *Annual Review of Psychology, 47*, 273–305.

Ericsson, K.A., & Simon, H.A. (1984). *Protocol analysis—verbal reports as data*. Cambridge, MA: MIT Press.

Erikson, E. H. (1982). *The life cycle completed: A review*. New York: Norton.

Etzioni, A. (1969). *The semi professions and their organisation: Teachers, nurses and social workers*. New York: Free Press.

Evans, G. (1991). Lesson cognitive demands and student processing in upper secondary mathematics. In G Evans (Ed.), *Learning and teaching cognitive skills*. Melbourne: ACER.

Evans, G., & Butler, J. (1992). Expert models and feedback processes in developing competence in industrial trade areas. *Australian Journal of TAFE Research, 8* (1), 13–32.

Eylon, B., & Linn, M.C. (1988). Learning and instruction: An examination of four research perspectives in science education. *Review of Educational Research, 58*, 251–301.

Ezzy, D. (1997). Subjectivity and the labour process: Conceptualising 'Good Work'. *Sociology, 31*(3), 427–444.

Fenwick, T. (1998). Women's development of self in the workplace. *International Journal of Lifelong Learning, 17*(3), 199–217.

Fenwick, T. (2002). Lady, Inc.: Women learning, negotiating subjectivity in entrepeneurial discourses. *International Journal of Lifelong Education, 21*(2), 162–177.

Fenwick, T. (2004). Learning in portfoliowork: Anchored innovation in and mobile identity. *Studies in Continuing Education, 26*(2), 229–246.

Fitts, P.M. (1964). Perceptual-motorskill learning. In A.W. Melton (Ed.), *Categories of human learning*. New York: Academic Press.

Forrester, K., Payne, J., & Ward, K. (1995). Lifelong education and the workplace: A critical analysis. *International Journal of Lifelong Education, 14*(4), 292–305.

Foucault, M. (1979). *Discipline and punishment*. New York: Vintage Books.

Foucault, M. (1986). *The care of the self: The history of sexuality, vol 3* (R. Hurley, Trans.). Harmsworth: Penguin.

Fuller, A., & Unwin, A. (2003). Fostering workplace learning: Looking through the lens of apprenticeships. *European Educational Research Journal, 2*(1), 41–55.

Fullarton, S. (1999). *Work experience and work placements in secondary school education*. Research Report Number 10. Camberwell, Victoria: ACER.

Flynn, P. (1988). *Facilitating technological change: The human resource challenge*. Cambridge, MA: Ballinger.

Garfinkel, H. (1990). The curious seriousness of professional sociology. In B. Conein, M. deFornel & L. Quere (Eds). *Forms of conversation Vol 1*. (69–78) Paris: CNET.

Gergen, K.J. (1994). *Realities and relationships: Soundings in social construction.* Cambridge, Mass: Harvard University Press.

Gergen, K.J. (2000). *The saturated self: Dilemmas of identity in contemporary life.* New York: Basic Books.

Giddens, A. (1984). *The constitution of society.* Cambridge: Polity Press.

Giddens, A. (1991). *Modernity and self-identity: Self and society in the late modern age.* Stanford: Stanford University Press.

Gimpel, J. (1961). *The cathedral builders.* New York: Grove Press.

Giraud, O. (2002). Firms' further training practices and social exclusion: Can industrial relations systems provide greater equality? Theoretical and empirical evidence from Germany and France. In K. Schoman & P. J. Connell (Eds.), *Education, training and employment dynamics: transitional labour markets in the European Union.* Cheltenham: Edward Elgar.

Glaser, R. (1990). Re-emergence of learning theory within instructional research. *American Psychologist, 45* (1), 29–39.

Glaser, R. (1984). Education and thinking—the role of knowledge. *American Psychologist, 39*(2), 93–104.

Goodnow, J.J. (1996). Collaborative rules: how are people supposed to work with one another? In P.B. Baltes & U.M. Staudinger (Eds.), *Interactive minds: Life-span perspectives on the social foundation of cognition* (pp. 163–197). Cambridge, UK: Cambridge University Press.

Goodnow, J.J. (1990). The socialisation of cognition: What's involved? In J.W. Stigler, R.A. Shweder & G. Herdt (Eds.), *Cultural Psychology* (pp. 259–286). Cambridge, UK: Cambridge University Press.

Goffman, E. (1990). *The presentation of self in everyday life.* London: Penguin Books.

Gorz, A. (1990). Have British workers been working harder in Thatcher's Britain? *British Journal of Industrial Relations, 28*(3), 293–312.

Gott, S. (1989). Apprenticeship instruction for real-world tasks: The co-ordination of procedures, mental models, and strategies. *Review of research in education, 15, 97–169.*

Greeno, J.G., & Simon, H.A. (1988). Problem solving and reasoning. In R.C. Aitkinson, R.J. Hormiston, G. Findeyez and R.D. Yulle (Eds.), *Steven's handbook of experimental psychology and education, Vol 2.* New York: Wiley.

Grey, C. (1994). Career as a project of the self and labour process discipline. *Sociology, 28*(2), 479–497.

Groen, G.J., & Patel, P. (1988). The relationship between comprehension and reasoning in medical expertise. In M. T. H. Chi, R. Glaser and R. Farr, *The Nature of Expertise.* New York: Erlbaum.

Grubb, W.N. (1996). *Working in the middle: Strengthening education and training for the mid-skilled labor force.* San Francisco: Jossey Bass.

Handel, M.J. (2005). Trends in perceived Job Quality, 1989 to 1998. *Work and Occupations, 32*(1), 66–94.

Handy, C. (1994). *The empty raincoat.* London: Hutchinson.

Harré, R. (1995). The necessity of personhood as embedded being. *Theory and Psychology, 5,* 369–373.

Harrison, B. (1997). *Lean and mean: Why corporations will continue to dominate the global economy.* New York: Guilford.

Hayes, J.R., Wheelwright, S., & Clark, K. (1988) *Dynamic manufacturing: Creating the learning organisation.* New York: The Free Press.

Heath, C., & Nicholls, G. (1997). Animated texts: Selective renditions of news stories. In L. Resnick, R. Saljo, C. Pontecorvo & B. Burge (Eds.), *Discourse, tools and reasoning: Essays on situated cognition.* (Vol. 63–86). Berlin: Springer Verlag.

Herzenberg, S., Alic, J., & Wial, H. (1998). *New rules for a new economy: Employment and opportunity in postindustrial America.* Ithaca: Cornell University/ILR Press.

Hodges, D.C. (1998). Participation as dis-identification with/in a community of practice. *Mind, Culture and Activity, 5*(4), 272–290.

Hodkinson, P.H., & Hodkinson, H. (2003). Individuals, communities of practice and the policy context. *Studies in Continuing Education, 25*(1), 3–21.

Hodkinson, P.H., & Hodkinson, H. (2004). The significance of individuals' dispositions in the workplace learning: A case study of two teachers. *Journal of Education and Work, 17*(2), 167–182.

Howard, A. (Ed). (1995). *The changing nature of work.* San Francisco: Jossey-Bass Publishers.

Hughes, K. & Bernhardt, A. (1999). *Market segmentation and the restructuring of banking jobs.* IEE Brief Number 24 February 1999. (pp. 1–4). New York: Institute on Education and the Economy.

Hull, G. (1997). Preface and Introduction. In G. Hull (Ed.), *Changing work, changing workers: Critical perspectives on language, literacy and skills.* (pp. 3–39). New York: State University of New York Press.

Jacobsen, J.P. (2004). *Women as labor force participants: Effects of family and organisational structure.* Paper presented at Reaching the Top: Challenges and Opportunities for Women Leaders conference, 3 March, 2004, Boston.

Kalleberg, A.L., Reskin, B.F., & Hudson, K. (2000). Bad jobs in America: Standard and nonstandard employment relations and job quality in the United States. *American Sociological Review, 65*(April), 256–278.

Kempnich, B., Butler, E., & Billett, S. (1999). *(Ir)reconcilable differences? Women and small business and the vocational education and training system.* Centre for Labour Studies, Department of Social Inquiry, University of Adelaide.

Knights, D., & Willmott, H. (1989). Power and subjectivity at work: From degradation to subjugation in social relations. *Sociology, 23*(4), 535–558.

Larkin, J., McDermott, J., Simon, D.P., & Simon, H.A. (1980). Expert and novice performance in solving physics problems. *Science, 208,* 1335–1342.

Lave, J. (1990). The culture of acquisition and the practice of understanding. In J.W. Stigler, R. A. Shweder & G. Herdt (Eds.), *Cultural psychology* (pp. 259–286). Cambridge, UK: Cambridge University Press.

Lave, J. (1993). The practice of learning. In S. Chaiklin & J. Lave (Eds.), *Understanding practice: Perspectives on activity and context* (pp. 3–32). Cambridge, UK: Cambridge University Press.

Lave, J., & Wenger, E. (1991). *Situated learning—legitimate peripheral participation.* Cambridge, UK: Cambridge University Press.

Lazonick, W. (1990). Competitive advantage on the shop floor. Cambridge, MA: Harvard University Press.

Leontyev, A.N. (1981). *Problems of the development of the mind.* Moscow: Progress Publishers.

Leicht, K.T. (1998). Work (if you can get it) and occupations (if there are any)? What social scientists can learn from predictions of the end of work and radical workplace change. *Work and Occupations, 25* (1), 36–48.

Lewis, J. (2005). Driver competence—Understanding 'hidden' knowledge through guided learning. Honors dissertation. Faculty of Education, Griffith University

Leuven, E., & Oosterbeek, H. (1999). The demand and supply of work related training: evidence from four countries. *Research in Labour Economics, 18*, 303–330.

Lipsig-Mumme, C. (1996). *Bridging the solitudes: Canadian perspectives on research partnerships in the New Work Order.* Keynote address presented at ANTARAC Annual Conference, 31 October–1 November 1996, Melbourne.

Livingstone, D. (2001). Expanding Notions of Work and Learning. In T. Fenwick (Ed.), *Sociocultural perspectives on learning through work* (pp. 19–30). San Francisco: Jossey Bass.

Livingstone, D., & Eichler, M. (2005). *Mapping the field of lifelong (formal and informal) learning and (paid and unpaid) work.* Joint Keynote Address presented at The Future of Lifelong Learning and Work, International Conference, June 20, 2005, Toronto.

Loutfi, M.F. (2001). Women, gender and work: An overview. In M. F. Loutfi (Ed.), *Women, gender and work* (pp. 3–20). Geneva: International Labour Organisation.

Maddison, A. (1982). *Phases of capitalist development.* Oxford: Oxford University Press.

Malle, B.F., Moses, L.J., & Baldwin, D.A. (2001). Introduction: The significance of intentionality. In B.F. Malle, L.J. Moses & D.A. Baldwin (Eds.), *Intentions and intentionality: Foundations of social cognition* (pp. 1–26). Cambridge, MA: The MIT Press.

Mansfield, N. (2000). *Subjectivity: Theories of the self from Freud to Haraway.* Sydney: Allen and Unwin.

Martin, L.M.W., & Scribner, S. (1991). Laboratory for cognitive studies of work: A case study of the intellectual implications of a new technology. *Teachers College Record, 92* (4), 582–602.

McBrier, D.B., & Wilson, G. (2004). Going down? Race and downward occupational mobility for white collar workers in the 1990s. *Work and Occupations, 31*(3), 283–322.

McGovern P. (1996). Trust, discretion and responsibility: The division of technical labour. *Work, Employment and Society, 10*(1), 85–103.

McGovern, P., Smeaton, D., & Hill, S. (2004). Bad jobs in Britian. *Work and Occupations, 31*(2), 225–249.

McNair, S., Flynn, M., Owen, L., Humphreys, C., & Woodfield, S. (2004). *Changing work in later life: A study of job transitions.* University of Surrey: Centre for Research into the Older Workforce.

Melkas, H., & Anker, R. (2001). Occupational segregation by sex in Nordic Countries: An empirical investigation. In M. F. Loutfi (Ed.), *Women, gender and work* (pp. 189–213). Geneva: International Labour Organisation.

Milkman, R. (1997). *Farewell to the factory: Auto Workers in the late twentieth century.* Berkeley: University of California Press.

Merrifield, J. (1997). If job training is the answer, what is the question? Research with displaced women textile workers. In G. Hull (Ed.), *Changing work, changing workers: Critical perspectives on language, literacy, and skills.* New York: State University of New York.

Mincer, J. (1989). Human capital and the labor market: A review of current research. *Educational Researcher, 18*(4), 27–34.

Neisser, U. (1976). *Cognition and reality.* San Francisco: W.H. Freeman.

Newman, D., Griffin, P., & Cole, M. (1989). *The construction zone: Working for cognitive change in schools.* Cambridge: Cambridge University Press.

Newell, A., & Simon, H.A. (1972). *Human problem solving.* Englewood Cliffs, N.J.: Prentice Hall.

Noon, M., & Blyton, P. (1997). *The Realities of Work.* Basingstoke, Hants: Macmillan.

O'Doherty, D., & Willmot, H. (2001). The question of subjectivity and the labor process. *International Studies of Management and Organisation, 30*(4), 112–133.

Organisation for Economic Cooperation and Development. (1998). *Lifelong learning: A monitoring framework and trends in participation.* Paris: Organisation for Economic Cooperation and Development.

Organisation for Economic Cooperation and Development. (2000). *Economics and finance of lifelong learning.* Paris: OECD.

O'Connell, P.J. (1999). *Adults in training: An international comparison of continuing education and training.* Paris: OECD

Owen, E., & Sweller, J. (1989). Should problem-solving be used as a learning device in mathematics? *Journal of Research in Mathematics Education, 20*(3), 321–8.

Patrickson, M., & Ranzijn, R. (2004). *Employability of older workers.* Adelaide: National Centre for Vocational Education Research.

Pea, R.D. (1993). Practices of distributed intelligence and designs for education. In G. Salomon (Ed.), *Distributed cognitions* (pp. 47–87). New York: Cambridge University Press.

Perkins, D., Jay, E., & Tishman, S. (1993a). Beyond abilities: A dispositional theory of thinking. *Merrill-Palmer Quarterly, 39*(1), 1–21.

Perkins, D., Jay, E., & Tishman, S. (1993b). New conceptions of thinking: From ontology to education. *Educational Psychologist, 28*(1), 67–85.

Perkins, D.N. & Salomon, G. (1989). Are cognitive skills context bound? *Educational Researcher, 18*(1), 16–25.

Piaget, J. (1968). *Structuralism.* (C. Maschler, trans. and ed.) London: Routledge and Kegan Paul.

Pusey, M. (2003). *The experience of middle Australia.* Cambridge, UK: Cambridge University Press.

Prawat, R.S. (1989). Promoting access to knowledge, strategy, and dispositions in students: A research synthesis. *Review of Educational Research, 59*(1), 1–41.

Quickie, J. (1999). *A curriculum for life: Schools for a democratic learning society.* Buckingham: Open University Press.

Ratner, C. (2000). Agency and culture. *Journal for the Theory of Social Behaviour, 30,* 413–434.

Rogoff, B. (1990). *Apprenticeship in thinking—cognitive development in social context.* New York: Oxford University Press.

Rogoff, B. (1995). Observing sociocultural activity on three planes: Participatory appropriation, guided participation, apprenticeship. In J.W. Wertsch, A. Alvarez & P. del Rio (Eds.), *Sociocultural studies of mind* (pp. 139–164). Cambridge, UK: Cambridge University Press.

Rose, N. (1990). *Governing the soul: The shaping of the private self.* London: Routledge.

Resnick, L.B., Säljö, R., Pontecorvo, C., & Burge, B. (1997). Introduction. In L. B. Resnick, C. Pontecorvo, R. Säljö & B. Burge (Eds.), *Discourse, tools and reasoning: Essays on Situated Cognition* (pp. 1–20). Berlin: Springer.

Rifkin, J. (1995). *The end of work: The decline of the global labor force and the dawn of the post- market era.* New York, NY: G.P. Putnam's Sons.

Ronnas, P. (1992). *Employment generation through private entrepreneurship in Vietnam.* Geneva: International Labour Organisation.

Rousseau, J.J. (1968). *The social contract.* London: Penguin.

Rowden, R. (1997). How attention to employee satisfaction through training and development helps small business maintain a competitive edge: A comparative case study. *Australian Vocational Education Review, 4*(2).

Rowden, R. (1995). The role of human resources development in successful small to mid-sized manufacturing businesses: A comparative case study. *Human Resource Development Quarterly, 6*(4), 335–373.

Salomon, G. (1997). *Distributed cognitions: Psychological and educational considerations.* Cambridge, UK: Cambridge University Press.

Sassen, S. (1991). *The global city: New York, London, Tokyo.* Princeton, NJ: Princeton University Press.

Savickas, M.L. (1999). *Career development and public policy: The role of values, theory and research.* Paper presented at the Making Ways: Career Development and Public Policy, International Symposia, Ottawa.

Scandura, J.M. (1980). Theoretical foundations of instruction: A systems alternative to cognitive psychology. *Journal of Structural Learning, 6*, 347–394.

Scott, A. (1994) *Willing Slaves? British workers under Human Resource Management.* Cambridge: Cambridge University Press.

Scribner, S. (1984). Studying working intelligence. In B. Rogoff & J. Lave (Eds.), *Everyday cognition: Its development in social context* (pp. 9–40). Cambridge, MA: Harvard University Press.

Scribner, S. (1985a). Knowledge at work. *Anthropology and Education Quarterly, 16*, 199–206.

Scribner, S. (1985b). Vygostky's use of history. In J.V. Wertsch (Ed.), *Culture, communication and cognition: Vygotskian perspectives* (pp. 119–145). Cambridge, UK: Cambridge University Press.

Scribner, S. (1997). A sociocultural approach to the study of mind. In E. Tobah, R.J. Falmagne, M.B. Parlee, L.M. Martin & E.A.S. Kapelman (Eds.), *Mind and social practice: Selected writings of Sylvia Scribner.* (pp. 266–280.). Cambridge, UK: Cambridge University Press.

Searle, J.R. (1995). *The construction of social reality.* London: Penguin.

Shah, C., & Burke, G. (2003). *Project 2000-02: Changing skill requirements in the Australian labour force in a knowledge economy.* Working Paper #48. Melbourne: Centre for the Economics of Education and Training.

Shima, S. (1998). Reconceptualizing part-time employment. *Work, Employment & Society, 12*(2), 375–378.

Sigelman, C.K. (1999). *Life-span human development* (Vol. 3). Pacific Grove: Brooks/Cole Publishing Company.

Skilbeck, M., Connell, H., Lowe, N., & Tait, K. (1994). *The vocational quest: New directions in education and training.* London: Routledge.

Skinner, C. (2004). The changing occupational structure of large metropolitan areas: Implications for the high school educated. *Journal of Urban Affairs, 26*(1), 67–88.

Skuratowicz, E., & Hunter, L.W. (2004). Where do women's jobs come from? *Work and Occupations, 31*(1), 73–110.

Smith, A., & Billett, S. (2003). *Enhancing employers' expenditure on training.* Adelaide: National Centre for Vocational Education Research.

Smith, R. J. (2004). *Necessity in action: The epistemological agency of the new employee.* Unpublished Master of Education thesis, Griffith University, Brisbane.

Solomon, N. (1999). Culture and difference in workplace learning. In D. Boud & D.J. Garrick (Eds.), *Understanding learning at work* (pp. 119–131). London: Routledge.

Somerville, M. (2002). *Changing masculine work cultures.* Paper presented at the Envisioning practice—Implementing change conference, Gold Coast.

Somerville, M. (2003). *Who Learns? Enriching learning cultures in aged care workplaces.* Paper presented at the 11th Annual International Conference on Post-compulsory Education and Training: Enriching learning cultures, Gold Coast.

Somerville, M., & Abrahamsson, L. (2003). Trainers and learners constructing a community of practice: Masculine work cultures and learning safety in the mining industry. *Studies in the Education of Adults, 35*(1), 19–34.

Somerville, M., & Bernoth, M. (2001). *Safe bodies: Solving a workplace learning dilemma.* Paper presented at the 9th Annual International Conference on Post-compulsory Education and Training: Knowledge Demands for the New Economy, Gold Coast.

Stasz, C. (1997) Do employers need the skills they want? Evidence from technical work. *Journal of Education and Work, 10*(3), 205–233.

Stevenson, J.C. (1991). Cognitive structures for the teaching of adaptability in vocational education. In G. Evans (Ed.), *Learning and teaching cognitive skills* (pp. 144–163). Victoria, Australia: ACER.

Suchman, L. (1996). Constituting shared workspaces. In Y. Engeström & D. Middleton (Eds.), *Cognition and communication at work* (pp. 35–60). Cambridge: Cambridge University Press.

Suchman, L. (1997a). Centers of coordination: A case and some themes. In L. B. Resnick, R. Saljo C. Pontecorvo, & P. Burge (Eds.), *Discourse, tools and reasoning: Essays on situated cognition* (pp. 41–62). Berlin: Springer.

Suchman, L. (1997b). *From interactions to integrations: A reflection on the future of HCI.* Keynote address presented at Interact 97—Discovering New Worlds of HCI, 16 July 1997. Available at www.acs.org.au/president/1997/intrct97/suchman.htm.

Sweller, J. (1989). Should problem solving be used as a learning device in mathematics? *Journal of Research into Mathematics Education, 20*(3), 321–28.

Tam, M. (1997). *Part-time employment: A bridge or a trap?* Brookfield, USA: Aldershot.

Tikkanen, T., Lahn, L., Ward, P., & Lyng, K. (2002). *Working life changes and training of older workers.* Trondheim: Vox.

Trogon, A., & Grusenmeyer, C. (1997). To resolve a technical problem through conversation. In L. Resnick, R. Saljo, C. Pontecorvo, & B. Burge (Eds.), *Discourse, tools and reasoning: Essays on situated cognition* (pp. 87–110). Berlin: Springer-Verlag.

US Department of Commerce. (1994, January 12). *Employment and Training Reporter,* 344.

United States Nuclear Regulatory Commission. (2004). *The accident at Three Mile Island.* Washington: United States Nuclear Regulatory Commission. http://www.nrc.gov/reading-rm/doc-collections/fact-sheets/3mile-isle.pdf (accessed on 7th November 2005).

Valsiner, J. (1994). Bi-directional cultural transmission and constructive sociogenesis. In W. de Graaf & R. Maier (Eds.), *Sociogenesis re-examined* (pp. 101–134). New York: Springer.

Valsiner, J. (1998). *The guided mind: A sociogenetic approach to personality.* Cambridge, MA: Harvard University Press.

Valsiner, J. (2000). *Culture and human development.* London: Sage Publications.

Valsiner, J., & van der Veer, R. (2000). *The social mind: The construction of an idea.* Cambridge, UK: Cambridge University Press.

Van Horn, C. (1996). Economic change and the American worker: A background paper. In *Twentieth century task force on retraining America's workforce: No one left behind.* New York: Twentieth Century Fund Press.

Van Lehn, V. (1989). Towards a theory of impasse-driven learning. In H. Mandl & A. Lesgold (Eds.), *Learning issues for intelligent tutoring systems.* (pp. 19–41). New York: Springer-Verlag.

Van de Ven, A.H., Delbecq, A.L., & Keonig, R. Jr. (1976). Determinants of co-ordination modes within organisations. *American Sociological Review, 41,* 322–338.

van Woerkom, M. (2003). *Critical reflection at work.* Enschede: Twente University.

von Glasersfeld, E. (1987). Learning as a constructive activity. In C. Janvier (Ed). *Problems of representation in the teaching and learning of mathematics.* Hillsdale, NJ: Lawrence Erlbaum.

Vygotsky, L.S. (1978). *Mind in society—the development of higher psychological processes.* Cambridge, MA: Harvard University Press.

Vygotsky, L.S. (1987). *Thought and language* (ed A. Kouzulin). Massachussets: The MIT Press.

Waddington, J., & Whitson, C. (1996). Empowerment versus intensification: Union perspectives of change at the workplace. In P. Ackers, C. Smith & P. Smith (Eds.). The new workplace and trade unionism. (pp. 149–77). London: Routledge.

Wall, T.D., & Jackson, P.R. (1995). New manufacturing initiatives and shopfloor job design. In Howard, A (Ed.), *The changing nature of work.* San Francisco: Jossey-Bass Publishers.

Waight, C., & Stewart, B. (2005). Valuing the adult learning in e-learning: Part two—Insights from four companies. *Journal of Workplace Learning, 17*(5/6), 398–414.

Waterhouse, P. (1998). *The changing nature and patterns of work and implications for VET.* Conference of the National Centre for Vocational Education Research (NCVER), July 1998, Charles Sturt University, Wagga Wagga.

Wenger, E. (1998). *Communities of practice: Learning, meaning, and identity.* Cambridge, UK: Cambridge University Press.

Whalley, P., & Barley, S.R. (1997). Technical work in the division of labor: Stalking the wily anomaly. In S.R. Barley & J.E. Orr (Eds.), *Between craft and science: Technical work in U.S. settings.* (pp. 24–52). Ithaca NY: Cornell University Press.

Wertsch, J.V. (Ed.). (1985). *Culture, communication and cognition: Vygotskian perspectives.* Cambridge, UK: Cambridge University Press.

Wertsch, J.V. (1991). A sociocultural approach to socially shared cognition. In L.B. Resnick, J.M. Levine & S.D. Teasley (Eds.), *Perspectives on socially shared cognition* (pp. 85–100). Washington DC: American Psychological Association.

Wertsch, J.V. (1998). *Mind as action.* New York: Oxford University Press.

Wright Mills, C. (1973). The meaning of work throughout history. In F. Best (Ed.), *The future of work.* Englewood Cliffs, NJ: Prentice Hall.

Zuboff, S. (1988). *In the age of the smart machine: The future of work and power.* New York: Basic Books.

Index